ZAGAT SURVEY®

2003/04

CHICAGO RESTAURANTS

Local Editor: Alice Van Housen

Local Coordinators: Carolyn McGuire and Jill Van Cleave

Editor: Daniel Simmons

Published and distributed by
ZAGAT SURVEY, LLC
4 Columbus Circle
New York, New York 10019
Tel: 212 977 6000
E-mail: chicago@zagat.com
Web site: www.zagat.com

Acknowledgments

We thank Lisa Futterman, Bill Rice, Brenda and Earl Shapiro, Laura Levy Shatkin and Tom Van Housen for their assistance.

This guide would not have been possible without the hard work of our staff, especially Betsy Andrews, Reni Chin, Anna Chlumsky, Larry Cohn, Griff Foxley, Schuyler Frazier, Curt Gathje, Katherine Harris, Natalie Lebert, Mike Liao, Dave Makulec, Donna Marino, Laura Mitchell, Emily Parsons, Rob Poole, Robert Seixas, Yoji Yamaguchi and Sharon Yates.

Second Printing
© 2003 Zagat Survey, LLC
ISBN 1-57006-521-7
Printed in the United States of America

Contents

About This Survey

For 24 years, Zagat Survey has reported on the shared experiences of diners like you. This *2003/04 Chicago Restaurant Survey* is an update reflecting significant developments since our last *Survey* was published. For example, we have added 156 places not in the previous edition, as well as indicating new addresses, phone numbers, chef changes, remodelings, etc. All told, this guide covers some 1,061 restaurants.

By regularly surveying large numbers of avid local restaurant-goers, we hope to have achieved a uniquely current and reliable guide. For this book, nearly 2,400 people participated. Since they dined out an average of 2.8 times per week, this *Survey* is based on nearly 350,000 meals annually. We sincerely thank each of these surveyors; this book is really "theirs."

Of course, we are especially grateful to our editor, Alice Van Housen, a freelance food writer and editor, and our coordinators, *Chicago Tribune* travel writer and editor Carolyn McGuire and cookbook author and food consultant Jill Van Cleave.

To help guide our readers to Chicago's best meals and best buys, we have prepared a number of lists. See Top Ratings, including Most Popular (pages 9-15), and Best Buys (page 16). In addition, we have provided 45 handy indexes and have tried to be concise. Finally, it should be noted that our editors have synopsized our surveyors' opinions, with their comments shown in quotation marks.

As companions to this guide, we also publish guides to nightlife, restaurants, hotels, resorts, spas, golf courses, shopping, movies, theater and, soon to be released, music. Most of these guides are also available on mobile devices and at **zagat.com,** where you can vote and shop as well.

To join any of our upcoming *Surveys,* just register at **zagat.com.** Each participant will receive a free copy of the resulting guide when it is published.

Your comments and even criticisms of this guide are also solicited. There is always room for improvement with your help. You can contact us at chicago@zagat.com or by mail at Zagat Survey, 4 Columbus Circle, New York, NY 10019. We look forward to hearing from you.

New York, NY
July 7, 2003

Nina and Tim

Nina and Tim Zagat

What's New

Chicago's year in the economic trenches brought closings – and rumors of closings – but there was plenty of good news, with lots of openings, as well.

Up and Running: Among the noteworthy newcomers, Lakeview landed Coobah, Monsoon and Platiyo; River North received Fogo de Chão and Pili.Pili; and Wicker Park won Lovitt and Ohba. Booming West Randolph Street added Azuré, d.kelly, Mar y Sol and Starfish (joining the sushi feeding frenzy, along with Coast Sushi Bar and Oysy). Other debuts were dotted democratically around the city and surrounding areas, playing into the national trend of close-to-home dining. Entries included Bistro Campagne, Follia, Glory, La Tache, Montage and Opera.

Up the Food Chain: Chef Mark Baker exited our top Food scorer, Seasons, making way for the estimable Robert Sulatycky. The Pump Room pumped out Andrew Coates, followed by Michael Gaspard, and pumped in Bernard Laskowski (ex Bin 36, mk North). Michael Dean Hazen rushed out of Rushmore, and John Coletta cut out for Carlucci Rosemont, replaced in the Caliterra kitchen by Rick Gresh (ex Green Dolphin Street). Jackie Shen left Lawry's for Red Light (replacing Paul Wildermuth, who's now singing at Opera), and Stephen Dunne joined the mk team.

Down Is Up: Determined restaurateurs brought business back with creativity, tweaking concepts and affording consumers unprecedented discounting via dining clubs and coupons, wine and spirits deals, and prix fixe meals. Strategic downscaling included the morphing of Aubriot into Escargot and Harvest on Huron into Allen's New American Cafe.

Up and Coming: Anticipated new arrivals include the Blackbird spin-off, avec/; Cortado, an Argentine entry from the Mas crowd; and the Bongo Room offshoot, Room 12. Chef-watchers await the return of Kelly Courtney with her seasonal American, Oakville, as well as a West Town newcomer-without-a-name from Shawn McClain (Spring). Another nameless hot prospect is gestating in the Loop's Hotel 71, and two super-sized sushi spots, Japonais and SushiSamba Rio, will be swimming upstream soon.

Up in Smoke: Of course, tough times took their toll. We regret the loss of Don Juan on Halsted; Flavor; Karizma; Lino's Ristorante; Mi Sueño, Su Realidad; Napa Valley Grille; Park Avenue Cafe; Rambutan; Rico's; Tanglewood; Trattoria Dinotto; Twelve 12; and Zinfandel.

Thumbs Up: It's no surprise that Chicago, as America's third-largest city, offers some of the country's best food. What *is* surprising is that the typical cost of a meal, $29.29, is almost our U.S. average of $28.78.

Chicago, IL   Alice Van Housen
July 7, 2003

Key to Ratings/Symbols

Name, Address & Phone Number

Zagat Ratings

Hours & Credit Cards

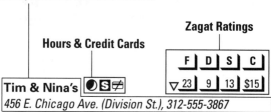

F	D	S	C
▽ 23	9	13	$15

Tim & Nina's ◑ⓈⒾ

456 E. Chicago Ave. (Division St.), 312-555-3867

◪ Hordes of "unkempt" U of C students have discovered this "never-closing" "eyesore", which "single-handedly" started the "deep-dish sushi pizza craze" that's "sweeping the Windy City" like a lake-effect storm; "try the eel-pepperoni-wasabi-mozzarella pie" – "it's to die for" (or from) – but bring cash, since "T & N never heard of credit cards or checks."

Review, with surveyors' comments in quotes

Restaurants with the highest overall ratings and greatest popularity and importance are printed in CAPITAL LETTERS.

Before reviews a symbol indicates whether responses were uniform ■ or mixed ◪.

Hours: ◑ serves after 11 PM
Ⓢ open on Sunday

Credit Cards: Ⓘ no credit cards accepted

Ratings: Food, Decor and Service are rated on a scale of **0** to **30**. The Cost (C) column reflects our surveyors' estimate of the price of dinner including one drink and tip.

F	Food	D	Decor	S	Service	C	Cost
23		9		13		$15	

0–9 poor to fair   **20–25** very good to excellent
10–15 fair to good   **26–30** extraordinary to perfection
16–19 good to very good   ▽ low response/less reliable

For places listed without ratings or a numerical cost estimate, such as an important newcomer or a popular write-in, the price range is indicated by the following symbols.

I	$15 and below	E	$31 to $50
M	$16 to $30	VE	$51 or more

Most Popular

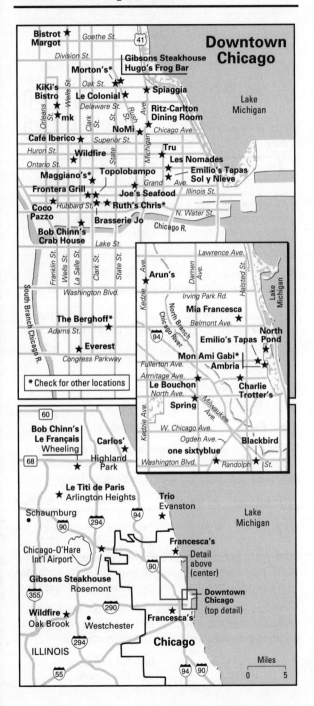

Downtown Chicago

- Bistrot Margot ★ — Goethe St. — 41
- Division St.
- Gibsons Steakhouse ★
- Hugo's Frog Bar
- Morton's* ★ — Oak St.
- KiKi's Bistro ★
- Le Colonial ★
- Spiaggia ★
- mk ★ — Delaware St.
- Ritz-Carlton Dining Room
- Café Iberico ★ — Superior St.
- NoMi ★ — Chicago Ave.
- Wildfire ★ — Huron St.
- Tru ★
- Ontario St.
- Les Nomades ★
- Maggiano's* ★
- Topolobampo ★
- Emilio's Tapas ★
- Sol y Nieve ★
- Frontera Grill ★ — Grand Ave.
- Joe's Seafood ★ — Illinois St.
- Coco Pazzo ★ — Hubbard St.
- Ruth's Chris* ★
- N. Water St.
- Brasserie Jo ★
- Chicago R.
- Bob Chinn's Crab House ★
- Lake St.
- Lake Michigan

Detail (center):

- Lawrence Ave.
- Arun's ★
- Irving Park Rd.
- Mia Francesca ★
- Belmont Ave.
- I-94
- Emilio's Tapas ★
- North Pond ★
- Mon Ami Gabi* ★
- Ambria ★
- Fullerton Ave.
- Armitage Ave.
- Le Bouchon ★
- North Ave.
- Charlie Trotter's ★
- Spring ★
- W. Chicago Ave.
- Ogden Ave.
- Blackbird ★
- one sixtyblue ★
- Washington Blvd. — Randolph St.

- The Berghoff* ★ — Adams St.
- Everest ★
- Congress Parkway

*Check for other locations

- 60
- Bob Chinn's ★
- Le Français — Wheeling
- 68
- Carlos' ★ — Highland Park
- Le Titi de Paris ★ — Arlington Heights
- Schaumburg ●
- Trio ★ — Evanston
- 90 / 294
- 94
- Lake Michigan
- Chicago-O'Hare Int'l Airport
- Francesca's ★
- Detail above (center)
- Gibsons Steakhouse ★ — Rosemont
- 355
- Downtown Chicago (top detail)
- Wildfire ★ — Oak Brook
- 290
- Westchester ●
- 294
- Francesca's ★
- Chicago
- ILLINOIS
- 55
- 94 / 90
- Miles 0 — 5

Top Ratings

Excluding places with low voting. An asterisked restaurant is tied with the one directly above it.

40 Most Popular

1. Tru
2. Charlie Trotter's
3. Ambria
4. Everest
5. mk
6. Frontera Grill
7. Mon Ami Gabi
8. Les Nomades
9. Gibsons Steakhse.
10. Wildfire
11. Topolobampo
12. Spiaggia
13. Blackbird
14. Spring
15. Maggiano's
16. Ritz-Carlton Din. Rm.
17. Arun's
18. Carlos'
19. KiKi's Bistro
20. Morton's
21. Coco Pazzo
22. Trio
23. Le Bouchon
24. Bob Chinn's
25. North Pond
26. NoMi
27. Joe's Seafood
28. Hugo's Frog Bar
29. Le Français
30. Berghoff, The
31. Café Iberico
32. Le Colonial
33. Le Titi de Paris
34. Francesca's
35. Emilio's Tapas
36. Ruth's Chris
37. Mia Francesca
38. one sixtyblue
39. Bistrot Margot
40. Brasserie Jo

It's obvious that many of the restaurants on the above list are among Chicago's most expensive, but if popularity were calibrated to price, we suspect that a number of other restaurants would join the above ranks. Given the fact that both our surveyors and readers love to discover dining bargains, we have added a list of 80 Best Buys on page 16. These are restaurants that give real quality at extremely reasonable prices. They are the places where you'll find Chicagoans and their families on Sunday nights or, for that matter, on any day when they are not on expense account.

Top Food

Top 40 Food

28 Seasons	Frontera Grill
Les Nomades	Retro Bistro
Ritz-Carlton Din. Rm.	**25** Blackbird
Charlie Trotter's	302 West
Le Titi de Paris	D & J Bistro
Carlos'	Avenues
Le Français	Salbute
Trio	Courtright's
27 Ambria	Gibsons Steakhse.
Tru	Joe's Seafood
Everest	Le Vichyssois
Tallgrass	Printer's Row
Spiaggia	Naha
Les Deux Gros	Le Bouchon
Topolobampo	**24** Barrington Bistro
Gabriel's	one sixtyblue
Arun's	Ritz-Carlton Café
26 mk	Café Spiaggia
Spring	Coco Pazzo
Morton's	Seasons Café

By Cuisine

American (New)
28 Seasons
Charlie Trotter's
26 mk
Spring
25 Blackbird

American (Regional)
24 Crofton on Wells
23 Meritage Cafe/Wine
22 Prairie
21 Soul Kitchen
20 Marion St. Grille▽

American (Traditional)
24 Ritz-Carlton Café
Seasons Café
23 Lawry's Prime Rib
Walker Bros.
Bongo Room

Asian
23 Le Colonial
Pasteur
Yoshi's Café
Catch 35
21 Red Light

French (Bistro)
26 Retro Bistro

Barbecue
21 Twin Anchors
20 Robinson's Ribs
Merle's Smokehse.
Smoke Daddy
Carson's Ribs

Cajun/Creole
20 Heaven on Seven
Wishbone
19 Davis St. Fishmarket
Pappadeaux Seafood
Dixie Kit./Bait Shop

Chinese
23 Hong Min
22 Phoenix
21 Emperor's Choice
20 Shine & Morida
Ben Pao

Eclectic
24 Stained Glass Wine
23 Room, The
21 Jane's
Deleece
She She
25 D & J Bistro
Le Bouchon

24 Barrington Bistro
Froggy's

French (Classic)
28 Le Titi de Paris
27 Les Deux Gros
25 Le Vichyssois
24 Oceanique
La Petite Folie

French (New)
28 Les Nomades
Ritz-Carlton Din. Rm.
Carlos'
Le Français
Trio

Greek
23 Costa's
20 Santorini
Parthenon
Pegasus
Greek Islands

Hamburgers
21 Pete Miller's Steak
19 Boston Blackie's
18 R.J. Grunt's
P.J. Clarke's
Twisted Spoke

Hot Dogs
22 Superdawg Drive-In
21 Wiener's Circle
19 Gold Coast Dogs
17 Fluky's

Indian
22 Tiffin
20 Viceroy of India
Gaylord India
Klay Oven
Indian Garden

Italian
27 Spiaggia
Gabriel's
24 Café Spiaggia
Coco Pazzo
Va Pensiero

Japanese
24 Mirai Sushi

Sushi Wabi
23 Bob San
Sushi Naniwa
Kuni's

Mediterranean
25 Avenues
Naha
22 Shallots
Lucca's
21 Tizi Melloul

Mexican
27 Topolobampo
26 Frontera Grill
25 Salbute
24 Cafe 28
23 Ixcapuzalco

Nuevo Latino
22 Mas
Nacional 27
21 Otro Mas
18 Mambo Grill

Pizza
21 Lou Malnati's
Pizza D.O.C.
Pizzeria Uno
20 Original Gino's East
Chicago Pizza/Grinder

Seafood
25 Joe's Seafood
24 Oceanique
Atlantique
Hugo's Frog Bar
Nick's Fishmarket

Spanish/Tapas
23 Mesón Sabika
22 Café Iberico
21 Emilio's Tapas
20 Cafe Ba-Ba-Reeba!
19 Tapas Barcelona

Steakhouses
26 Morton's
25 Gibsons Steakhse.
24 Ruth's Chris
Chicago Chop Hse.
Las Tablas

Top Food

Thai
27 Arun's
22 Thai Pastry
21 Vong's
19 Star of Siam
18 P.S. Bangkok

Vegetarian
19 Reza's
18 Chicago Diner
    Blind Faith Café
16 Heartland Cafe
14 Slice of Life

By Special Feature

Breakfast†
23 Walker Bros.
22 Original Pancake
21 Ina's
20 John's Place
    Lou Mitchell's

Brunch
28 Seasons
    Ritz-Carlton Din. Rm.
26 Frontera Grill
24 North Pond
23 MOD.

Business Dining
28 Seasons
    Les Nomades
    Ritz-Carlton Din. Rm.
    Charlie Trotter's
    Le Titi de Paris

BYO
24 Las Tablas (Lincoln Park)
23 Hong Min (Chinatown)
    Room, The
    Tre Kronor
22 Thai Pastry

Hotel Dining
28 Seasons
    Four Seasons
    Ritz-Carlton Din. Rm.
    Ritz-Carlton
    Trio
    Homestead
27 Ambria
    Belden Stratford
25 Gibsons Steakhse.
    Doubletree

Late Dining
25 Gibsons Steakhse.
24 Hugo's Frog Bar
23 Hong Min (Chinatown)
    Rosebud Steakhse.
22 Superdawg Drive-In

Meet for a Drink
26 mk
    Frontera Grill
25 Gibsons Steakhse.
    Joe's Seafood
    Naha

Newcomers
    Bistro Campagne
    Monsoon
    Opera
    Platiyo
    West Town Tavern

People-Watching
25 Blackbird
    Gibsons Steakhse.
24 Mirai Sushi
23 MOD.
    Nine

Worth a Trip
28 Le Titi de Paris
    Arlington Heights
    Carlos'
    Highland Park
    Le Français
    Wheeling
    Trio
    Evanston
27 Tallgrass
    Lockport

† Other than hotels

By Location

Andersonville/Edgewater
- **24** Atlantique
  - Francesca's
- **23** Pasteur
  - Room, The
- **20** Tomboy

Bucktown
- **25** Le Bouchon
- **24** Café Absinthe
- **23** Meritage Cafe/Wine
  - Margie's Candies
  - Cafe Matou

Chinatown
- **23** Hong Min
- **22** Phoenix
- **21** Emperor's Choice
- **19** Penang

Gold Coast
- **27** Spiaggia
- **25** Gibsons Steakhse.
- **24** Café Spiaggia
  - Hugo's Frog Bar
- **23** Le Colonial

Lakeview/Wrigleyville
- **24** Cafe 28
  - Mia Francesca
- **23** Yoshi's Café
  - erwin, american cafe
- **22** Matsuya

Lincoln Park/DePaul
- **28** Charlie Trotter's
- **27** Ambria
- **24** North Pond
  - Las Tablas
- **23** Via Carducci

Little Italy/University Village
- **24** Francesca's
- **23** Chez Joel
- **21** Tufano's Vernon Park
  - Tuscany
  - Rosebud on Rush

Loop
- **27** Everest
- **24** Nick's Fishmkt.
- **23** Catch 35
  - Vivere
- **22** Trattoria No. 10

Market District
- **24** one sixtyblue
  - Sushi Wabi
- **23** Rushmore
- **22** La Sardine
- **21** Marché

Near North
- **28** Seasons
- **26** Morton's
- **25** Avenues
  - Joe's Seafood
- **24** Seasons Café

River North
- **27** Topolobampo
- **26** mk
  - Frontera Grill
- **25** Naha
- **24** Coco Pazzo

Streeterville
- **28** Les Nomades
  - Ritz-Carlton Din. Rm.
- **27** Tru
- **24** Ritz-Carlton Café
  - Caliterra

Suburban North
- **28** Carlos'
  - Trio
- **27** Gabriel's
- **24** Froggy's
  - Va Pensiero

Uptown/Lincoln Square
- **22** Thai Pastry
- **21** Pizza D.O.C.
  - La Bocca della Verità
  - She She
- **19** Andies

West Loop
- **25** Blackbird
- **23** Nine
- **22** Carmichael's Steak
- **20** Lou Mitchell's
  - Wishbone

Wicker Park
- **26** Spring
- **24** Mirai Sushi
- **23** MOD.
  - Bob San
  - Bongo Room

Top 40 Decor

27 Spiaggia
Ritz-Carlton Din. Rm.
Everest
Tru
Seasons
26 Ambria
NoMi
Charlie Trotter's
Signature Room
Les Nomades
Le Français
RL
Avenues
Seasons Café
25 Courtright's
Tizi Melloul
Trio
Nine
302 West
Spring

Pump Room
Carlos'
120 Ocean Place
Le Titi de Paris
North Pond
Tallgrass
24 mk
Le Colonial
Atwood Cafe
Ritz-Carlton Café
Café Spiaggia
Arun's
Naha
Topolobampo
Lovell's/Lake Forest
one sixtyblue
Gabriel's
23 Zealous
Vivere
Red Light

Outdoors

Athena
Green Dolphin St.
Kamehachi
Meritage Cafe/Wine
NoMi
Pegasus

Puck's at the MCA
Smith & Wollensky
South Gate Cafe
Tavern on Rush
Thyme
Topo Gigio

Romance

Ambria
Biggs Steakhse.
Café Absinthe
Chez Joel
Everest
Geja's Cafe
Gioco

KiKi's Bistro
Le Bouchon
Le Colonial
Spring
302 West
Tizi Melloul
Va Pensiero

Rooms

Blackbird
Le Colonial
Marché
Nine
NoMi
North Pond
one sixtyblue

RL
Spiaggia
Spring
Tizi Melloul
Tru
Wave
Zealous

Views

Cité
Everest
Lobby, The
Mill Race Inn
NoMi
North Pond

Oak Terrace
Riva
Seasons
Signature Room
Spiaggia
Tasting Room

Top 40 Service

28	Charlie Trotter's	**24**	302 West
	Ritz-Carlton Din. Rm.		Froggy's
	Trio		Morton's
	Everest		Ritz-Carlton Café
27	Tru		Courtright's
	Seasons		Joe's Seafood
	Le Français	**23**	Gibsons Steakhse.
	Les Nomades		Va Pensiero
	Ambria		D & J Bistro
	Carlos'		Stained Glass Wine
	Le Titi de Paris		Cafe Pyrenees
	Tallgrass		Le Vichyssois
26	Gabriel's		NoMi
	Spiaggia		Bistro Banlieue
	Arun's		Nick's Fishmarket
25	Avenues		Printer's Row
	Seasons Café		Les Deux Gros
	Topolobampo		Retro Bistro
	Spring		Hugo's Frog Bar
	mk		Café Spiaggia

Best Buys

Top 40 Bangs for the Buck

1. Superdawg Drive-In
2. Margie's Candies
3. Potbelly Sandwich
4. Fluky's
5. Wiener's Circle
6. Gold Coast Dogs
7. Walker Bros.
8. Salt & Pepper Diner
9. Original Pancake
10. Artopolis Bakery
11. Sarkis Grill
12. Breakfast Club
13. Penny's Noodle Shop
14. Billy Goat Tavern
15. Orange
16. Johnny Rockets
17. Manny's Café
18. Lou Mitchell's
19. Chipotle Mexican
20. Bongo Room
21. Cafe Nordstrom
22. Chicago Flat Sammies
23. Nuevo Leon
24. Leo's Lunchroom
25. Moody's Pub
26. Nookies
27. Tre Kronor
28. Ann Sather
29. Corner Bakery
30. Cosí
31. Zoom Kitchen
32. Toast
33. Cross-Rhodes
34. Lucky Platter
35. Kitsch'n on Roscoe
36. Russell's BBQ
37. Tempo
38. My Pie Pizza
39. Aurelio's Pizza
40. Hilary's Urban Eatery

Other Good Values

Addis Abeba
Amitabul
Andies
Army & Lou's
Athenian Room
Bijan's Bistro
Bite
BJ's Market & Bakery
Chicago Diner
Cold Comfort Cafe
Dell Rhea's Chicken
Edna's
El Nandu
Ethiopian Diamond
Flo
Flying Chicken
Gladys Luncheonette
Hashalom
Hot Doug's
Jambalaya's

Jang Mo Nim
Joy Yee's Noodle
La Cazuela Mariscos
Lem's BBQ
Lincoln Noodle Hse.
Lou Malnati's
LuLu's Dim Sum
Lutz Café & Pastry
Noon-O-Kabab
Pasta Palazzo
Red Lion Pub
Ruby of Siam
San Soo Gab San
Silver Seafood
Thai Little Home
Thai Pastry
Twisted Spoke
Udupi Palace
Uncommon Ground
Victory's Banner

Restaurant Directory

Abbey Pub & Restaurant S —| —| —| M
(fka Lambay Island at the Abbey Pub)
3420 W. Grace St. (Elston Ave.), 773-463-5808
Tucked behind the green-and-white awning of a somewhat divey Northwest Side pub is this small but striking dining room appointed with evocative photographs of the Gaelic countryside; the menu is straight from the Old Sod, as well – Irish breakfast, shepherd's pie and beer-battered fish and chips to be enjoyed with a pint of stout or a Black & Tan; N.B. the Abbey offers live music seven nights a week.

Abril ◑ S 17| 13| 16| $17
2607 N. Milwaukee Ave. (bet. Kedzie Ave. & Logan Blvd.), 773-227-7252
☑ Paisanos are polarized over this Logan Square "Mex cafe", so it's your call whether it offers "authentic", "tasty" food, "congenial" service and a "good bang for your peso", or just "typical" south-of-the-border fare slung by "rude" servers in a "shabby" space; respondents agree, however, that the "mega-margaritas" are "fantastic"; N.B. the kitchen stays open till 3 AM on weekends.

Addis Abeba S 20| 11| 16| $16
3521 N. Clark St. (bet. Addison St. & Newport Ave.), 773-929-9383
■ "Adventurous palates" head to Wrigleyville for "Chicago's best Ethiopian" dining – "authentic", "slyly spicy" and "a bargain", to boot; the "friendly" service can be "slow at times", but "you get to eat with your hands" (staffers wear T-shirts bearing the international symbol for 'no flatware'), "a fun experience" that enlivens the otherwise "sparse", "non-glamorous atmosphere."

Adobo Grill S 19| 18| 18| $29
1610 N. Wells St. (North Ave.), 312-266-7999
■ Surveyors swoon for the "magnificent margaritas and godly guacamole" "made tableside" at this "hip" Old Town three-year-old where the "inventive", "eclectic" fare "is some of the freshest in town"; it can get so "noisy" that you might have to "forget conversation", but with "personable" servers and a "fun atmosphere", the "see-and-be-seen" crowd doesn't seem fazed in the least.

Akai Hana ▽ 25| 15| 22| $21
848 N. State St. (Chestnut St.), 312-787-4881
3223 W. Lake Ave. (Skokie Blvd.), Wilmette, 847-251-0384 S
■ "In-the-know" folks "go" to these Gold Coast and North Suburban "real Japanese" "favorites" for "reliable" "and affordable" "fine food" including a "range of appetizers" and "fresh" "bargain sushi that doesn't taste like a bargain"; "always mobbed", they feature "cheerful decor and staff" and a "kid-friendly", "family atmosphere", though there are beer and wine for the big folks.

A La Turka [S] 18 | 18 | 20 | $22

3134 N. Lincoln Ave. (Belmont Ave.), 773-935-6447

■ The "nicest-ever" servers are "thankful you came" to this "charming" Lakeview Turkish with an "authentic feel" behind its "blah storefront"; "for the best experience", "sit on the floor at the rotating tables" to enjoy the "exotic" food, which is also a "great value"; P.S. young turks visiting on Friday or Saturday nights appreciate that "the belly dancer is neither old nor fat."

Albert's Café & Patisserie [S] 19 | 18 | 18 | $19

52 W. Elm St. (bet. Clark & Dearborn Sts.), 312-751-0666

■ "Indulge" in "old-world charm" at this "quaint" and "conservative" Gold Coast cafe/bakery that's a bastion of "the Left Bank in Chicago"; with "good food" (including "excellent pastries") and "consistent quality and service", it's "pleasant" for a "breakfast with a European feel", a "casual" lunch, a "ladies' brunch" or a "great break from Michigan Avenue" shopping.

Allen's New American Cafe - | - | - | E

217 W. Huron St. (bet. Franklin & Wells Sts.), 312-587-9600

Chef-owner Allen Sternweiler has morphed his former Harvest on Huron into this somewhat down-scaled River Norther serving a seasonal New American menu with global influences (and an emphasis on game and seafood) paired with a 200-bottle wine list; a remodeling has resulted in the addition of a communal table and a noise-muffling divider between dining room and lounge.

Always Thai ▽ 18 | 11 | 16 | $16

1825 W. Irving Park Rd. (bet. Ashland & Damen Aves.), 773-929-0100

◪ "Always a reliable choice", this Lakeview Thai is a "find" for "tasty, fresh food" ("try the chive dumplings") at "reasonable prices", even if the "menu is limited"; since its "less-than-stimulating decor" is "nothing to write home about", many view it as a "great take-out option."

Amarind's [S] ▽ 20 | 14 | 17 | $22

6822 W. North Ave. (Oak Park Ave.), 773-889-9999

◪ Siam-savvy surveyors say it's "well worth a long trip" to this "artistic" Thai yearling on the border of Oak Park and Chicago, where a "dedicated chef" creates "fine cuisine", including "offbeat selections"; foes feel, though, that "the food is the only thing that shines", saying service can be uneven and the decor "depressing."

AMBRIA 27 | 26 | 27 | $68

Belden Stratford Hotel, 2300 N. Lincoln Park W. (Belden Ave.), 773-472-5959

■ "No superlative is enough" to convey the "polished" "excellence" of Lettuce Entertain You's "pure luxe" Lincoln

Park "grande dame", a "romantic" "special-occasion" spot "suited for classicists"; it's "always a divine experience" "worth every dollar" thanks to chef-owner Gabino Sotelino and chef de cuisine Anselmo Ruiz's "fabulous" New French dishes, an "outstanding sommelier", "servers who appear as if by magic" and an atmosphere of "hushed elegance."

American Girl Place Cafe S | 13 | 23 | 21 | $23 |
American Girl Pl., 111 E. Chicago Ave. (bet. Michigan Ave. & Rush St.), 312-943-9400
☒ A "must-see" "fantasy" for young ladies from "5 to 105", this "amusing" "theme restaurant" on the Mag Mile is a "sweet place to take your little princess and her doll", as the poppet playmates "are catered to" with their own "special seating and dishware"; be warned, though, that most "boys are entirely bored" by the proceedings and "no one goes for" the "marginal", "production-line" food.

Amitabul S | ▽ 19 | 9 | 16 | $14 |
6207 N. Milwaukee Ave. (Nagle Ave.), 773-774-0276
■ Vegetarians and even some "steak lovers" laud the "healing qualities" of this "unique Korean vegan" on the Northwest Side, "a welcome departure from the typical" and "one of the best options" for "fresh and spicy" animal-free cuisine that's "not dressed up like it's got meat in it"; the ambiance may be (pardon the allusion) "bare-bones", but it's got a "peaceful vibe."

Ammo S | - | - | - | I |
2601 W. Leland Ave. (Rockwell St.), 773-478-2666
The kitchen of this tiny corner cafe serves up creative, low-priced New American breakfasts, lunches and now dinners to Lincoln Square locals; pale pink walls and pretty chairs in black-and-white stripes and toile add color and charm to the sunny room; N.B. it's BYO at present, with a liquor license in the works.

Andies S | 19 | 16 | 17 | $19 |
1467 W. Montrose Ave. (Greenview Ave.), 773-348-0654
5253 N. Clark St. (Berwyn Ave.), 773-784-8616 ☽
■ A "favorite" pair of "local quickies", these two Middle Eastern–Meds serve up "big menus" of "inexpensive", "healthy" food with enough "variety for everyone's tastes", including "lots of options for vegetarians"; both offer a "laid-back" "neighborhood" atmosphere, but most say the "Clark Street location has the nicer room."

Angelina Ristorante S | 20 | 18 | 20 | $25 |
3561 N. Broadway (Addison St.), 773-935-5933
☒ Nestled behind a "quaint storefront" "in the Boys Town area", this "ol' reliable" delivers "substantial" and "tasty" (if "somewhat predictable") Southern Italian fare, including "delicious" "fresh pastas", served by a "staff that gets to

know you by name"; though "romantics" rate it "cute" and "cozy", expansive eaters warn that the "comfortable interior feels a touch claustrophobic when crowded."

Anna Maria Pasteria [S] 18 | 15 | 18 | $22
3953 N. Broadway (Irving Park Rd.), 773-929-6363
■ Pasta-loving pen pals praise this "solid, basic Italian" as the "mama's kitchen" of Lakeview for its "big portions" of "traditional, consistently good" "stick-to-your-ribs" "home cooking" served "at reasonable prices" by a "friendly" staff in a "charming" "storefront" setting; P.S. no longer just a "great BYO" spot, it now serves beer and wine.

Ann Sather [S] 17 | 13 | 17 | $14
5207 N. Clark St. (Foster St.), 773-271-6677
929 W. Belmont Ave. (Sheffield Ave.), 773-348-2378
Ann Sather Café [S]
3411 N. Broadway (Roscoe St.), 773-305-0024
1448 N. Milwaukee Ave. (North Ave.), 773-394-1812
3416 N. Southport Ave. (Roscoe St.), 773-404-4475
■ This family of "solid Swedish" spots has been a Chicago "constant over the years", best beloved for its "mind-blowing", "sinful" cinnamon rolls, hearty "hangover" breakfasts and "cheap", "tasty, old-fashioned" eats; the "people-watching is a show" and the "friendly" staffers act "like they've known you all your life", so expect "long waits" on "crowded weekends."

Antico Posto [S] 20 | 20 | 20 | $27
Oakbrook Center Mall, 118 Oakbrook Ctr. (Rte. 83), Oak Brook, 630-586-9200
■ Even "from a distance you can smell the [scent of] garlic" wafting from this Lettuce Entertain You outpost in the Western Suburbs; "surprisingly good for a mall restaurant", it boasts "comfortable tables" and "melt-in-your-mouth" "Italian staples" served by an "aware" staff in a "warm", "sedate" atmosphere; as suggested by the "racks that greet you when you walk in", there's also a "great wine program."

Arco de Cuchilleros [S] 18 | 14 | 16 | $22
3445 N. Halsted St. (bet. Addison & Belmont Aves.), 773-296-6046
■ Tapas tasters graze upon "lots of little nibbly things" at this Boys Town "best-kept secret", "especially in summer", when they can be sampled on the "wonderful garden-oasis" "patio in back" rather than at one of the "tables crammed into" the "small", "unassuming" interior; either way, wash them down with "excellent sangria" or a "great margarita."

Aria [S] – | – | – | E
Fairmont Chicago Hotel, 200 N. Columbus Dr. (bet. Randolph & South Water Sts.), 312-444-9494
Set in the Loop's former Entre Nous and Metropole spaces, this hip venue bypasses the Fairmont hotel's lobby with a

separate entrance that leads to a spacious lounge and crescent-shaped dining room decked with tapestries and sparkling mosaics; its Eclectic menu tempts with the riches of faraway lands including freshly baked naan from the tandoor, savory flatbread pizzas from the brick oven and entrées such as the featured roast of the day.

Army & Lou's S

▽ | 20 | 14 | 21 | $16

422 E. 75th St. (King Dr.), 773-483-3100

■ Though most "Lincoln Park flannel-shirt frat boys are too chicken to come on down", Southern-savvy surveyors "get to this" "inexpensive and dependable" "diner-type" destination on the Far South Side for "fantastic soul food"; it's "not for dieters", but trenchermen "die for" the "catfish (yow!)" or "down-home chitterlings" ("wow!") and always "save room for" the "great peach cobbler."

Art of Pizza, The S

– | – | – | I

3033 N. Ashland Ave. (Nelson St.), 773-327-5600

The "excellent stuffed pizza" at this Lakeview purveyor represents "a solid pie" to critics who comprehend the aesthetics of dough, sauce and toppings; owner Art (pun intended) Shabez prides himself on providing "fresh, well-prepared" 'za – "as well as delicious chicken parmesan, lasagna and salads" – and "great service" to the patrons who pack the "few tables" and stools in his "tiny place."

Artopolis Bakery & Cafe S

20 | 19 | 19 | $15

306 S. Halsted St. (Jackson St.), 312-559-9000

■ "Fast food with class", "flair and taste" is on the "creative menu" at this "upscale Greektown cafe and bakery" that's "great for grazers", since it's "lighter and fresher than your mainstay" Hellenic; fans "love the artopita" sandwiches, "amazing soups" and "delicious pastries", and "friendly service" adds to the "good vibe" of its "light and airy" space; P.S. it's "easy on the wallet" too.

ARUN'S S

27 | 24 | 26 | VE

4156 N. Kedzie Ave. (bet. Belle Plaine & Berteau Aves.), 773-539-1909

■ Showcasing Arun Sampanthavivat's "culinary genius", this "intimate" and "beautiful" Albany Park "haute" Thai "temple" "satisfies all the senses" with "superior" service and "one aphrodisiac after another"; "set aside a full evening" for the "leisurely" (and obligatory) $85 prix fixe menu, as "each of the 12 courses is a treat" "to eat and behold", featuring "artistic presentations" and a "gradual escalation of spice levels."

a tavola

22 | 19 | 22 | $36

2148 W. Chicago Ave. (bet. Hoyne Ave. & Leavitt St.), 773-276-7567

■ Though "it's small", many judge this "gem" of a Northern Italian in Ukrainian Village the "gnumber-one spot for gnocchi" that "melts in your mouth" – just one of the "pricey pastas" on its "limited menu" of "simple, elegant" fare offered in an "unusually intimate" and "serene dining" room; with "terrific service" from a staff that "cares enough to get it right", it "often surprises and always delights."

Athena ●S | 20 | 20 | 18 | $24 |
212 S. Halsted St. (Adams St.), 312-655-0000
■ "In the heart of Greektown", this "good establishment" is a "favorite" for its "solid" Athenian "standards" and "consistent service"; still, some say "the main attraction here" is "fun outdoor dining in the summer", since the "lovely patio" not only "rocks" with "great city views" but also offers a breather from the "hubbub like a Mykonos windmill" generated within by the "boisterous" clientele and "chatty waiters."

Athenian Room S | 18 | 10 | 17 | $16 |
807 W. Webster Ave. (Halsted St.), 773-348-5155
■ "Greektown comes to Lincoln Park" at this "diner-ish" (some say "dump"-ish) "institution", a "dependable" and "nostalgic" favorite for its "terrific chicken" Kalamata and an "easy stop for a gyro" or a "reliably good burger" (they serve American dishes too), all at "bargain prices" that add to the "value."

Atlantique S | 24 | 20 | 23 | $40 |
5101 N. Clark St. (bet. Carmen & Foster Aves.), 773-275-9191
■ Most mariners consider this Andersonville seafooder a prize "catch" for chef Jared Wentworth's "imaginative", "beautiful presentations" of "fine, fresh fish" and other "well-prepared" delights (owner "Jack Jones is a genius!"), complemented by a "thoughtfully assembled" wine list; the "civilized", "softly lit" room with an "ocean motif" affords "intimate", "leisurely" dining, abetted by "on-the-ball" service from a "friendly staff."

Atwater's S | ▽ 19 | 23 | 21 | $37 |
Herrington Inn, 15 S. River Ln. (State St.), Geneva, 630-208-7433
◪ A "small dining room" of "understated elegance" "with a view" of the "lovely Fox River" "makes the drive worthwhile" to this "upscale" West Suburban New French–American set in the Herrington Inn; "knowledgeable servers" enhance the experience, though the "imaginative menu" strikes some world-weary wayfarers as "a bit too pricey" and even sometimes a little "disappointing."

Atwood Cafe S | 21 | 24 | 20 | $32 |
Hotel Burnham, 1 W. Washington St. (State St.), 312-368-1900
■ A "shining star on State Street", this "exquisite" "architectural gem" within the "beautifully restored" Hotel Burnham serves "cozy" American "comfort food"

such as "famous pot pies" and "divine bread pudding"; it's "a hot spot for a Loop lunch" ("if you can snag a table") and "a great location for pre-theatre dining"; P.S. "big windows" and a new patio afford "great people-watching."

Aurelio's Pizza S 18 | 12 | 16 | $15

Centennial Plaza, 1455 W. Lake St. (Lombard Rd.), Addison, 630-889-9560
1509 W. Sibley Blvd. (bet. Bensley & Calhoun Aves.), Calumet City, 708-730-1400
1545 S. Western Ave. (15th St.), Chicago Heights, 708-481-5040
1002 Warren Ave. (Highland Ave.), Downers Grove, 630-810-0078
13001 W. 143rd St. (Bell Rd.), Homer Glen, 708-645-4400
18162 Harwood Ave. (183rd St.), Homewood, 708-798-8050
17 W. 711 Roosevelt Rd. (Summit Rd.), Oak Brook, 630-629-3200
6543 W. 127th St. (Ridgeland Ave.), Palos Heights, 708-389-5170
601 E. 170th St. (Cottage Grove Ave.), South Holland, 708-333-0310
15901 Oak Park Ave. (Rte. 6), Tinley Park, 708-429-4600

■ Pie-faces fawn over this chain of "family-favorite" suburban staples (especially the "flagship Homewood" location) and its "authentic Chicago-style pizza", praising everything from the "sweet", "tomatoey sauce" to the "thin-and-crispy crust" (its "Super Six [selection] is an institution"); so what if the "typical decor" is "nothing special"? – you can always "order for delivery."

Avenue Ale House ●S ▽ 15 | 18 | 15 | $21

825 S. Oak Park Ave. (bet. Harrison & Jackson Sts.), Oak Park, 708-848-2801

■ West Suburban sports fans give a "thumbs-up" to this "friendly neighborhood" "bar/restaurant" year-round – "in summer" they "like the rooftop cafe" with its "skyline views", "in winter it's a cozy spot for dinner" and anytime it's a "place to watch the game" or hear some "ok bands" while chowing down on a "good burger" or other "typical bar food" and chugging one of their 70-plus beers.

AVENUES S 25 | 26 | 25 | $70

Peninsula Chicago, 108 E. Superior St. (bet. Michigan Ave. & Rush St.), 312-573-6754

■ It's "high-end all the way" at this "perfect! perfect! perfect!" Peninsula hotel venue, a Near Norther with a New French–Med "seafood-intensive" menu compliments of chef de cuisine David Hayden; expect "mighty-fine fine dining" in a "posh, proper" and perhaps just a soupçon "snobby" setting (the "gold color scheme is apt" given the "top prices"), where an "outstanding" staff "gives it their all"; N.B. Sunday brunch is now served.

Azuré – | – | – | M

832 W. Randolph St. (Green St.), 312-455-1400
Set in the Market District's former Millennium Steaks & Chops space, this Cal-Ital concept offers prime cuts and

short ribs along with creative salads, pastas, and entrées amid toffee-and-orange decor featuring a two-story wine rack and walls of windows that open to an outdoor dining area; N.B. the first floor lounge serves lighter fare.

Babaluci Italian Eatery S 18 | 15 | 16 | $23
2152 N. Damen Ave. (Webster Ave.), 773-486-5300
1001 W. Golf Rd. (bet. Gannon Dr. & Higgins Rd.),
Hoffman Estates, 847-843-3663
■ City or suburb, this pair of Italian sisters is a "sure thing" for "big portions" of "great", "basic stuff to fill you up", all "at a decent price"; what's "fun" and "funky" for some might be "a little noisy" for others, but either way the "festive ambiance" is "good for large groups."

Bacchanalia S⌷ 22 | 15 | 22 | $27
2413 S. Oakley Ave. (bet. 24th & 25th Sts.), 773-254-6555
☑ "Thankfully un-trendy", this Heart of Italy "oldie but goodie" is a "traditional" "Italian neighborhood spot" where "garlic is king" and the "homestyle cooking" (such as "great chicken Vesuvio") is as "real" as the "generous" staff; there are a few complaints, however, about "tight quarters" that some say are "in need of updating" and a "cash-only" policy that credit-card carriers find "a pain."

Bacino's 17 | 12 | 14 | $17
2204 N. Lincoln Ave. (Webster Ave.), 773-472-7400 S
118 S. Clinton St. (Adams St.), 312-876-1188
Bacino's Trattoria S
1504 N. Naper Blvd. (Ogden Ave.), Naperville, 630-505-0600
Ravinia Plaza, 15256 S. La Grange Rd. (153rd St.), Orland Park,
708-403-3535
■ In the "best deep-dish" campaign of Chicago's pizza wars, allies admire this chain for "awesome stuffed" pies that are "really loaded", like the signature "healthy spinach option"; there's also "good" "cheesy" flat 'za and other "standard Italian fare", but "inconsistent service" and "modest surroundings" draw some barbs.

Bada Bing S – | – | – | M
1840 W. North Ave. (bet. Honore St. & Wolcott Ave.), 773-395-1000
Calzones, antipasti, meatball sandwiches and stuffed shells satiate the hungry patrons of this airy Wicker Park self-serve eatery; velvet curtains line the French doors that swing open to a sunny patio in finer weather, and a rooftop deck is promised for summer.

Bagel, The S ∇ 23 | 16 | 21 | $15
3107 N. Broadway St. (Belmont Ave.), 773-477-0300
Old Orchard Shopping Ctr., 50 Old Orchard Ctr. (Old Orchard Rd.),
Skokie, 847-677-0100
■ A taste of "New York in Lakeview" and the Northern Suburbs, these "traditional delis" – part of "a dying breed" –

"delight diners" with a "wide variety" of "some of the best Jewish food around" (including "good bagels" and "great matzo ball soup"); rapacious reviewers report that "huge servings" make it "the place to go for an eatfest."

Balagio — — — E
19917 S. LaGrange Rd. (Pleasant Hill Rd.), Frankfort, 815-469-2204 S
18042 Martin Ave. (Ridge Rd.), Homewood, 708-957-1650
"Sophisticated" for the Southwest Suburbs, these sister spots are "reliable dining choices" cradling "kitchens that produce consistently good-quality", "huge portions" of "great" Italian food, served in a "friendly" manner within "gorgeous" interiors featuring "beautiful frescoes."

Bandera S 19 | 18 | 18 | $26
535 N. Michigan Ave., 2nd fl. (bet. Grand Ave. & Ohio St.), 312-644-3524
■ The "great smell" of "excellent rotisserie chicken" draws "crowds" to this "consistent and comforting" Streeterville American offering Mag Mile views and "hearty, affordable" fare with "Southwest flair" (raves for the "great jalapeño cornbread"); daters dig the "cave-like", "sexy" atmosphere and nightly "live jazz", though certified city-dwellers suggest it's "a touch of the suburbs on Michigan Avenue."

Bangkok S ∇ 19 | 15 | 16 | $17
3542 N. Halsted St. (Addison St.), 773-327-2870
■ Partisans praise this "somewhat cramped" Wrigleyville "nook" known for its "good takeout" and "authentic" Siamese spices as "one of the more creative Thais in the city", but naysayers note "lots of competition" in the field and claim "there is better" to be found than its "predictable" entrées or "adequate all-you-can-eat [lunch] buffet"; still, most agree it "will do in a pinch."

Bank Lane Bistro ∇ 16 | 16 | 17 | $29
655 Bank Ln. (bet. Deer Path & Westminster Rds.), Lake Forest, 847-234-8802
■ This "pleasant" North Suburban boîte decorated with "imposing Parisian posters" strikes surveyors as a bit "erratic", with New American and French "bistro-type food" that's sometimes "satisfying" but sometimes not, service that swings from "good" to just "fair" and an interior that some find "romantic" but others call "uncomfortable."

Bar Louie ◑S 14 | 13 | 14 | $18
3545 N. Clark St. (Addison St.), 773-296-2500
1704 N. Damen Ave. (Wabansia St.), 773-645-7500
123 N. Halsted St. (Randolph St.), 312-207-0500
5500 S. Shore Dr. (55th St.), 773-363-5300
226 W. Chicago Ave. (Franklin St.), 312-337-3313
47 W. Polk St. (Dearborn St.), 312-347-0000

(continued)

Bar Louie

1321 W. Taylor St. (Loomis St.), 312-633-9393
1520 N. Sherman Ave. (Grove St.), Evanston, 847-733-8300
22 E. Chicago Ave. (Washington St.), Naperville, 630-983-1600
913 N. Milwaukee Ave. (Lake Cook Rd.), Wheeling, 847-279-1199

Louie on the Park ◑ⓈＳ

1816 N. Lincoln Ave. (Clark St.), 312-337-9800

◪ "Late-night" Louie lovers find "big fun" at the "many locations" of this "dependable chain" of "noisy", "upbeat" "hipster and yupster hangouts" and swear they're "not just for getting smashed" in, thanks to "above-average bar food"; others say they serve "middling pub grub", "forgot about service as they expanded" and are "too smoky"; N.B. the Hyde Park location opened post-*Survey*.

Barn of Barrington Ｓ | 16 | 19 | 17 | $32 |

1415 S. Barrington Rd. (¼ mi. north of Dundee Rd.), Barrington, 847-381-8585

◪ Its "memorable setting" is the main draw of this "dated" Northwest "Suburban eatery" in a "pretty" "antique-filled barn", not its "sometimes disappointing service" or menu of "good" but "uninspired" Traditional American dishes; still, "blue hairs" and spring chickens alike "go for the Sunday champagne brunch", one reason this "landmark" has "staying power."

BARRINGTON | 24 | 21 | 22 | $36 |
COUNTRY BISTRO Ｓ

Foundry Shopping Ctr., 700 W. Northwest Hwy. (Hart Rd.), Barrington, 847-842-1300

■ "Inventive" and "unfailingly excellent", this "great French bistro" in a "relaxing country setting" is "worth a drive" to the Northwest Suburbs for its "delicious" and "authentic" food, including "delightful rabbit and osso buco"; "owners Jean-Pierre and Denise [Leroux] make it feel like home", and the "first-rate" "waiters' knowledge" about the "extensive wine list" is an added "thrill."

Barro Cantina Ｓ | – | – | – | M |

163 W. North Ave. (Wells St.), 312-266-2484

Set in the former Trattoria Dinotto space in Old Town, this welcoming cantina serves Nuevo Latino tapas and a smattering of entrée-sized dishes (including various ceviche, chili and empanadas); the intimate space is warmed by sunny yellow walls, bright artwork and terra cotta plates on white paper-covered tables; tipples range from South American wines to Latin cocktails.

Basta Pasta Ｓ | 18 | 16 | 18 | $25 |

6733 N. Olmsted Ave. (Northwest Hwy.), 773-763-0667

◪ "Don't eat for two days before" a visit to this "lively", "high-decibel" Edison Park "neighborhood spot" "where the fun" and "good Southern Italian food" "come in troughs", the "friendly" staff really "works hard" and "the price is right"; it's a place "for eaters, not nitpicky diners" of the sort who might snort 'basta!' about such "basic" fare and "nothing-fancy" ambiance.

BD's Mongolian Barbeque 🅂   15 | 13 | 15 | $17

3330 N. Clark St. (bet. Belmont Ave. & Roscoe St.), 773-325-2300
221 S. Washington St. (Jefferson Ave.), Naperville, 630-428-0300
445 E. Townline Rd. (Milwaukee Ave.), Vernon Hills,
847-247-9600
■ "Design your own dinner" at this "festive" stir-fry smorgasbord in Wrigleyville, where you "choose your own ingredients" from "many options" then hand them off to a "stand-up comedian cook" who sets them a-sizzling on the "communal wok"; the servers may be "inexperienced", but "they want you to have fun" – and "kids love it"; N.B. the West and Northwest Suburban branches are unrated.

BeccoD'Oro 🅂   21 | 20 | 20 | $41

Radisson Hotel & Suites, 160 E. Huron St. (St. Clair St.),
312-787-1300
Northbrook Court Mall, 2124 Northbrook Ct. (Red Oak Ln.),
Northbrook, 847-272-9003
■ Fans of this "distinctive" Streeterville Italian in the Radisson Hotel & Suites say it's "better than its more pretentious competitors" thanks to a "talented" and "accommodating chef" who turns out "superior pasta" and other "imaginative" fare; a "refined" interior and "great service" make for "an exceptional experience" that should "impress the most demanding clients"; N.B. the Suburban North branch opened post-*Survey*.

bella! Bacino's 🅂   – | – | – | M

75 E. Wacker Dr. (Michigan Ave.), 312-263-2350
36 S. La Grange Rd. (Harris Ave.), La Grange, 708-352-8882
More bella than ever since the Bacino's folks renovated and upgraded their Loop and Suburban West locations, these comfy, rustic Italians cover the antipasti, insalata, pizza and panini menu categories, plus a handful of pasta offerings and entrées (naturally, die-hards can still get the signature stuffed spinach 'za, too), all paired with a value-priced wine list and full bar service.

Bella Notte 🅂   21 | 16 | 19 | $27

1372 W. Grand Ave. (Noble St.), 312-733-5136
■ There's "always a doggy bag" after a visit to this "old-style" Near West "gem" with "reliable service" and a "*Sopranos*-like supper-club" feel; "gargantuan portions" of "can't-lose specials" and other "consistently good", "straight-on" Southern Italian selections made with "fresh, flavorful and tasty ingredients" draw raves, despite the "cramped dining room."

Benihana of Tokyo 🅂
18 | 17 | 20 | $31

*Fitzpatrick Hotel, 166 E. Superior St. (Michigan Ave.),
312-664-9643*
*747 E. Butterfield Rd. (bet. Highland Ave. & Meyers Rd.),
Lombard, 630-571-4440*
1200 E. Higgins Rd. (Meacham Rd.), Schaumburg, 847-995-8201
150 N. Milwaukee Ave. (Dundee Rd.), Wheeling, 847-465-6021

◪ Go for "dinner and a show" to this Japanese teppanyaki chain known for "communal tables", a "convivial" vibe and "great antics" from "tableside chefs" who "cook to entertain"; though the "theme-park" concept may be "a bit hackneyed", locals say it's "not just for tourists" but "for groups" or a "family night out"; the downside: expect to "leave smelling like stir-fry."

Ben Pao 🅂
20 | 23 | 20 | $28

52 W. Illinois St. (Dearborn St.), 312-222-1888

◪ Lettuce Entertain You's River North outpost for lotus-eaters draws a "Ben wow!" for "sinfully sensual decor" and a "unique", "chic Chinese" menu that's "not authentic but awesome" nonetheless; fans give a "pow!" to the "terrific" black-pepper scallops, "fabulous cherry bomb shrimp", "peppy staff" and "cool cocktails", even if the disappointed denounce the place as "gimmicky" and "uneven."

BERGHOFF, THE
19 | 19 | 19 | $22

O'Hare Int'l Airport, Concourse C (I-90), 773-601-9180 🅂
17 W. Adams St. (bet. Dearborn & State Sts.), 312-427-3170

■ "Great Wiener schnitzel" scarfers are "always looking for an excuse to go to this "indestructible" Loop "landmark", a "sentimental favorite" for "solid German" fare and house-brewed beer served amid "old-world" "wood-paneled glory"; regulars report that "half the fun" is the "consistently surly" "100-year-old waiters" ("you can't get any more Chicago"); N.B. the O'Hare outpost has a lighter cafe menu.

Best Hunan 🅂
17 | 14 | 18 | $20

*Hawthorn Fashion Sq., 700 N. Milwaukee Ave. (Rte. 60),
Vernon Hills, 847-680-8855*

■ "Despite the strip-mall feel", this "traditional Chinese" in the Northwest Suburbs has some surveyors swearing it's still aptly named, with "good", "fresh, reliable" fare such as "spicy crispy chicken" and a staff that "treats you like family"; another bonus: you "can get Peking duck without ordering in advance."

Bêtise, A Bistro on the Lake 🅂
19 | 21 | 20 | $33

*Plaza del Lago, 1515 Sheridan Rd. (Lake Ave.), Wilmette,
847-853-1711*

◪ Bistro-goers battle it out over this informal French "serving a North Shore clientele" in the Plaza del Lago shopping center near, though *not* on, Lake Michigan; pros praise the "warm" and "charming" decor, "considerate service", "reliable entrées" and "specials [that] are really special"; nevertheless, cantankerous cons cavil that it's "somewhat pricey", "predictable" and "pedestrian."

Biaggio's 🅂   20 | 18 | 18 | $30
28 S. Orland Square Dr. (bet. La Grange Rd. & 149th St.), Orland Park, 708-460-9600
10296 S. 78th Ave. (west of Harlem Ave.), Palos Hills, 708-237-1050
■ The "chef is not afraid of garlic" at this South Suburban Italian offering "high quality standards" and "obliging" service in a "homey" setting; pugilism proponents are pleased to report having "met Muhammad Ali while dining on linguine" – which is no tall tale since The Champ's "charming daughter" Rasheda Ali-Walsh is co-owner; N.B. the Southwest Suburban location opened post-*Survey*.

Bice Grill 🅂   18 | 18 | 18 | $28
158 E. Ontario St. (bet. Michigan Ave. & St. Clair St.), 312-664-1474
■ "If you can't afford Bice, try the next best" thing advise Grill-goers who groove on the "good, solid" and "price-worthy" fare at this Streeterville Northern Italian "adjacent" to its "big brother"; it's a "good spot for a casual", "light dinner" and "great for local workers" in search of a "quick", albeit "crowded, lunch."

Bice Ristorante 🅂   20 | 20 | 19 | $39
158 E. Ontario St. (bet. Michigan Ave. & St. Clair St.), 312-664-1474
☑ Taken "all together", the "friendly staffers", "trendy" "Eurotrash clientele", "mouthwatering menu" and "great wine selection" at this Streeterville Northern Italian (offspring of a prolific Milanese mamma) make for what most call a "satisfying" experience; "many tempting choices" are served in a setting of "considerable style", though some still say this "sophisticated" spot is "not worth the high tariff" and "falls short of its pretense."

Big Bowl 🅂   18 | 17 | 17 | $20
6 E. Cedar St. (State St.), 312-640-8888
60 E. Ohio St. (Rush St.), 312-951-1888
215 Parkway Dr. (Deerfield Rd.), Lincolnshire, 847-808-8880
1950 E. Higgins Rd. (Rte. 53), Schaumburg, 847-517-8881
☑ Bowled-over boosters declare "the bowl is, in fact, big", as are the "big food and big fun", at this "Americanized" Asian chain of "always lively" "fast-food heavens"; the "noodles are great" and you can "get things the way you want them" at the stir-fry bars, but bummed bowlers say they strike out with "dependable but uninspired" fare.

Biggs Steakhouse & Wine Cellar 🅂   – | – | – | E
1150 N. Dearborn St. (bet. Division & Elm Sts.), 312-787-0900
Set in a fireplace-filled Gold Coast landmark mansion that once hosted the '70s French venue Biggs, this elegant

entry has kept its predecessor's name but been reborn as a refined, contemporary steakhouse overseen by chef Frederic Boyer (ex The Pump Room); in addition to installing hardwood floors and repainting the interior, the new owners have created an exposed-brick, cellar-level wine bar (with a grazing menu and no by-the-glass markup).

Bijan's Bistro ●🅢　　　－｜－｜－｜M

663 N. State St. (Erie St.), 312-202-1904

River North's casual American bistro and late-night mainstay went away for a while, but it's back in its former location (in a new building), sporting a spiffed up decor of dark wood, concrete flooring, accents of copper tile and vintage-inspired light fixtures; the prices, however, are decidedly retro (entrées average under $15); N.B. plans are underway for brunch, outdoor dining and a coveted 4:00 AM liquor license (for now, the bar closes at 2:00 AM).

Billy Goat Tavern　　14｜11｜13｜$10

Navy Pier, 600 E. Grand Ave. (Illinois St.), 312-670-8789 🅢
3516 N. Clark St. (Addison St.), 773-327-4361 🅢⇸
430 N. Michigan Ave. (Wacker Dr.), 312-222-1525 ●🅢⇸
O'Hare Field Terminal 1, Concourse C, Gate 18 (I-90), 773-462-9368 🅢
330 S. Wells St. (Van Buren St.), 312-554-0297 ⇸
1535 W. Madison St. (Ogden Ave.), 312-733-9132 🅢⇸
309 W. Washington Blvd. (Franklin St.), 312-899-1873 ⇸

■ The Goats are multiplying thanks to the success of the "under-the-city" original on lower Michigan, "a Chicago icon ('nuff said)" whose gruff staffers were the inspiration for *SNL*'s famed "cheezborger, cheezborger, cheezborger" skit; "bring antacid" for the "cheap hangover food" at this "real guys' place" where "lack of decor *is* the decor."

Bin 36 🅢　　　21｜21｜19｜$38

339 N. Dearborn St. (bet. Kinzie St. & Wacker Dr.), 312-755-9463 ●
275 Parkway Dr. (Aptakisic Rd.), Lincolnshire, 847-808-9463

◪ Oenophiles enjoy this "hopping" River North "shrine to wine" where "fanciful, flirtatious" flights flank "swank" New American dishes on an "awesome tasting menu"; the "airy, bright" space is "hip without the gotta-wear-black attitude", and the "knowledgeable" staff "guides without pushing"; still, some are sour on the "stark" decor and "deafening din"; N.B. the Food rating may not reflect a mid-*Survey* chef change, and the Suburban North branch opened post-*Survey*.

Bistro Banlieue 🅢　　24｜22｜23｜$36

44 Yorktown Convenience Ctr. (bet. Butterfield Rd. & Highland Ave.), Lombard, 630-629-6560

■ "A hint of Paris in the [Western] Suburbs", this French "bistro *magnifique*" offers "comforting food" "bountifully plated with taste to match"; the "understated" digs are "cozy", even if some consider the "strip-mall location" "bizarre", and the "accommodating" staff provides "super service"; P.S. calorie- or cost-conscious customers will appreciate that they "offer entrées in two sizes."

Bistro Campagne 🅂   –|–|–| M
4518 N. Lincoln Ave. (bet. Sunnyside & Wilson Aves.), 773-271-6100
Chef-owner Michael Altenberg (Campagnola) brings classic bistro fare to the burgeoning Lincoln Square scene; design details left over from its predecessor, the former Villa Kula, include etched leaded glass, elaborate mosaics and murals and a recessed bronze ceiling over the dark-wood bar, plus the pleasant garden.

Bistro Marbuzet 🅂   23|21|19|$38
7600 W. Madison St. (Des Plaines Ave.), Forest Park, 708-366-9090
■ The "West Suburban crowd" savors a "taste of the city" at Jack Jones' "elegant French" and New American bistro, an "unexpected find for Forest Park" where "healthy portions" of "innovative, delicious food" get "stylish presentations" in a "lovely setting"; even those who say the "unpolished" "service needs to catch up" to the clever cuisine concede it's unquestionably "friendly."

Bistro 110 🅂   21|20|19|$35
110 E. Pearson St. (bet. Michigan Ave. & Rush St.), 312-266-3110
■ There's an air of "joie de vivre" at this "bustling" Near North bistro that's "very French in a very American (friendly) way"; "known for wood-roasted dishes" and "awesome garlic", it's "always a safe bet" in a "great location for shoppers" just "off the Mag Mile", even if some respondents reckon it's "past its prime"; P.S. the "Sunday jazz brunch" is a "favorite."

BISTROT MARGOT 🅂   21|20|20|$35
1437 N. Wells St. (Schiller St.), 312-587-3660
■ A "bit of Paris" in Old Town, this "romantic", "bustling bistro" is the "*parfait*" place for "a good honest meal" of "authentic" French fare with "suave service"; in fact, some supporters who're "sorry it's been discovered" by the "lively" "crowds" choose to forgo its "cramped" interior – "like dining in a phone booth with 50 of your closest friends" – in favor of its sidewalk cafe.

Bistrot Zinc 🅂   19|20|19|$31
1131 N. State St. (bet. Cedar & Elm Sts.), 312-337-1131
■ Now soloing since its Southport sibling's shuttering, this "solid" State Street staple with a "genuine" French bistro feel is prized for its "always-charming" atmosphere, as well

as "traditional and consistent fare" like "wonderful *poulet grand-mère*"; it'll "tide you over 'til your next trip to Europe", and it's also "reasonably priced for the Gold Coast."

Bistro Ultra S | 20 | 17 | 20 | $30
2239 N. Clybourn Ave. (Webster Ave.), 773-529-3300
▰ A "happy find" "hidden" in the Clybourn corridor, this "intimate" bistro beckons with "personable service", a "diverse wine list" and chef Juan Hurtado's "consistently good" (if "limited") menu of French fare at "fair prices"; though many applaud it for "avoiding getting sucked into trendiness", skeptics are "not sure what the fuss is about" and say there's "nothing distinctive" about its "small space."

Bite ●S | ▽ 18 | 12 | 13 | $14
1039 N. Western Ave. (Cortez St.), 773-395-2483
■ "Great for a cheap date", this "hip" Ukrainian Village Eclectic "with a funky beat" plates "unpretentious" eats that are "a cut above fast food"; still, some slam the "spotty service" and say the decor "could use a bump", since a "high number of body piercings per server" isn't everyone's idea of ambiance; P.S. it's "BYO, baby!"

BJ's Market & Bakery S | ▽ 22 | 12 | 19 | $13
8734 S. Stony Island Ave. (87th St.), 773-374-4700
■ Dixie devotees declare that you should "forget your diet and go" for "tasty" "home cooking" served "cafeteria-style" "from the Southern kitchen" of this soulful Far South Sider, favored more for its "small prices" and "the most heavenly, awe-inspiring piece of catfish you'll ever eat" than the "nothing-fancy" decor.

BLACKBIRD | 25 | 19 | 23 | $48
619 W. Randolph St. (bet. Desplaines & Jefferson Sts.), 312-715-0708
■ "Wear black" within the "white surroundings" of this "see-and-be-scene" West Loop New American where "brilliant" chef Paul Kahan employs French influences to take you on "a wonderful journey of amazing flavors" and "knowledgeable" servers "match the food" with "great wine selections"; "go with people you like", though, "because you'll be squeezed in tight" in a "minimalist" room that strikes some as "elegantly stark", others as "antiseptic."

Black Duck Tavern & Grille S | 14 | 16 | 14 | $26
1800 N. Halsted St. (Willow St.), 312-664-1801
▰ Some say this Lincoln Park American is "more of a bar than a restaurant" thanks to "crowds" of "singles" in search of "eye candy", while others opine it's "becoming a real neighborhood place" and a "nice" "post-Steppenwolf spot"; either way, most agree the "fair-to-good food" from a "menu that's going in too many directions" "could be better" and "is secondary to the scene."

Blind Faith Café Ⓢ
18 | 13 | 16 | $17

525 Dempster St. (Chicago Ave.), Evanston, 847-328-6875
☒ Evanston's "veggie heaven" is "true to the faith", luring "a beautiful following" of "dedicated vegetarians" and "people with special dietary needs" with "innovative", "eclectic" fare that converts claim "even meat lovers will love"; still, a few heretics harrumph that the "homey" environment is a bit "bare-bones" and the "sincere", "groovy crew" is sometimes "spacey."

Blue Bayou Ⓢ
– – – M

3734 N. Southport Ave. (bet. Grace St. & Waveland Ave.), 773-871-3300
Parisian chandeliers from the '20s hang from the high pressed-tin ceiling and French quarter memorabilia crams the walls of this Lakeview New Orleans–style bar and grill; look for a lengthy menu of moderately priced Cajun-Creole faves and a cozy upstairs bar, paneled in antique wood (from an old barn) and featuring French doors opening onto a balcony, à la Bourbon Street.

Bluefin
▽ 19 | 14 | 18 | $29

1952 W. North Ave. (Milwaukee Ave.), 773-394-7373
☒ Schools of thought swim separately on whether the "creative preparations" from the "mainly sushi menu" at this Bucktown Japanese are "artistic" or "strange, but they work" fans say, thanks to fin fare so "amazingly fresh" it's "still gasping"; critics carp that the servers are "nice" but "forgetful" and claim the room "looks like a warehouse."

Blue Line Club Car
– – – I

1548 N. Damen Ave. (bet. North & Pierce Aves.), 773-395-3700
Under the rattling El, at the bustling six-way intersection that defines Wicker Park, this sleek, dimly lit refuge features martinis, burgers and other all-American entrées at low prices; leather booths, metal trim, club-car curtains and retro light fixtures add to the railroad-car feel.

Bluepoint Oyster Bar ⓈS
19 | 18 | 18 | $37

741 W. Randolph St. (Halsted St.), 312-207-1222
☒ Despite its location "in landlocked Chicago", this Market District shellfish haven has a "great variety" of "expensive-but-worth-it oysters and clams", "huge shrimp and crab legs" and other "good seafood"; the "dark", "cozy" room is "classy and relaxing" to some seafarers, though others warn it's "not for a quiet night"; P.S. landlubbers who detest the denizens of the deep may dig the "excellent steaks."

BOB CHINN'S CRAB HOUSE ⓈS
21 | 13 | 18 | $33

315 N. LaSalle Dr. (Wacker Dr.), 312-822-0100
393 S. Milwaukee Ave. (Dundee Rd.), Wheeling, 847-520-3633
☒ If you're "in the mood for raucousness" and "awesome" seafood, "join the herd" of Northwest "Suburbanites" and

"tourists" who "stampede" this "big, noisy barn" seating 650; though the "good mai tais" "help with the wait", many "don't care for being" "shuffled, seated, served and shown the door" and wonder "why the crowds" "line up"; N.B. the River North outpost opened post-*Survey*.

Bob San ●S · 23 · 20 · 20 · $34

1805 W. Division St. (Wood St.), 773-235-8888

■ Specializing in "top-notch, fresh sushi" that's "some of the best in the city", this Wicker Park "hipster" hawks "delicious" "Japanese cuisine matched" with a "fantastic wine list"; restaurateur Bob Bee, "the owner, makes you feel at home", and his "friendly" staff provides "fast service" in a "funky" setting with a "great vibe"; P.S. it's "open late."

Bogart's Charhouse S · 15 · 15 · 14 · $27

18225 Dixie Hwy. (183rd St.), Homewood, 708-798-2000
17344 Oak Park Ave. (171st St.), Tinley Park, 708-532-5592

◪ South and Southwest Suburban boosters of these "decent family steakhouses" with a "catchy name" and "semblances of Bogie" throughout say "get there early" to avoid "long waits" for a "real deal" on slabs so "huge" they're practically a "side of beef"; the "disappointed" are "at a loss to understand their popularity", humphing that this is not the beginning of a beautiful friendship.

Bone Daddy ●S · 16 · 13 · 16 · $20

551 N. Ogden Ave. (Grand Ave.), 312-226-6666

◪ Expect "smoky ribs and a smoky bar" at this Near West Twisted Spoke spin-off that fans call the "daddy of all comfort-food spots" for its "tasty dry-rub" varieties ("not the 'fall-off-the-bone' type") and "good pulled-pork BBQ" at "bargain" prices; those who "expected more" declare the "unimaginative food" "just ok" and add "once was enough."

Bongo Room S · 23 · 18 · 17 · $16

1470 N. Milwaukee Ave. (Honore St.), 773-489-0690

■ Surveyors serve up a staggering stack of superlatives for the "delicious" "gourmet pancakes" and "unique omelets" at this "breakfast favorite", an "inventive yet consistent" Wicker Park American that's "so good it should be cloned"; there's "always" a "trendy crowd" hanging around "for a seat" in the "hip, flaky" space, so "be prepared to wait and wait" ("it's worth it"); N.B. the kitchen closes at 2:30 PM.

Boston Blackie's · 19 · 13 · 17 · $17

164 E. Grand Ave. (St. Clair St.), 312-938-8700 S
120 S. Riverside Plaza (bet. Adams & Monroe Sts.), 312-382-0700
405 Lake Cook Rd. (Waukegan Rd.), Deerfield, 847-418-3400 S
Hubbard Woods Plaza, 73 Green Bay Rd. (Scott St.),
Glencoe, 847-242-9400 S

◪ Many folks' "burger of choice" graces the grills of this Streeterville "hamburger saloon" and its three younger brothers, all of whom "do well at what they set out to do" – serve "bar food with class", such as "tender chicken sandwiches" and "good salads", at "cheap prices"; still, some say they "lack atmosphere", especially the original Grand Avenue outpost with its "depressing" "'70s" decor.

Boulevard Café 🄢   – | – | – | M
3137 W. Logan Blvd. (Milwaukee Ave.), 773-384-8600
Logan Square has embraced this comfy American cafe done in warm earth tones with plush horseshoe booths; fare includes artichoke ravioli, chicken pot pie and apple strudel, and a late menu is served until 2:00 AM – a boost for fans of the live entertainment most nights (including a Grateful Dead jam on Sundays).

BRASSERIE JO 🄢   21 | 21 | 20 | $35
59 W. Hubbard St. (bet. Clark & Dearborn Sts.), 312-595-0800
☑ "All you need is the Eiffel Tower" to complete the "authentic Parisian experience" at this "true brasserie" in River North, where there's "always an 'up' feeling"; "legendary chef" Jean Joho fashions "French comfort food" with an "Alsatian influence, something different from the standard", though curmudgeons claim it's "not as special as Jo thinks"; still, many midday *mangeurs* are "sorry they've closed for lunch."

Breakfast Club, The 🄢⊘   20 | 13 | 17 | $13
1381 W. Hubbard St. (Noble St.), 312-666-3166
■ Join the clubbers who "crawl out of bed and go" to this Near West "neighborhood treasure" in a "crowded" but "cute pink cottage" for "good, honest" "Traditional [American] breakfast food" "and plenty of it", such as "wonderful French toast" and "great omelets"; factor in "friendly", "fast-paced" service and it's definitely "worth the hunt"; N.B. there's lunch too, but no dinner.

Brett's Café Americain 🄢   20 | 16 | 19 | $26
2011 W. Roscoe St. (Damen Ave.), 773-248-0999
☑ When not in the kitchen crafting "elevated comfort food", chef-owner Brett Knobel might be found "chatting with customers" at this "eclectic" New American in Roscoe Village; supporters savor her "elegant twist on brunch" and "heavenly baked goods", saying this "fine" "sleeper" "should be busier" despite decor that's a trifle "tired" and service that seesaws between "amiable" and "brusque."

Bricks 🄢   19 | 14 | 18 | $17
1909 N. Lincoln Ave. (Wisconsin St.), 312-255-0851
■ The "awesome", "creative" thin-crust pizza with "gourmet ingredients" (like "good BBQ chicken" and "pureed artichoke sauce") "melts in your mouth" at this "small, dark" "subterranean gem" in Lincoln Park, where

"accommodating service" means "crowded" can be "fun"; P.S. the "young crowd loves it" and dubs it "da bomb."

Bruna's Ristorante S   21 15 19 $26
2424 S. Oakley Ave. (24th Pl.), 773-254-5550
■ "*Buono, buono, buono!*" shout supporters of the "simply prepared" "classic Italian dishes" at this "charming" "family-run" Heart of Italy "neighborhood standby" that makes "you feel like an old friend"; though some say the "homey" interior "needs a face-lift", regulars "love" that this "blast from the past" "hasn't changed in years."

Bubba Gump Shrimp Co. S   13 14 15 $23
Navy Pier, 700 E. Grand Ave. (Lake Shore Dr.), 312-252-4867
◪ Aptly "located at Navy Pier", this "kid-friendly" *Gump*-themed seafooder serves up "lots of fried stuff" in a "cute" nautical room or "outdoor dining" space that's "fun" for "people-watching"; but grumps who grumble the "concept is lame" feel "Forrest would frown" at this "tourist trap's" "chain food, chain ambiance" and "gimmicky service."

Buca di Beppo S   16 19 18 $23
2941 N. Clark St. (bet. Oakdale & Wellington Aves.), 773-348-7673
521 Rush St. (Grand Ave.), 312-396-0001
90 Yorktown Shopping Ctr. (bet. Butterfield Rd. & Highland Ave.), Lombard, 630-932-7673
15350 S. 94th Ave. (159th St.), Orland Park, 708-349-6542
604 N. Milwaukee Ave. (Lake Cook Rd.), Wheeling, 847-808-9898
◪ "Come hungry and expect noise" at these "crazy, cozy, kitschy" and "crowded" chain outposts where the "campy" "conglomerations of memorabilia" look "like an Italian grandmother's house exploded"; portions are so "huge" "you could open a shelter" with the leftovers, but purists posit that quantity and "lots of garlic" can't compensate for "unimaginative", "blah" dishes; N.B. the Near North branch opened post-*Survey.*

Buona Terra Ristorante S   – – – M
2535 N. California Ave. (Logan Blvd.), 773-289-3800
Exposed brick and murals of the Tuscan countryside lend a cozy air to this reasonably priced Logan Square trattoria, which offers simple, earthy Italian fare and a fine view of the changing neighborhood's comings and goings.

BUtterfield 8 ●   – – – E
713 N. Wells St. (Superior St.), 312-327-0940
Restaurateur Demetri Alexander star-69s that classic Liz-Taylor-as-classy-call-girl flick with this River North reinvention of his former Lola's space (with Savarin sandwiched briefly between); the glam factor runs high (lit Plexiglas floor, white leather and butter-yellow velvet

appointments), and the cuisine harks back to haute American fare of yore (chilled tomato juice, turtle soup, beef Wellington, chicken Kiev) accompanied by cocktails coyly called 'Pillow Talk' and 'Hollywood Swinger.'

Cab's Wine Bar Bistro S ▽ 20 20 21 $35
430 N. Main St. (Duane St.), Glen Ellyn, 630-942-9463
■ Life is a Cabernet at this "romantic" "class act" in the Western Suburbs, a "pleasant place" where it's "great to try a flight" from the "excellent [Cab-focused] wine list" thanks to "knowledgeable servers" whose "good recommendations" will help you "pair" "sophisticated selections" with "interesting choices" from its "consistently good" New American menu; all in all, it's "a lucky find that you'll want to share with friends."

Café Absinthe S 24 21 21 $40
1954 W. North Ave. (Damen Ave.), 773-278-4488
■ Bucktown's "favorite" "hidden gem" is "still hip", but "at least you can get in now" ("if you can find the door", that is) to savor the "fresh take on interesting ingredients" of its "consistently creative" "but not too froufrou" seasonally changing New American menu; conversationalists comment that it can be "noisy", but canoodling "couples" covet the "clandestine" quality of its "intimate, dark" digs.

Cafe Ba-Ba-Reeba! S 20 20 18 $27
2024 N. Halsted St. (bet. Armitage & Fullerton Aves.), 773-935-5000
☑ There's "something on the menu for everyone" at Lincoln Park's "tasty" tapas "pioneer", a Lettuce Entertain You Spanish "favorite" that's remained "a constant over the years" as a "fun place" to visit "with friends" or "a date" (as long as you don't mind "long waits" and "little elbow room"); still, the jaded jab it's "lost steam" to the competition.

Café Bernard S 20 17 19 $32
2100 N. Halsted St. (Dickens Ave.), 773-871-2100
■ "One of the oldest" in town, this "humble", "homey" bistro on a "quiet little corner" in Lincoln Park may still be "unknown" to some, "but it's not unloved" by the "habitués" who haunt it; owner "Bernard [LeCoq] cares about every plate" of "classic", "reasonably priced" French fare "going out of" his "consistent" kitchen, though some wish he'd concern himself with the "quaint", somewhat "tired" decor.

Cafe Bolero S ▽ 19 14 17 $21
2252 N. Western Ave. (south of Fullerton Ave.), 773-227-9000
■ For "easy Cuban eating" (a cuisine "not readily found in Chicago"), this "lively" Bucktown "neighborhood spot" run by "friendly owners" is "exceptionally good", including "tropical" "favorites" like "fantastic ceviche"; you get "so much for so little" that "a meal can be had on appetizers

alone", and this place was serving "mojitos long before they became drink of the year."

Cafe Borgia S — | — | — | M
17923 Torrence Ave. (179th St.), Lansing, 708-474-5515
South Suburban Lansing's long-lived Italian cafe is revered for its attentive service, reasonable prices and robust, authentic food (such as roast lamb shank, polenta torte with goat cheese, and penne with porcini cream sauce); the intimate space with open kitchen and colorful artwork expands to a seasonal patio; N.B. reservations are for large parties only, and bar offerings are limited to beer and wine.

Cafe Central S 21 | 18 | 21 | $32
455 Central Ave. (Green Bay Rd.), Highland Park, 847-266-7878
■ This "lovely, casual" "little sister" of the "famous Carlos'" is a North Suburban natural for "huge plates" of "hearty", "dependable bistro food" that's "well worth trying" and "reasonably priced"; "hands-on owners" "Carlos and Debbie [Nieto] consistently" ensure a "good experience" within a "charming" "Parisian interior" that's "comfortable" to some, a bit "cramped" to others; P.S. save room for the "excellent desserts."

Café des Architectes S — | — | — | E
Sofitel Chicago Water Tower, 20 E. Chestnut St. (Wabash Ave.), 312-324-4000
Gallic touches, modern French furniture and nods to Chicago's architectural legacy abound at the stylish, light-filled lobby cafe of the Gold Coast's striking new prism-shaped Sofitel Hotel; a thoughtful Franco-American wine list complements the upscale French-Med menu.

CAFÉ IBERICO ●S 22 | 17 | 17 | $23
739 N. La Salle Blvd. (bet. Chicago Ave. & Superior St.), 312-573-1510
■ Regulars report this "hopping" "hangout" in River North is "jammed solid for a reason" – namely, "delicious Spanish tapas" "as they were meant to be", except perhaps for the "large portions" ("no tiny ones here!") at "reasonable prices" that make for "good value"; the "to-die-for sangria" makes the "long waits" "worth it", but the "great energy" generated by the "pulsing crowd" can be "ear-splitting."

Café La Cave S 22 | 23 | 22 | $43
2777 Mannheim Rd. (bet. Higgins Rd. & Touhy Ave.), Des Plaines, 847-827-7818
■ "Fall in love" at this "old-line Continental" O'Hare-area "expense-accounter" that "still has class" and "deserves its good reputation"; whether you "dine in the cave" (a "romantic simulated" grotto) or formal dining room (a "great throwback" to a more "elegant" time), you'll find tables

"well spaced" "for a proposal", "social dinner or client" tête-à-tête and "rich cuisine" like "excellent Dover sole" and "must-have bananas Foster."

Café Le Loup [S] ▽ 18 | 14 | 17 | $26

3348 N. Sheffield Ave. (bet. Belmont Ave. & Roscoe St.), 773-248-1830

◪ Windy Cityites wolf down "good bistro fare" at this "family-run" Lakeview "casual French" whose "small", "quirky", "cozy quarters" feature lupine "prints" and posters; while all agree it's "economical", hecklers howl about "uninspiring food", "enthusiastic but eccentric service" and a "so-so inside" area, preferring the "great patio that's heated in winter."

Café Luciano [S] 19 | 19 | 20 | $28

871 N. Rush St. (Chestnut St.), 312-266-1414
2676 Green Bay Rd. (bet. Central Ave. & Isabella St.), Evanston, 847-864-6060

◪ "Solid Italian comfort food" is the draw at this duo of "intimate cafes", "favorites with locals" who call them "dependable" for "consistent quality", "friendly service" and "comfortable" environs; the "unimpressed", though, find the "not-very-inventive menu" a bit "old-fashioned" and "ordinary"; P.S. speaking of "pedestrian", the Gold Coast branch's sidewalk seating affords "great people-watching."

Cafe Matou [S] 23 | 20 | 22 | $36

1846 N. Milwaukee Ave. (bet. Armitage & North Aves.), 773-384-8911

■ "Serene and satisfying", this "under-appreciated" bistro "sleeper" on the fringe of Bucktown is "wonderful by all available standards", offering an "adventurous menu" of "French food well prepared" by chef Charlie Socher, an "excellent wine list" and "outstanding service" in a "modern yet charming" space; its "low profile" and "secluded" location help it "keep a good clientele."

Cafe Nordstrom [S] 19 | 17 | 17 | $15

Nordstrom, 55 E. Grand Ave. (Michigan Ave.), 312-464-1515
10 Oakbrook Ctr. (bet. Butterfield & Spring Rds.), Oak Brook, 630-571-2121
Woodfield Shopping Ctr., 6 Woodfield Shopping Ctr. (bet. Higgins Rd. & Rte. 53), Schaumburg, 847-605-2121
Old Orchard Ctr., 77 Old Orchard Shopping Ctr. (bet. Golf Rd. & Skokie Blvd.), Skokie, 847-677-2121

■ "Get stoked to go shopping" at these "classy" yet "casual" cafes that are "fun on the run" and "a welcome relief from bad mall food", offering up a "fast and healthy" assortment of Eclectic "pick-me-up" fare with "great children's selections"; not only are these "shoppers' heavens" "perfect for a mother and daughter after a huge spree", but "guys like them" too.

Cafe Pyrenees
23 | 18 | 23 | $37

River Tree Court Mall, Rte. 60 & Milwaukee Ave. (Rte. 21), Vernon Hills, 847-918-8850

■ "Don't tell" Downtown dwellers about this "culinary treasure in a strip mall" say selfish West Suburbanites who call this "classic French" bistro "a real find" for its "artfully prepared" fare ("every meal is excellent"); despite their best efforts, savvy city surveyors have discovered that its "delicious food" and "gracious" service more than make up for its "unlikely setting."

Cafe Selmarie S
19 | 15 | 17 | $18

4729 N. Lincoln Ave. (bet. Giddings St. & Western Ave.), 773-989-5595

◪ "Is it a great bakery that serves" "good food", or is it a "good" New American "restaurant with a great bakery attached"? query quibblers confused by this "quaint" Lincoln Square "dessert mecca"; still, with goodies "worthy of a trip to the gym", sweet-toothed surveyors suggest you "decide for yourself"; P.S. it's also a "nice place" to "meet a friend for lunch" or a "yummy Sunday brunch."

CAFÉ SPIAGGIA S
24 | 24 | 23 | $39

980 N. Michigan Ave., 2nd fl. (Oak St.), 312-280-2750

■ Not only is this "high-style" Mag Mile Italian eatery "terrific" for a shopping break, respondents report it's also "more fun" and "personal" than its "serious big brother, Spiaggia", offering the same chef (though a "different menu") "and same view for less money"; Tony Mantuano's "top-notch" food is "beautifully presented", and the "attentive servers" provide "great service" within an "elegant", "conversation-friendly atmosphere."

Café 36 S
24 | 20 | 22 | $39

22-24 W. Calendar Ct. (La Grange Rd.), La Grange, 708-354-5722

■ Find "France in La Grange" at this "West Suburban heaven" of a French bistro whose "creative" menu of "outstanding" food (including "interesting selections of game") "never disappoints", and whose "charming" staff offers "professional service"; though the thrifty think it's a little "pricey for the area", most say "the extra dollars are well worth it."

Cafe 28 S
24 | 17 | 20 | $25

1800 W. Irving Park Rd. (Ravenswood Ave.), 773-528-2883

■ Latin lovers laud this "locationally challenged" Lakeview Cuban-Mexican, a "little place with a big kick" and a "fun drink list", where "fabulous flavors bursting" from "creative dishes make for exciting and satisfying" dining; those who "avoid the weekend crowds", saying it's becoming "too popular" and "loud", may feel less squeezed since a post-*Survey* expansion; P.S. you'll be "treated like family" at the "innovative [Sunday] brunch."

Caffé La Scala [S] | – | – | – | M

626 S. Racine Ave. (Harrison St.), 312-421-7262
Now under new ownership, the formerly old-school Rico's boasts a spiffed-up dining room that resounds with recorded arias (and often a few live tunes from exuberant tenors visiting the bar); the menu, however, still offers dependable Little Italy standards.

California Pizza Kitchen [S] | 16 | 13 | 16 | $18

52 E. Ohio St. (bet. Rush St. & Wabash Ave.), 312-787-6075
Water Tower Pl., 835 N. Michigan Ave., 7th fl. (bet. Chestnut & Pearson Sts.), 312-787-7300
939 W. North Ave. (Sheffield Ave.), 312-337-1281
Arlington Town Square, 3 S. Evergreen Ave. (Campbell St.), Arlington Heights, 847-598-0801
Oakbrook Center Mall, 551 Oakbrook Ctr., 2nd level (Rte. 83), Oak Brook, 630-571-7800
Old Orchard Mall, 374 Old Orchard Ctr. (Old Orchard Rd.), Skokie, 847-673-1144
Woodfield Village Green, 1550 E. Golf Rd. (Meacham Rd.), Schaumburg, 847-413-9200
◪ The "creative spin" on "designer pizza" at these "busy" city and suburban outposts of a national chain is "never a bummer" to aficionados of their "excellent topping combinations"; naysayers find them "noisy" and "nothing special", but however you slice it they're "dependable" "places for kids where adults can still eat well"; N.B. Deer Park and Geneva branches are slated to open in 2003.

Caliterra Bar & Grille ◐ [S] | 24 | 21 | 22 | $43

Wyndham Hotel, 633 N. St. Clair St. (Erie St.), 312-274-4444
■ Expect "consistently inventive" Cal-Ital fare at this "gem" in Streeterville whose "seasonally obsessed" "monthly menus offer great variety"; the "beautiful room" is so "civilized" and the service so "down to earth" you'll "forget it's in a hotel", and don't miss the "awesome brunch" buffet on Sundays; N.B. the Food rating may not reflect the post-*Survey* arrival of chef Rick Gresh (ex Green Dolphin Street).

Calypso Cafe [S] | 19 | 17 | 17 | $23

Harper Ct., 5211 S. Harper Ave. (53rd St.), 773-955-0229
■ "Don't forget to bring your sunscreen" to this "upbeat" Hyde Park Caribbean where an "inventive" menu offers "authentic fare from the islands" like "good jerk chicken wings" and "sweet plantains" at a "great bang for the buck"; escapists "never feel rushed" in the "smart, bright" room, a "one-of-a-kind place" that's especially "fun" "on a cold, snowy day."

Campagnola [S] | 24 | 20 | 22 | $40

815 Chicago Ave. (Main St.), Evanston, 847-475-6100
■ "Affable" chef-owner Michael Altenberg "continues to amaze" at this two-tier Italian in the North Suburbs where

the "creative yet refined cuisine" showcases "top-shelf organic ingredients" that are "fresh! fresh! fresh!" and the "intelligent staff" provides "sincere hospitality"; surveyors split over the duo of dining levels — some like the "rustic first floor", others "prefer the more-expensive upstairs" that features "excellent-value tasting dinners."

Cannella's on Grand S | 18 | 12 | 19 | $29

1132 W. Grand Ave. (May St.), 312-433-9400
◪ Fans of Steven Cannella's defunct digs on Wells Street and West Huron are still relishing the "rebirth of an old favorite"; like its old-guard Italian predecessors, this "friendly" "Grand Avenue restaurant" is known for "large portions" of "good hearty food" at "reasonable prices", though cutting-edge culinary critics complain the fare's as "ordinary" as the "decor is bland."

Cantare S | ▽ 22 | 21 | 21 | $40

200 E. Chestnut St. (Mies van der Rohe Way), 312-266-4500
■ A relatively "new favorite" for "tasty [Northern] Italian off the Mag Mile", this "friendly" Streeterville spot – the "lesser-known" sibling of Volare – is known for "good service" and "creative" interpretations of "classic" dishes; N.B. the Food score may not reflect the departure of chef Edward Leonard and the introduction of a new menu.

Cape Cod Room S | 22 | 22 | 22 | $45

Drake Hotel, 140 E. Walton Pl. (Michigan Ave.), 312-787-2200
◪ "Savor a trip down memory lane" at this Streeterville "landmark" "in the Drake" Hotel, a "stiff-upper-lip" "old-school seafood" spot (you "can't beat the oysters" and "awesome bookbinder soup") with a "dark" "New England" feel; the experience is "expensive but worth it" to fans but "pricey" to those who say it's "lost its luster"; N.B. jackets are preferred at dinner.

Capital Grille S | 23 | 23 | 22 | $46

633 N. St. Clair St. (Ontario St.), 312-337-9400
■ Streeterville's "sophisticated steakhouse" is a "carnivore heaven" replete "with cigars" and "testosterone", where "high-quality beef" and "lobsters the size of Trident submarines" make for "great power lunches" as well as "expense-account" dinners; yes, "it's a chain, but it feels local" say capital-ists who compliment its "classy", "clubby atmosphere" and appreciate the "A-1 treatment" from its "top-notch" staff.

CARLOS' S | 28 | 25 | 27 | $68

429 Temple Ave. (Highwood Ave.), Highland Park, 847-432-0770
■ "Worth the drive at twice the distance", this North Suburban veteran is "always a sure bet" for "a special

night out" thanks to "outstanding", "palate-pleasing" New French cuisine that's so "dependably wonderful" devotees "dream about" it; "invisible attention" from a "stellar staff" overseen by "superb hosts Carlos and Debbie Nieto" is another hallmark of its "small and comfortable" room; P.S. the "great wine list" boasts 1,500 bottles.

Carlucci S — 20 | 20 | 19 | $35

250 Marriott Dr. (Milwaukee Ave.), Lincolnshire, 847-478-0990
6111 N. River Rd. (Higgins Rd.), Rosemont, 847-518-0990
◪ Cronies say these "old-fashioned" "Italian restaurants for Italians" in the Northwest Suburbs are "always reliable" for "well-prepared" fare, though some dubious diners are "disappointed" by what they deem "ordinary" output and call them "pricey for pasta"; still, the River Road sibling is a "good place to meet a friend passing through O'Hare"; N.B. a Downers Grove location is slated to open mid-2003.

Carmichael's Chicago Steak House S — 22 | 20 | 21 | $38

1052 W. Monroe St. (bet. Morgan St. & Racine Ave.), 312-433-0025
■ To fans, the "terrific cuts" "rank with the best" at this "unpretentious" West Loop "steak-and-cigar stop" in a "good location" near the United Center, a "great before-the-game place" where you might just "catch" sight of a few "celebrity locals and athletes"; "it feels like everyone knows your name" within its "cavernous but comfortable" confines, though some prefer the "super outside seating"; N.B. the Food score may not reflect the post-*Survey* arrival of chef Nick Zarzecki.

Carmine's S — 20 | 18 | 18 | $34

1043 N. Rush St. (bet. Bellevue Pl. & Cedar St.), 312-988-7676
◪ "Plentiful" portions of "tasty" "true Italian food" lure the loyal to this "reliable Rosebud" restaurant, a "popular hangout" in a part of the Gold Coast cards have christened the "Viagra triangle"; it's a "place to be seen" ("go early to avoid long waits"), with "great people-watching" and "fabulous alfresco dining", "weather permitting", though wafflers wonder "what's the hype about?"

Carson's Ribs S — 20 | 13 | 17 | $26

5970 N. Ridge Ave. (Clark St.), 773-271-4000
612 N. Wells St. (Ontario St.), 312-280-9200
200 N. Waukegan Rd. (bet. Deerfield & Lake Cook Rds.), Deerfield, 847-374-8500
5050 N. Harlem Ave. (Foster Ave.), Harwood Heights, 708-867-4200
◪ "Still the standard" to many, these city and suburban BBQ "classics" give you an "honest slab at an honest price", with "meaty", "macho ribs" that are "consistently tender" and served in "artery-clogging abundance" (though some prefer the "awesome pork chops"); still, the quarrelsome

question the "frayed decor", quipping "the setting of natural Formica is perfect for takeaway."

Catch 35 S   23 | 21 | 21 | $39
Leo Burnett Bldg., 35 W. Wacker Dr. (bet. Dearborn & State Sts.), 312-346-3500
■ "Interesting preparations" of "Asian-influenced" seafood "subtly enhanced by light sauces" make for the "freshest catch in the Loop" at this "unique", "contemporary" spot where a "personable and knowledgeable" staff helps patrons navigate the "vast menu"; a "favorite" "for business lunches" and tête-à-têtes of "the well-heeled", it's also "well situated for Goodman Theater"–goers.

Cerise S   ∇ 21 | 21 | 19 | $46
Le Méridien Hotel, 521 N. Rush St., 5th fl. (Grand Ave.), 312-645-1500
☑ "One of the best restaurants no one seems to know about", this "upscale" Near North bistro "hidden" in the Le Méridien Hotel is "hard to find" but "worth the search" say fans of its French-Med fare; foes of this "fledgling" two-year-old feel the "disappointing service" "needs work."

Charlie's Ale House S   15 | 15 | 15 | $19
Navy Pier, 700 E. Grand Ave. (Lake Shore Dr.), 312-595-1440
5308 N. Clark St. (Berwyn Ave.), 773-751-0140
1224 W. Webster Ave. (Magnolia Ave.), 773-871-1440
☑ "The '60s live on" at these "cozy" pubs that may be "more bar than restaurant" but are "good" for "a brew and a burger", as well as other "decent", "traditional" American "bar food"; besides, folks "love the beer garden" at the DePaul location and the Navy Pier branch's "fun patio"; N.B. the Andersonville outpost opened post-*Survey*.

CHARLIE TROTTER'S   28 | 26 | 28 | VE
816 W. Armitage Ave. (Halsted St.), 773-248-6228
■ Possessed of a "perfectionist's zeal", chef-owner Charlie Trotter "overlooks no detail" at this "world-class" Lincoln Park New American "innovator", "an epicurean's idea of heaven" where "creative cooking", "a well-chosen wine list", "flawless service" (rated No. 1 in our *Survey*) and "lovely atmosphere" add up to an "exhilarating", "one-of-a-kind culinary experience."

Cheesecake Factory S   20 | 18 | 17 | $22
John Hancock Ctr., 875 N. Michigan Ave., lower level (Chestnut St.), 312-337-1101 ●
Woodfield Mall, 53 Woodfield Rd. (Plum Grove Rd.), Schaumburg, 847-619-1090
Old Orchard Ctr., 374 Old Orchard Ctr. (Skokie Blvd.), Skokie, 847-329-8077
☑ "The menu is almost as long as the wait" at these "cavernous" chainsters, each a "guilty pleasure" where

the "giant portions" of "consistently good" American fare just might "leave no room for" the "decadent" and "dreamy cheesecakes" (it's "hard to pick just one flavor"); still, some fuddy-duddies frown about the "fantasy" decor and the "smiley" staffers who "can't keep up with the tourists."

Chef's Station S ▽ 26 | 21 | 22 | $33

Davis Street Metra Station, 915 Davis St. (Church St.), Evanston, 847-570-9821

■ Though it's "hard to find your way" to the "unexpected location" of this "easy-to-overlook" North Suburban in Evanston's historic "Davis Street Metra Station", those who do report it's "a top-quality surprise" that gives the "gourmet treatment" to "innovative" New American dishes at "reasonable prices"; "great service" and a tasting menu that's "a steal" add to the appeal; N.B. patio seating is now available.

Chez François – | – | – | M

14 S. Third St. (State St.), Geneva, 630-262-1000

Born in Spain but raised in France, aptly named chef-owner François Sanchez has opted for nurture over nature, transforming his former West Suburban tapas restaurant, Granada, into this Southern French bistro with earthy regional specialties – a representative signature dish is duck breast and duck ravioli with red cabbage in a red-wine-and-fig sauce – served in a colorful dining room that evokes the sensuous, sunny Gallic countryside.

Chez Joel S 23 | 20 | 22 | $36

1119 W. Taylor St. (Racine Ave.), 312-226-6479

■ A "surprisingly good" "French gem" set "amid all the red-sauce Italians" in Little Italy, this "always-pleasing" "standout" of a bistro offers "food prepared with care and skill" in a "low-key", "homey" environment that some say is a bit too "cozy" thanks to "tables crammed" "so close you dine with your neighbors" – no wonder the claustrophobic covet an "outdoor summer seat" in the "great garden."

Chicago Chop House S 24 | 19 | 22 | $44

60 W. Ontario St. (bet. Clark & Dearborn Sts.), 312-787-7100

◪ "Here's the beef" brags the brotherhood of "good ol' boys", "big-city movers and shakers" and "conventioneers" who descend upon the "dark" dining rooms of this River North "Chicago landmark", a "classy" steak-and-chop shop known for "great meat" "without all the pretension"; a word to the wise: "if you want a little quiet, ask to be seated upstairs", as the "first-floor piano bar is raucous."

Chicago Diner S 18 | 13 | 16 | $16

3411 N. Halsted St. (Roscoe St.), 773-935-6696

◪ "Interesting" and "inventive" flesh-free fare ranging from "healthy tofu stir-fries" to "delicious 'meat' dishes (without the meat)" that "even a carnivore would love" have fans fawning over this "casual" Wrigleyville "vegetarian nirvana"; still, the "loveless" complain of "bland results" and "hole-in-the-wall" surroundings.

Chicago Firehouse Restaurant S 19 | 21 | 19 | $36

1401 S. Michigan Ave. (14th St.), 312-786-1401

◪ Expect no alarms at this "dignified" South Loop pioneer in an "authentic two-story firehouse", as the only thing "smokin'" is the "hearty American fare" ("move over, mom!") served either in its "quiet, civilized" dining rooms or on its "lovely patio"; some wet blankets, though, say it's "a little expensive" for this "neighborhood-in-progress"; N.B. the Food score may not reflect the post-*Survey* arrival of chef Jeff Boerst (ex Tavern on Rush).

Chicago Flat Sammies S 16 | 12 | 13 | $12

163 E. Pearson St. (Michigan Ave.), 312-664-2733

■ "When shopping on Michigan Avenue", "snack"-ers stop into this "crowded" Gold Coast Lettuce Entertain You spot in the historic Pumping Station for a "quick", "cheap lunch" of "surprisingly good" "gourmet-ish fast food" such as the eponymous "flavorful sandwich", "good salads and flatbread" pizzas and "excellent milkshakes."

Chicago Kalbi ◗S – | – | – | M

3752 W. Lawrence Ave. (Hamlin Ave.), 773-604-8183

This Northwest Sider is an "excellent place for Korean BBQ" where "friendly service" outshines the plain decor; the namesake dish – marinated ribs wrapped with rice and bean paste in a lettuce leaf – is especially "fun" when you "cook it yourself" using "fresh ingredients" over a wood-fired tabletop grill; P.S. "get a private" booth.

Chicago Pizza & Oven Grinder Co. S⊄ 20 | 16 | 16 | $19

2121 N. Clark St. (bet. Dickens & Webster Aves.), 773-248-2570

◪ A "great twist on the typical pizzeria", this "affordable" Lincoln Park "classic" serves up "unique sandwiches" and "amazing pizza pot pies" ("an upside-down treat"); doubters dismiss the latter as "bizarre" and "not really" 'za and ponder the propriety of its "unorganized waiting list" that "isn't written down"; P.S. "cash only."

Chicago Prime Steakhouse ◗S – | – | – | E

1370 Bank Dr. (Meacham Dr.), Schaumburg, 847-969-9900

Hidden near Schaumburg's Woodfield Mall, this tasteful and relaxing Suburban Northwest steakhouse oasis indeed serve prime beef (take your pick from the hunks on the raw-meat tray) and traditional steakhouse fare, with a few surprises for good measure; prime rib is a specialty, but they recommend reserving it in advance; N.B. live jazz makes for a mellow mood Thursday–Saturday nights.

CHIC Cafe S

21 | 14 | 18 | E

Cooking and Hospitality Institute of Chicago, 361 W. Chestnut St. (Orleans St.), 312-873-2032

■ "Students cook and serve" at this River North BYO in the Cooking and Hospitality Institute of Chicago, where "guinea pigs" gladly gather for an "ever-changing" and "always surprising" Eclectic–Contemporary French menu that's not only a "delicious" "delight" but an "excellent value" as well (lunches are just $15 , while dinners are only $25), even though "you're really eating someone's homework."

Chief O'Neill's Pub S

18 | 20 | 17 | $19

3471 N. Elston Ave. (Addison St.), 773-583-3066

■ Denizens of this "wonderfully friendly" "local pub" on the Northwest Side claim you'll "leave with an Irish accent", so "authentic" are its "cute atmosphere" (with a "great beer garden") and "generous portions" of "hearty", "traditional" fare – from "burgers and brew" to "fantastic fish 'n' chips"; curmudgeonly crawlers, however, call the food a bit "bland" ("pass the salt" "and pepper").

Chilpancingo S

23 | 21 | 20 | $36

358 W. Ontario St. (Orleans St.), 312-266-9525

■ "Holy mole!" exclaim enthusiasts of "Frontera Grill alum" Geno Bahena's "festive and lively" River Norther ("sister of Ixcapuzalco") where "sophisticated", "creative regional Mexican cuisine" is paired with "sexy straight-up margaritas" or pours from an "outstanding wine list"; the "exotic" space features "authentic" folk art and "vivid paintings that reflect the vivid flavors", including "works by the chef-owner" himself.

Chinn's 34th St. Fishery S

21 | 13 | 18 | $29

3011 W. Ogden Ave. (bet. Fender Ave. & Naper Blvd.), Lisle, 630-637-1777

☑ You "must go early for a table", as there's "almost always a wait" at this West Suburban seafooder serving "a whole lotta fresh fish" and "garlic-butter rolls to die for" at "reasonable prices"; critics concede it's "not as crowded as Bob Chinn's" Crab House, its Wheeling cousin, but complain that its "smaller" setting is just as "noisy" and "needs better decor."

Chinoiserie S⊅

20 | 12 | 15 | $26

509 Fourth St. (Linden Ave.), Wilmette, 847-256-0306

☑ Champions cheer this North Suburban Eclectic-Asian as "a mixed marriage that works", praising the "creative" interplay of "interesting Chinese and French" influences in its "mouthwatering" fare; dissenters dismiss the menu, though, as an "inauthentic" and "odd mixture" that's "pricey for a casual restaurant", adding the service is "earnest" but "disjointed" and the decor is "disappointing"; P.S. it's "BYO" and "cash only."

Chipotle Mexican Grill   15 | 11 | 13 | $11

10 E. Jackson Blvd. (State St.), 312-566-0308
291 E. Ontario St. (Fairbanks Ct.), 312-587-7753 **S**
3181 N. Broadway (Belmont Ave.), 773-525-5250 **S**
2000 N. Clybourn Ave. (Cortland St.), 773-935-5710 **S**
316 N. Michigan Ave. (bet. Wacker Dr. & Water St.),
312-578-0950 **S**
2256 N. Orchard Ave. (Lincoln Ave.), 773-935-6744 **S**
1166 N. State St. (Division St.), 312-654-8637 **S**
610 W. Diversey Pkwy. (Clark St.), 773-281-1492 **S**
711 Church St. (bet. Orrington & Sherman Aves.), Evanston,
847-425-3959 **S**
1132 W. Lake St. (Harlem Ave.), Oak Park,
708-524-8211 **S**
Additional locations throughout the Chicago area

Amigos who approve of this McDonald's-owned Mexican chain say it serves "good fast food" in the form of "cheap", "healthy" "throw-pillow-size burritos" made from "fresh ingredients" "you choose yourself" (plus "knock-your-socks-off margaritas" at most branches); desperados dismiss them as "bland", "gringo-style" "McBurritos", though, and slam the "stark" "warehouse" surroundings.

Cielo **S**   ▽ 19 | 22 | 19 | $34

Omni Chicago Hotel, 676 N. Michigan Ave., 4th fl. (Huron St.),
312-944-7676

"Everything about this fine restaurant is understated" – including its "hidden" location on the fourth floor of Near North's Omni Chicago Hotel – but undaunted acolytes advise it's worth seeking out for its "high-quality" New American and Northern Italian fare and "stately", "modern" room with a "great ceiling" graced by an "awesome" trompe l'oeil sky mural and "huge windows" offering "fantastic views of bustling Michigan Avenue."

Cité **S**   18 | 23 | 19 | $59

Lake Point Tower, 505 N. Lake Shore Dr., 70th fl. (Navy Pier),
312-644-4050

High atop Lake Point Tower, this celestial 70th-story Streeterville stalwart draws raves for its "romantic" room and one of the "best views in Chicago" ("although you pay for it"); the starry-eyed say its "excellent" American–New French menu and "great service" add up to an "exquisite night on the town", though the earthbound earmark the "food good but" "overpriced" and the servers "snooty."

Cloud 9 ●**S**   – | – | – | M

1944 N. Oakley St. (Armitage Ave.), 773-486-3900
Antique light fixtures, upholstered chairs and a dreamy paint job set the scene at this former Bucktown corner tavern, but despite the glowing, atmospheric setting, the restaurant's menu is firmly grounded in reasonably priced contemporary American dishes.

Clubhouse, The S
19 | 21 | 19 | $30

Oakbrook Center Mall, 298 Oakbrook Ctr. (Rte. 83), Oak Brook, 630-472-0600

☑ Though it's closed its onsite golf pro shop, Oak Brook's "trendy" yet "classy" "meet market" is still a sweet spot; members of the gallery consider it "a club I'd actually join", with "great people-watching" and "generous portions" of Traditional American fare in a "good-looking", "high-energy setting"; holdouts hint the "manly" meals are "good but inconsistent" and favor the "quieter upstairs" over the "noisy" main floor.

Club Lucky S
19 | 18 | 18 | $26

1824 W. Wabansia St. (bet. Ashland & Damen Aves.), 773-227-2300

☑ Mixing "martinis and meatballs" for a "young, hip crowd", this "swinging" "supper club" "led the Bucktown restaurant surge" more than a decade ago and is still serving traditional Italian "comfort food" ("nothing fancy – just good, large portions") in a setting that's a "retro throwback to the '40s and '50s"; still, "long waits" have some gamblers trying their luck at "plenty of better places."

Coast Sushi Bar ●S
– | – | – | M

2045 N. Damen Ave. (bet. Dickens & McLean Aves.), 773-235-5775

More mod sushi, with the curb appeal of a hip Bucktown boutique; the menu marries the familiar and the creative from both sushi bar and kitchen, with some intriguing signature maki and unusual Japanese dishes such as exotic tempura (taro, lotus root, edible flowers) and a spicy tamarind duck entrée; the decor is ultra-minimal, with widely spaced tables, webbed leather chairs and a painted concrete floor; N.B. it's BYO for now.

Cochon Sauvage S
▽ 22 | 19 | 20 | $39

1060 College Ave. (President St.), Wheaton, 630-784-8015

☑ Hog-wild Western Suburbanites "can't believe" this "great bistro" is "tucked away in Wheaton", yet there it is – a "wonderful find" for "excellent French cuisine" that's not as rustic as the name would imply"; still, not everyone "can't wait to go again", as some squeal about "inconsistent service" and grunt that it's "not as good as Les Deux Gros", its Glen Ellyn littermate; N.B. the Food score may not reflect the post-*Survey* arrival of chef Famous Jefferson.

COCO PAZZO S
24 | 22 | 23 | $42

300 W. Hubbard St. (Franklin St.), 312-836-0900

■ "It feels like Italy" at this "polished" "NYC import" in River North where the "top-of-the-line" Northern Italian cuisine combines "innovative choices with classic favorites" ("chef Tony Priolo is a master of risotto"); "beautiful lighting" enlivens the "warm atmosphere" of its "handsome" "loft space", and "mature service" means it's "outstanding" for "personal entertaining" or a "power lunch."

Coco Pazzo Cafe S   22 | 20 | 21 | $33
Red Roof Inn, 636 N. St. Clair St. (Ontario St.), 312-664-2777
■ "The 'crazy chef' is right on target" at Streeterville's "more casual", "more affordable" "version of Coco Pazzo" (restaurateur Pino Luongo's popular River North eatery), where the "beautiful people" congregate for "inventive" Northern Italian "comfort food" in a "relaxed", "European setting" complete with some of the "best outdoor dining" in town.

CoCoRo/East S   ▽ 20 | 14 | 18 | $30
668 N. Wells St. (bet. Erie & Huron Sts.), 312-943-2220
☑ Shabu-shabu seekers and sushi searchers are split over this "small and comfortable" River North Japanese: some swear the fare is "authentic", "fresh and delicious", while others find it "disappointing"; service remarks are similarly skewed, ranging from regrettably "rushed" to favorably "fast"; nevertheless, everyone agrees there's a "nice selection of sakes"; N.B. at press time, a shortening of the name to 'East' was planned.

Cold Comfort Cafe & Deli S   ▽ 18 | 12 | 12 | $11
2211 W. North Ave. (Leavitt St.), 773-772-4552
☑ "No more trips to the kosher deli in the suburbs" for some thanks to this "quaint" and (name notwithstanding) "cozy" spot set in a Bucktown building that dates to 1886; a "well-kept secret" for "mouthwatering sandwiches" to take out or eat in, and "killer breakfasts", it's a "fun place" featuring a "friendly staff" that "tries hard" – still, some surveyors say it "needs more waiters."

Como S   – | – | – | E
695 N. Milwaukee Ave. (Huron St.), 312-733-7400
In a nod to their famed, now-defunct Como Inn, the Marchetti family has revived the name for a new generation at this old-guard Italian on the Near West site of their former Fahrenheit; the menu reads like a roll call of classic pasta, meat and chicken dishes, and the updated loftlike space sports creamy walls, a draped ceiling with a chandelier and canopied booths, plus a patio for warm-weather dining.

Convito Italiano S   19 | 15 | 17 | $23
Plaza del Lago, 1515 Sheridan Rd. (north of Lake Ave.), Wilmette, 847-251-3654
☑ "Always yummy" to loyalists, this North Shore market and trattoria is a "great spot" for "simple", "reliable" Italian fare that's "less than cutting-edge but still a fine meal"; contrarians who're convinced it's become "complacent" cite "basic decor" and "service [that] can be a little cold" as reasons to "pick up a picnic" or "bring home dinner."

Coobah ◖ S
−|−|−| M

3423 N. Southport Ave. (bet. Newport Ave. & Roscoe St.), 773-528-2226

There's atmosphere to spare at this lively Latin Lakeview latecomer, a noisy bar/restaurant with terra cotta walls, huge cast-iron light fixtures and a green high-gloss poured-epoxy floor; cooking till at least 1 AM nightly, its kitchen creates chile-spiked Eclectic fare comprising elements of Spanish, Filipino, Colombian, Brazilian and Cuban cuisines, which is paired with a plethora of specialty drinks (including mojitos, of course) and a comprehensive Iberian and South American wine list.

Copa Cubana S
▽ 19 | 17 | 19 | $23

224 S. Main St. (bet. Jackson & Jefferson Sts.), Naperville, 630-983-2672

☑ "For something a little different", a "swelling crowd" of Naperville natives coos over the "creative" yet "authentic" Cuban fare at this "real gem" located in a former laundromat that's now a "fun, festive" brick-and-stucco room flecked with vintage photos of Havana; some dissidents declare that they're "not crazy about the food" but wonder "where else can you get plantains in the [Western] Suburbs?"

Cornelia's Restaurant S
19 | 18 | 19 | $29

750 W. Cornelia Ave. (bet. Broadway & Halsted St.), 773-248-8333

■ Gone is the "kitschy name" of this former 'Roosterant' in Boys Town, and with it the chicken-centric focus and farm-implement motif; what remains is a "sweet date place" for couples (including some of the "*Will & Grace*" variety) where they "take great care" with "innovative" Italian dishes and American "comfort food" like "nice pork chops"; P.S. certain "spotlighted artworks" on the walls are for sale.

Corner Bakery
17 | 13 | 13 | $13

35 E. Monroe St. (Wabash Ave.), 312-372-0072 S
Field Museum, 1400 S. Lake Shore Dr. (opp. Soldier Field Stadium), 312-588-1040 S
Goodman Theatre, 56 W. Randolph St. (Dearborn St.), 312-346-9492 S
Market Bldg., 140 S. Dearborn St. (Marble Pl.), 312-920-9100
516 N. Clark St. (Grand Ave.), 312-644-8100 S
360 N. Michigan Ave. (bet. Wacker Dr. & Water St.), 312-236-2400 S
676 N. St. Clair St. (Erie St.), 312-266-2570 S
1121 N. State St. (Cedar St.), 312-787-1969 S
Sears Tower, 233 S. Wacker Dr. (Adams St.), 312-466-0200
224 S. Michigan Ave. (Adams St.), 312-431-7600 S
Additional locations throughout the Chicago area

☑ "Proving fast food can be good", this expanding chain of "quick pick-me-up stops" draws crowds of "carb lovers" with its "relatively healthy" menu of "consistently good sandwiches, pizzas, breads and pastries"; critics complain of "assembly-line" fare and "confusing, chaotic, cafeteria-style ordering", contending they're "not as special" now that "there's one on every corner."

Cosí
15 | 14 | 12 | $13

57 E. Grand Ave. (Rush St.), 312-321-1990 🆂
*28 E. Jackson Blvd. (bet. State St. & Wabash Ave.),
312-939-2674*
*Illinois Center, 233 N. Michigan Ave. (bet. Lake St. &
Wacker Pl.), 312-938-3200*
203 N. La Salle Blvd. (Lake St.), 312-368-4400
*116 S. Michigan Ave. (bet. Adams & Monroe Sts.),
312-223-1061* 🆂
230 W. Monroe St. (Franklin St.), 312-782-4755
230 W. Washington St. (Franklin St.), 312-422-1002
*25 E. Hinsdale Ave. (Garfield Ave.), Hinsdale,
630-654-5033* 🆂
1101 Lake St. (Harlem Ave.), Oak Park, 708-524-8412 🆂
*15139 La Grange Rd. (151st St.), Orland Park,
708-364-6600* 🆂
Additional locations throughout the Chicago area
◪ Though this "corporate" chain offers "many choices" of "unique salads" as well as "creative sandwiches" on "delicious bread", raters resent paying "NYC prices" ("it should be called 'Costlí'") for what some call "forgettable food" and add "too bad they don't have the service thing down"; N.B. some locations offer an expanded dinner menu served by waiters.

Costa's 🆂
23 | 21 | 22 | $28

340 S. Halsted St. (Van Buren St.), 312-263-9700
*1 S. 130 Summit Ave. (Roosevelt Rd.), Oakbrook Terrace,
630-620-1100*
■ A Greek chorus of connoisseurs cries "opa!" for these "favorite" Gemini twins, together rated "the best" in our *Survey* for their nationality's cuisine; whether dining at the "elegant Greektown" original "or the West Suburban" spinoff, expect these brothers to deliver a "welcoming atmosphere" "as charming as Athens", with "savory" "upscale" specialties presented on "white tablecloths" by "knowledgeable" servers.

COURTRIGHT'S 🆂
25 | 25 | 24 | $49

*8989 S. Archer Ave. (Willow Springs Rd.), Willow Springs,
708-839-8000*
■ You'll "feel like you're at your rich uncle's house" when visiting this "elegant yet exceedingly comfortable" New American retreat, a "'downtown' spot in the Southwest Suburbs" whose "high quality standards", "amazing wine cellar" and "beautiful" "parklike" "setting on the [Cook County] Forest Preserve" "complement its wonderful" cuisine; N.B. the Food rating may not reflect the post-*Survey* arrival of chef Jonathan Harootunian (ex Vivere).

Cousin's S
18 | 15 | 14 | $18

2833 N. Broadway (Diversey Pkwy.), 773-880-0063

☑ The "delicious aromas" of "flavorful", "familiar Med" favorites "with an exotic Turkish twist" prompt the faithful to "grab a floor pillow" at this "comfy", "vegetarian-friendly" Lakeview spot, the sole survivor of an erstwhile North Side trio; still, "friendly but haphazard service" that can be "painfully slow" has doubters declaring they "wouldn't recommend that [their] cousins go there"; N.B. the Decor score may not reflect a post-*Survey* redecoration.

Cristiano's S
– | – | – | E

2001 Rand Rd. (Hicks Rd.), Palatine, 847-776-0100

Passionate Lombardy native Cristiano Bassani (ex Coco Pazzo, Bice) makes himself at home in the Northwest Suburbs, where he has settled in to deliver his upscale Northern Italian fare including artichoke carpaccio, enticing ravioli and risotto specialties, and whole-roasted market fish, all paired with a predominantly Italian wine list; the refined, white-tablecloth decor artfully blends touches of old and new.

Crofton on Wells
24 | 20 | 22 | $45

535 N. Wells St. (bet. Grand Ave. & Ohio St.), 312-755-1790

■ "Suzy can cook" say "fine-dining" fans who "go often to Crofton" to "treasure" the "adventure" of its "creative" eponymous chef-owner's seasonally changing menu of "excellent" Regional American fare; the "minimalist" decor of this "quiet haven" in River North strikes some as "sleek" and "romantic", but others deem the "drop-ceiling"-ed digs a bit "dull" and wish "she would pretty up the place."

Cross-Rhodes S≠
19 | 9 | 17 | $14

913 Chicago Ave. (Main St.), Evanston, 847-475-4475

■ Scholars of "classic cheap Greek" give extra credit to this "reliably good" North Suburban offering "comfort food" like "great gyros, chicken and fries at great prices"; "fast service" from a "friendly" crew makes it a "favorite family place" despite a decidedly "no-frills atmosphere" that has some saying "don't bother eating in"; speaking of credit, cancel the cards 'cause it's "cash only."

Cru Café & Wine Bar ●S
17 | 19 | 16 | $26

888 N. Wabash Ave. (Delaware Pl.), 312-337-4001

☑ Swirl-and-sippers say a "vino paradise" awaits at this "totally Euro", "hip-and-comfortable" Gold Coaster that's "mostly for nibbles" and "great flights" of wine; the "cozy and classy" atmosphere "with chandeliers and couches" makes it a "nice" "place for a date" or "to meet after work for drinks", but off-put oenophiles object to "sporadic service" and call it "average for the price."

Cucina Bella Osteria & Wine Bar S | 18 | 17 | 19 | $27 |
1612 N. Sedgwick Ave. (North Ave.), 312-274-1119
Cucina Bella Trattoria S
Days Inn Lincoln Park North, 642 W. Diversey Pkwy. (bet. Clark & Halsted Sts.), 773-868-1119

■ These 'beautiful kitchens' in Old Town and Lincoln Park are each a "homey" "neighborhood place to meet friends" over "so much" "authentic Italian" food you'll have "enough for seconds", though detractors damn with faint praise, labeling the fare "pretty good"; still, pet people are pleased that you can "bring your dog and sit outside"; N.B. the Decor score may not reflect the trattoria's post-*Survey* relocation.

Cullen's Bar & Grill S | – | – | – | M |
3741 N. Southport Ave. (bet. Addison St. & Irving Park Rd.), 773-975-0600

"Small and often crowded", this American version of a "classic Irish pub" in Lakeview is "popular with the bar crowd" for its "great atmosphere", expansive patio and "good food and drink" including "homespun meatloaf and mashed potatoes", "great onion rings" and, of course, Guinness; it's also a "fun" pre- or post-play stop for stage-struck visitors to owner-impresario Michael Cullen's adjacent Mercury Theater.

Currents ● | – | – | – | E |
Swissôtel, 323 E. Wacker Dr. (Columbus Dr.), 312-565-2665
The name hints at seafood, but this handsome, upscale spot in the lower level of the Loop's Swissôtel serves a seasonal menu of creative, contemporary American cuisine with a Med accent (and a limited menu of panini, burgers and pizzas until 1:00 AM), with a grappa bar offering about 50 selections; N.B. the menu informs the hotel's international business audience that 'all prices are quoted in U.S. Dollar.'

Cyrano's Bistrot & Wine Bar | 21 | 20 | 20 | $34 |
546 N. Wells St. (Ohio St.), 312-467-0546
■ "Roxanne would approve" of the "good, honest French cooking" "done right" "without breaking the bank" at this "funky but chic" bistro boasting "comfortable" environs that are "surprisingly quaint" for River North; headed by a "warm and friendly" "husband-and-wife team" (chef Didier Durand and wine cellar master Jamie Pellar), the "polite staff" will "make you feel right at home"; N.B. live music is now offered on Friday and Saturday nights.

Cy's Crabhouse S | 16 | 14 | 16 | $26 |
3819 N. Ashland Ave. (Grace St.), 773-883-8900
933 N. Milwaukee Ave. (Lake Cook Rd.), Wheeling, 847-279-1700
■ Those with "a taste for crab" can't concur on this city and suburban duo: some say they're "nice", "family-oriented" places where you "can go in jeans" for a "great value on fresh seafood" and "Middle Eastern dishes"; others yawn

"ho-hum", admitting that the "fair" fare will do "in a pinch"
but dinging the "disappointing service" and dismissing the
decor as "lacking."

Czech Plaza ⓢ⊄   ▽ 20 | 9 | 21 | $15

7016 W. Cermak Rd. (Home Ave.), Berwyn, 708-795-6555

☑ Czech out the "big portions" of "simple, tasty, rib-sticking"
"Bohemian" dishes (some for "less than a sawbuck")
recalling "grandma's good food" at this "old-world" outpost
in the Western Suburbs; the service is "quick and no-
nonsense", but most warn "don't go for the ambiance
'cause there ain't any"; P.S. another "problem: they don't
accept credit cards."

D & J BISTRO ⓢ   25 | 21 | 23 | $35

*First Bank Business Ctr., 466 S. Rand Rd. (Rte. 22), Lake Zurich,
847-438-8001*

∎ Allies who "have never had a bad meal" at this Northwest
Suburban spot applaud its "authentic" French bistro
"comfort food prepared in an upscale way"; "urban
sophistication with rural charm" makes it "feel like Paris
despite the strip-mall" setting, and if it's a little "crowded",
it may be because the "consistency is excellent" and the
"price is right."

Dave & Buster's ◗ⓢ   12 | 14 | 13 | $20

1030 N. Clark St. (bet. Maple & Oak Sts.), 312-943-5151
*1155 N. Swift Rd. (bet. Army Trail Rd. & Lake St.), Addison,
630-543-5151*

☑ "Fun is key" at these Gold Coast and Suburban Northwest
outposts of a national chain of "family places" whose
"mass appeal" is gazillions of games; still, arcade-ians
who berate the "blah bar food" "wish the chow was as
good as" (and not just "a break from") the "entertaining"
trivial pursuits; as is, some say "it's hard to believe anyone
without kids would set foot" in them.

Dave's Italian Kitchen ⓢ   18 | 13 | 17 | $17

*1635 Chicago Ave. (bet. Church & Davis Sts.), Evanston,
847-864-6000*

∎ "An Evanston tradition", this "college haunt" is a
"bargain" in a "basement", with "good Italian fare" like
"satisfying pastas and thin-crust pizzas" at "1960s prices";
the decor is "nothing fancy" and "noisy students" can
make it "hard to have a conversation" here, but fans find it
so "quirky and endearing" that some are shouting "Dave,
open one in Chicago!"

David's Bistro ⓢ   ▽ 28 | 20 | 25 | $34

*Norwood Plaza, 623 N. Wolf Rd. (Central Ave.), Des Plaines,
847-803-3233*

∎ A "small storefront" in the Northwest Suburban Norwood
Plaza strip mall is home to this "chef-owned" bistro where

the eponymous David Maish gives "excellent presentation" to the "outstanding", "innovative" and reasonably priced New American fare on his "unique menu"; with a "friendly" staff and a cozy space replete with "beautiful wood walls" of bird's-eye maple and red oak, it's "a great hideaway."

Davis Street Fishmarket 🗷   19 15 17 $25
501 Davis St. (Hinman Ave.), Evanston, 847-869-3474
🗹 "Happy faces" hint at the "chaotic fun" of Evanston's "seafood lover's heaven", which afishionados say is "always spot-on" for its "large selection" of "fresh" fin food with Cajun-Creole flare and "fabulous oyster bar", all offered in a "down-to-earth" "neighborhood atmosphere" "reminiscent of the East Coast"; still, critics crab about "long waits", "noise" and "spotty service."

Dee's Mandarin 🗷   21 16 17 $23
1114 Armitage Ave. (Seminary Ave.), 773-477-1500
■ Good fortune for Lincoln Parkers – this "gourmet Chinese" is "a bright spot" in the neighborhood for "flavorful, generous servings" of "good but not flashy" Mandarin cuisine, "fantastic Szechuan" specialties and sushi, all made from "quality ingredients and unusual recipes" and "seemingly lighter and healthier than" some competitors' fare; P.S. there's "reliable carry-out" and delivery too.

Deleece 🗷   21 17 20 $26
4004 N. Southport Ave. (Irving Park Rd.), 773-325-1710
■ "Deleece is always delish" declare devotees of the "eclectic and tasty" New American cuisine prepared "with culinary flair" and "smartly served" at this "casual" Wrigleyville "restaurant that you'll wish was in *your* neighborhood"; "filled with regulars", its "unassuming" interior strikes many as "inviting" and "cozy", though a few find its "decor lacking" and say it's "noisy" when "crowded"; P.S. the Sunday "brunch is lovely."

Dell Rhea's Chicken Basket 🗷   19 13 16 $16
645 Joliet Rd. (Frontage Rd.), Willowbrook, 630-325-0780
■ For a "nostalgic" "no-frills family dinner" of "fried chicken the way it used to be", the faithful flock to this "classic roadhouse" (circa 1946) in the Southwest Suburbs, a "time warp that transports you" "back to the days of Route 66"; "hard to find but worth the search", it's a "favorite standby" that's "holding up after all these years"; N.B. the Decor score may not reflect a renovation in progress at press time.

Del Rio   19 17 21 $30
228 Green Bay Rd. (Rte. 22), Highwood, 847-432-4608
■ "You're never a stranger" at this North Suburban "classic", a "throwback to Highwood's yesteryears" where the kitchen reassures with "consistently good" "solid [Northern] Italian cooking" supported by a "vast

wine list" and delivered with "personal service" in a "crowded but fun" "atmosphere from the past"; "don't expect cutting-edge", just "rich" dining that's "old-fashioned, in a good way."

Dick's Last Resort S   12 13 13 $20
River East Plaza, 435 E. Illinois St. (bet. Lake Shore Dr. & McClurg Ct.), 312-836-7870
☑ Gluttons for punishment "wear old clothes" to this "dockside" Navy Pier "tourist place" (part of a "chain" that prides itself on having "no class whatsoever") to "get sloppy" over "messy BBQ" and seafood while enduring "obnoxious" barbs from a "deliberately insulting staff"; those who don't "like the abuse" or the "rowdy", "raunchy" revelry "stay away in droves", suggesting you "make it your last resort" as well.

Dinotto Ristorante S   _ _ _ M
215 W. North Ave. (Wells St.), 312-787-3345
Offshoot of the shuttered Trattoria Dinotto, this family-owned Southern Italian keeps the flame alive in Old Town with traditional fare at moderate prices and a Boot-centric wine list; the space is less intimate than its predecessor's, but distressed yellow walls and ceramics add warmth; N.B. the kitchen closes at midnight on weekends, and al fresco patio dining is a warm-weather treat.

Dionises ⌀   _ _ _ M
510 N. Western Ave. (Grand St.), 312-243-7330
A gritty stretch of Western Avenue outside contrasts with the spacious white-tablecloth dining room and grotto bar in this notch-above Mexican restaurant in Ukrainian Village; the space's nightclub feel heats up after 10 PM, when folks head to the dance floor to kick up their heels.

Dixie Kitchen & Bait Shop S   19 18 17 $19
Harper Ct., 5225 S. Harper Ave. (53rd St.), 773-363-4943
825 Church St. (Benson Ave.), Evanston, 847-733-9030
■ Whether at the "Hyde Park haven" or the "Evanston eatery", these "cute" soul sisters seduce with "abundant" portions of "tasty" Cajun, Creole and "Southern cuisine" ("love those fried green tomatoes") that "hit the spot" for most, though holdouts hint the food's "good for a fix but not like home cookin'"; either way, "you have to love" these "Dixie" chicks' "diverse clientele and servers."

d.kelly   _ _ _ E
623 W. Randolph St. (bet. Desplaines & Jefferson Sts.), 312-628-0755
Co-owner spouses Maria Ambriz and chef Daniel Kelly (a 12-year veteran of the Hyatt Hotel chain) have transformed the West Loop former Grace dining room – rearranging furniture, reupholstering banquettes, exposing brick walls

and adding black-and-white photography throughout – to create this elegant, upscale New American whose menu is full of fresh twists on classic fare such as pan-seared chicken breast stuffed with Maine lobster.

Domaine [S] – | – | – | E

1045 N. Rush St. (Cedar St.), 312-397-1045

Let them eat caviar at this trendy, Versailles-inspired nightclub, where sharing portions of 'plateaux' and a since-opening addition of full-size American entrées power the Gold Coast glitterati for a turn on the dance floor – or a trip up the grand staircase; the licentious, luxe decor appeals to well-heeled locals looking for a little naughty with their nosh and nightcap; N.B. entertainment includes DJs and live performances (with cover charge Thursday–Saturday).

Don Juan [S] 21 | 18 | 19 | $29

6730 N. Northwest Hwy. (bet. Devon & Touhy Aves.), 773-775-6438

■ The "original" half of an erstwhile duo – and the sole survivor since the shuttering of its upstart sibling "on Halsted" in Lincoln Park – this family-owned "Edison Park location" is known for the "ultra-fresh, bright flavors" of its "wonderful", "innovative Mexican cuisine" (plus "fabulous margaritas"); N.B. two environments and two menus (overseen by the family's star chef, Patrick Concannon) offer a choice of traditional or fine dining.

Don Roth's Blackhawk [S] 22 | 20 | 21 | $33

61 N. Milwaukee Ave. (Dundee Rd.), Wheeling, 847-537-5800

■ A steak-and-seafooder serving substantially the "same menu as 30 years ago", this "traditional, old-style" "Chicago classic" in the Northwest Suburbs is a "step back in time, but a pleasant one" "for meat lovers" thanks to a "consistent" kitchen serving up "no surprises"; the "kitschy spinning salad bowl" "may be a gimmick", but some consider it "worth the trip."

Don's Fishmarket & Tavern [S] 19 | 18 | 19 | $30

9335 Skokie Blvd. (south of Golf Rd.), Skokie, 847-677-3424

◪ North Suburban mariners maintain that this "local hangout" is a "worthwhile" "oldie but goodie" for "reliable seafood" "done every way you want", with "old-fashioned service", to boot; still, some perceive the provender as "plain", "predictable" and "pedestrian"; N.B. a renovation of its dining room and tavern is planned for 2003.

Dover Straits [S] 21 | 19 | 20 | $30

1149 W. Golf Rd. (Gannon Dr.), Hoffman Estates, 847-884-3900
890 US Hwy. 45 (Rte. 83), Mundelein, 847-949-1550

■ These "always-dependable" Northwest Suburban seafood siblings are "traditional" "favorites" of a "generally older crowd" that "skips the fancy stuff" at other spots in favor of their "great early-bird" specials and "really good, basic fish menu", including "excellent Dover sole"; another "big plus" is their "dance floors with live bands" some nights (varies by location); those "into trying something new", though, may be "disappointed."

Duke of Perth §

17	17	18	$17

2913 N. Clark St. (Oakdale Ave.), 773-477-1741

■ Lakeview locals feel "lucky to have" this Scottish-American pub "in the neighborhood"; it's "the real thing", with "cozy, authentic decor" that makes you "feel like you're eating in Glasgow" and "celestial fish and chips" aided by a "good choice of UK ales" and an "amazing" selection of scotches; one complaint from the kilt-clad, though – it "should offer haggis!"

D'Vine Restaurant & Wine Bar §

18	16	18	$38

1950 W. North Ave. (Damen Ave.), 773-235-5700

◪ A "creative" New French–New American menu and a "trendy" vibe render this Wicker Parker a "romantic date place", and it's also a "good spot for late-night" weekends thanks to a DJ spinning Brazilian jazz or ambient house tunes and a 2 AM kitchen closing Fridays and Saturdays; dissenters dismiss it as "pretentious", though, citing less-than-divine service from a "full-of-themselves staff"; N.B. dinner only, closed Monday and Tuesday.

Eclectic

∇ 21	18	19	$39

117 E. North Ave. (Main St.), Barrington, 847-277-7300

■ Set in a historic schoolhouse (the former site of the now-defunct Greenery), this – you guessed it – Eclectic eatery in the Northwest Suburbs is helmed by "innovative chef" and owner Patrick Cassata, who employs "various global influences" to create a "gourmet dining experience" in a "intimate setting" where you'll get "personal attention."

Edelweiss §

∇ 21	20	20	$28

7650 W. Irving Park Rd. (Cumberland Ave.), Norridge, 708-452-6040

■ As Chicago's selection of traditional Teutonics shrinks, surveyors "in an oompah mood" give this "solid" "classic" a ratings boost for its "good German food" and service with "just enough schmaltz"; it's a "bit out of the way", but "if you like heavy" fare such as "great schnitzel" supplemented by an "excellent beer selection", there's no place better" in the Northwestern Suburbs.

Edna's §

–	–	–	I

3175 W. Madison St. (Kedzie Ave.), 773-638-7079

The down-home soul food is just what you'd expect at this thirtysomething Far West diner that sports a long Formica counter and vinyl stools – the perfect setting for generous servings of hot homemade biscuits, fried chicken, collard greens and ham hocks on rice, followed by pies and peach cobbler; N.B. closed on Monday, no liquor served.

Edwardo's S   18 | 11 | 14 | $16

1321 E. 57th St. (bet. Kenwood & Kimbark Aves.), 773-241-7960
1212 N. Dearborn St. (Division St.), 312-337-4490
2662 N. Halsted St. (1 block south of Diversey Pkwy.), 773-871-3400
521 S. Dearborn St. (bet. Congress Pkwy. & Harrison St.), 312-939-3366
904 W. Army Trail Rd. (County Farm Rd.), Carol Stream, 630-830-9600
6831 North Ave. (Grove Ave.), Oak Park, 708-524-2400
9300 Skokie Blvd. (Gross Point Rd.), Skokie, 847-674-0008
401 E. Dundee Rd. (east of Milwaukee Ave.), Wheeling, 847-520-0666

◪ Going "head to head" in a category crowded with "too many chains", this group gets its slice of the praise pie for "some of the best pizzas around", especially the "great stuffed spinach" variety (with a "dandy thin-crust" version too), made with "all-natural" "fresh ingredients"; many addicts "always take out", though, as there's little to "no atmosphere"; N.B. alcohol service varies by location.

EJ's Place S   21 | 17 | 19 | $37

10027 Skokie Blvd. (Old Orchard Rd.), Skokie, 847-933-9800

◪ Lots of North Suburban "locals" like this "steady" Italian steakhouse "related to Erie Cafe and Gene & Georgetti" through family (though all are separately owned), calling it "ideal" for its "great steaks and fresh fish" served in a "clubby", "cozy cabin atmosphere"; nevertheless, less laudatory participants pronounce it "pricey for Skokie" and pan a few worrisome "waiters with New York attitude."

Elaine   ▽ 21 | 18 | 20 | $35

10 W. Jackson Ave. (Washington St.), Naperville, 630-548-3100

◪ "Popular in the Western Suburbs", this "hip", "stylish" two-year-old set in a "lovely old house in Naperville" offers an "inventive American" menu; with "so much potential", though, it's yet to live up to the high expectations of some surveyors who cite "ups and downs" in food and service.

Eli's the Place for Steaks S   21 | 18 | 21 | $42

215 E. Chicago Ave. (Michigan Ave.), 312-642-1393

◪ Diehard fans of this "old-fashioned" Streeterville chop shop delight in its "huge portions" of "top-notch" beef and "amazing cheesecake" served in a "manly", "relaxed dining room" by a staff that "treats you courteously"; a younger generation grumbles it's "your father's idea of a steakhouse" and "needs a face-lift", but those who think it serves "yesteryear's food" should check out the new menu from chef Michael Tsonton (ex Courtright's), whose post-*Survey* arrival may not be reflected in the Food rating.

El Jardin S
| 15 | 13 | 14 | $20 |

3335 N. Clark St. (bet. Addison St. & Belmont Ave.), 773-528-6775
Surveyors say the "average food" at this "reliable" Wrigleyville Mexican pales in comparison to its "killer – and I mean killer – margaritas" ("what's in those, anyway?"), but at least its "brunch is the best hangover cure around", as long as you avoid its "great outdoor seating areas", which can be "too loud and crowded even for the Cubs and college crowds."

El Nandu S
| ∇ 19 | 14 | 19 | $18 |

2731 W. Fullerton Ave. (bet. California & Fairfield Aves.), 773-278-0900
Fans fancy this "cozy" "haunt" in Logan Square for "*el yummo*" Argentinean fare such as "excellent beef", "delicious chimichurri dishes" and "great empanadas" washed down with "best-kept-secret sangria"; there's "not much for the vegetarians", but carnivores appreciate getting "good food for the dollar"; N.B. a guitarist spices up the night Friday and Saturday.

El Presidente ◑S
| ∇ 14 | 10 | 14 | $15 |

2558 N. Ashland Ave. (Wrightwood Ave.), 773-525-7938
"Where else can you get chilaquiles at 3 AM on Xmas?" – so surveyors sum up the appeal of this "24-hour" spot serving "cheap" and "basic Mexican" fare on "busy Ashland Avenue" at the Northwest edge of Lincoln Park; still, the peevish protest about "run-of-the-mill" food and "vinyl decor" that amounts to "zero atmosphere."

EMILIO'S TAPAS S
| 21 | 19 | 19 | $27 |

444 W. Fullerton Pkwy. (Clark St.), 773-327-5100
4100 W. Roosevelt Rd. (Manheim Rd.), Hillside, 708-547-7177
EMILIO'S TAPAS SOL Y NIEVE S
215 E. Ohio St. (bet. Fairbanks Ct. & St. Clair St.), 312-467-7177
EMILIO'S TAPAS LA RIOJA S
230 W. Front St. (Wheaton Ave.), Wheaton, 630-653-7177
Each of Emilio Gervilla's tapas spots has its loyalists, but a quorum clamors for the "huge variety" of their "intensely flavored" and "authentically Spanish" "grazing goodies" (including "daily specials that yield tasty treasures"), all "reasonably priced" and served in "lively" yet "relaxing" settings that add up to "an utterly charming experience."

Emperor's Choice ◑S
| 21 | 13 | 18 | $24 |

2238 S. Wentworth Ave. (Cermak Rd.), 312-225-8800
Though some would "prefer to keep this place a secret", word is out that this Chinatown "classic" Cantonese-

Mandarin offers "always-fresh" "Chinese seafood like no other" – including what some say is the "best Peking lobster" around – in a "noisy, authentic" atmosphere; the emperor's new naysayers, though, deem it "not so choice anymore" and decry the "dreary", "dated" decor.

Enoteca Piattini ● | – | – | – | M |
934 W. Webster Ave. (bet. Bissell St. & Sheffield Ave.),
773-281-3898
Dimly lit, peppered with candles and rich in dark woods, this spacious Lincoln Park *vino* venue pairs a sophisticated list of wines with an ample choice of Italian small plates (hence the name) ranging from antipasti and pastas to meat and seafood dishes; in keeping with the theme of tasting and sharing, its extensive by-the-glass roster generally offers about 30 options.

Erawan Royal Thai Cuisine S | ▽ 23 | 25 | 26 | $52 |
729 N. Clark St. (Superior St.), 312-642-6888
■ River North's "high-end" Siamese is "pricey but well worth it", considering the "quality ingredients and creative presentations" of its "super meals" from two menus (one traditional, the other "Thai-Western fusion"), both supported by a "terrific wine list"; the "elegant", "beautiful decor" and "polite service" also help ensure a "great night out"; N.B. both owner and chef are veterans of top-rated Arun's.

Erie Cafe S | 21 | 19 | 22 | $39 |
536 W. Erie St. (Kingsbury St.), 312-266-2300
◪ "Now *this* is a steakhouse!" cry cronies of River North's cousin of Gene & Georgetti and EJ's Place (separately owned by members of one *famiglia*), an "old-school" spot "for schmoozing with clients and associates", where the "simple" Italian "man's food" is "top-quality", the service is "pro" and the location "looks like a movie set"; still, the "uninspired" say it "lacks charm."

erwin, an american cafe & bar S | 23 | 21 | 23 | $36 |
2925 N. Halsted St. (Oakdale Ave.), 773-528-7200
■ "They care and it shows" at this "quiet charmer" in Lakeview, where chef-owner Erwin Drechsler's "deft touch" yields "outstanding" New American cuisine that's "uncomplicated" yet "sophisticated" and offered on "seasonal menus as varied as the Chicago weather", making it "worth many visits"; the "neighborhood feel" may "lack buzz" ("this isn't see-and-be-seen"), but it's "warm, cozy" and "without pretense."

Escargot S | – | – | – | M |
1962 N. Halsted St. (Armitage Ave.), 773-281-4211
Lincoln Park's former Aubriot has been reconceived by chef-owner Eric Aubriot, who scaled it back in price and complexity (entrées are now all under $20) while remaining

true to his French culinary roots and stellar training; decor
changes are minor, and the upstairs lounge, Eau, continues
to offer wine, light fare and ambient music.

ESPN Zone S
12 | 19 | 13 | $20

43 E. Ohio St. (Wabash Ave.), 312-644-3776

◪ Sideliners kick back at this "big, boisterous interactive-
games" chain outpost in River North, calling it a "sports-
lovers' paradise" with American fare that's "better than
the ballpark (and more fun)" and predicting you'll come
away with a case of "tube envy from so many big TVs";
spoilsports say it's a "sensory-overload" "spectacle only",
as the "typical" bar food is "better left to the tourists."

Ethiopian Diamond S
▽ 21 | 12 | 17 | $17

6120 N. Broadway (Glen Lake Ave.), 773-338-6100

■ When white-bread Midwesterners wish for "food like
somebody *else's* mom used to make", they head to this
"feisty", "fun" spot in Edgewater for "tasty and unique"
Ethiopian dishes – including many "healthy vegetarian
choices" – that are not only "authentic" and "spicy" (i.e.
"not Americanized") but a "value" too; good thing, since
the draw is definitely "not the decor."

Ethiopian Village S
▽ 14 | 10 | 15 | $17

(aka Ethio Cafe)

3462 N. Clark St. (bet. Cornelia & Newport Aves.), 773-929-8300

◪ This Wrigleyville restaurant may have two names, but
it serves just one cuisine – "authentic Ethiopian"; the
"communal eating" makes it "fun" "for a group", and its
"interesting buffet" [Thursday–Sunday] is a "good way to
try this food" for first-timers (with lots of choices "for
vegetarians"); nevertheless, many are "lukewarm" toward
the "disappointing food."

EVEREST
27 | 27 | 28 | $74

*One Financial Pl., 440 S. La Salle Blvd., 40th fl. (Congress Pkwy.),
312-663-8920*

■ "Dress to the teeth and allow lots of time" for a "prime-
dining" "splurge" at this "heavenly" "high-end" haven 40
floors above the Loop; chef Jean "Joho has the touch",
turning out "breathtaking" New "French haute cuisine"
with "an emphasis on Alsatian" flavors "backed" by an
"amazing" "booklike wine list" and "superior service"; the
"opulent" "safari" interior has detractors, but all are awed
by its "stellar views."

Evergreen ●S
– | – | – | M

2411 S. Wentworth Ave. (24th St.), 312-225-8898

More upscale than most of its neighbors on this stretch
of Wentworth in Chinatown, this charming Cantonese-
Mandarin standout is an evergreen favorite for Hong Su
chicken and kung pao beef, along with a few seafood

surprises like clams in black bean sauce, served on white tablecloths in a large and attractive room.

Ezuli ●⬤S ▽ 20 | 16 | 16 | $22
1415 N. Milwaukee Ave. (Wood St.), 773-227-8200
■ Named after a Haitian love goddess, this "fun, electric place" in Wicker Park attracts worshipers with "wonderful Caribbean cuisine" such as "awesome jerk chicken", "piña colada bread pudding to die for" and other "flavorful", "interesting food"; the setting is "hip" and "trendy but not pretentious", and a "hostess dancing" to DJ music six nights a week adds to the "cool atmosphere."

Fadó Irish Pub S 13 | 19 | 14 | $21
100 W. Grand Ave. (Clark St.), 312-836-0066
☑ "Good times" are reported at this "fun" River North link in an Irish-themed "national chain" by fans who call it a "favorite watering hole" with "great music and decor", an "interesting" layout that "lends itself to socializing" and some "decent" "pub grub"; separatists say "go for the Guinness, not the food", claiming that the long-ago "authentic feel" is actually "manufactured for tourists."

Famous Dave's S 18 | 16 | 16 | $20
1631 W. Lake St. (½ mi. east of Hwy. 53), Addison, 630-261-0100
113 S. Western Ave. (south of Main St.), Carpentersville, 847-428-9190
Yorktown Ctr., 206B Yorktown Ctr. (Highland Ave.), Lombard, 630-620-6363
1126 E. Ogden Ave. (Burlington Ave.), Naperville, 630-428-3500
7201 W. 25th St. (bet. Cermak Rd. & 26th St.), North Riverside, 708-447-8848
15657 S. Harlem Ave. (bet. 156th & 157th Sts.), Orland Park, 708-532-7850
1101 E. Dundee Rd. (Rand Rd.), Palatine, 847-202-2213
948 S. Barrington Rd. (Ramblewood Dr.), Streamwood, 630-483-2480
99 Townline Rd. (bet. Aspen & Deerpath Drs.), Vernon Hills, 847-549-9933
☑ "Tasty" ribs are the business of this "fun, casual" "roadhouse" chain in the Northwest and West Suburbs where the tickled tell us the "finger-licking food" "done right at the right price" is "worth its weight in BBQ sauce"; the fickle find fault with the "formula" feel, "ordinary" output and "iffy" service.

Father & Son Pizza ●S 17 | 13 | 16 | $19
5691 N. Milwaukee Ave. (Markham Ave.), 773-774-2620
2475 N. Milwaukee Ave. (Sacramento Blvd.), 773-252-2620
Marcello's Father & Son Pizza ●S
645 W. North Ave. (bet. Halsted & Larrabee Sts.), 312-654-2550
☑ These "informal" fraternal Logan Square and Northwest Side pizza-and-Italian places have partialists who prize

their signature thin-and-crispy 'za and other "Italian food at value" prices, though panners pooh-pooh the product as "passable" and the pies as "just adequate"; similarly, some say Marcello's is a "good, inexpensive restaurant", while others say it's "trying to be upscale" but missing the mark.

Feast S 20 18 17 $27
1616 N. Damen Ave. (North Ave.), 773-772-7100
■ Feasters fawn over this "hip" Bucktown New American, saying it's "a good local place that's just fancy enough"; chef Debra Sharpe brings "a touch of whimsy" to her "creative" yet "down-home" fare, which is served up in an "inviting" and "funky atmosphere" – in short, "for both the eyes and the palate, the name says it all!"; P.S. there's "delightful" outdoor dining too.

Ferrari Ristorante S – – – E
2360 N. Clybourn Ave. (bet. Ashland & Fullerton Aves.), 773-348-2450
In revamping his former Lincoln Park fave, Marco!, chef-owner Marco Conti doubled the seating capacity (by annexing the building next door), swapped cozy for chic (blood-red banquettes now line the pure white walls and Versace chargers grace each tabletop) and invited toque Massimo Ferrari to join him in the partially glassed-in open kitchen (hence the new name); the cuisine is still authentic Italian, though, including house-made pastas and risottos, both specialties of the more-rustic prior incarnation.

Filippo's S 22 16 20 $27
2211 N. Clybourn Ave. (Webster Ave.), 773-528-2211
■ Greedy gluttons are "glad no one knows this" "cozy" Clybourn Corridor Southern "Italian eatery", "one of the undiscovered treasures" in town that "carefully prepares" "terrific", "dependable" dishes, including "some of best pastas in Chicago"; a "friendly staff" and "comfortable prices" contribute to the "homey feeling"; P.S. the kitchen's "very accommodating with special requests."

Firefly ◑S – – – M
3335 N. Halsted St. (bet. Belmont & Cornelia Aves.), 773-525-2505
Restaurant baron Dion Antic has transformed his Boys Town corner boîte (formerly Deville) into an intimate cafe; the simple snacky menu features bistro-style classics, but the emphasis is on martinis, conversation and peeking into the curtained booths that line one side of the snug space.

Fireplace Inn, The ◑S 18 16 17 $26
1448 N. Wells St. (bet. North Ave. & Schiller St.), 312-664-5264
◪ It may be "nothing fancy", but loyalists nevertheless "love those ribs" at this Old Town BBQ "joint" that's been "packing them in like sardines" since 1969; a few firebrands grumble over "generic" grub, "dark" digs and "slow"

service, but the "nice outdoor garden" and sports on TV
help keep it a "neighborhood favorite."

Flat Top Grill S   18 | 14 | 15 | $19

3200 N. Southport Ave. (Belmont Ave.), 773-665-8100
319 W. North Ave. (Orleans St.), 312-787-7676
1000 W. Washington Blvd. (Carpenter St.), 312-829-4800
707 Church St. (bet. Orrington & Sherman Aves.), Evanston, 847-570-0100
726 Lake St. (Oak Park Ave.), Oak Park, 708-358-8200
☑ "Go hungry" and "choose your own fresh ingredients,
then watch 'em cook it all up" at this "fun" (if "hectic")
chain of Asian-American stir-fry stops where "lots of good
choices" and a "helpful staff" allow inter-activists to be as
"creative as they want"; flat-liners flame the "DIY" concept,
claiming it "all tastes the same", but admit it's "a great
place for kids"; N.B. the Decor score may not reflect a
post-*Survey* remodeling of the Evanston branch.

Flo S   – | – | – | I

1434 W. Chicago Ave. (bet. Bishop & Noble Sts.), 312-243-0477
This girl is a Wicker Park woman now, maturing beyond her
breakfast-brunch-lunch limitations to serve dinner Tuesday–
Saturday (and soon to sport a very grown-up liquor license);
the bargain-priced fare exhibits Southwestern influences
in such dishes as Frito pie, roasted chicken with mole, and
shrimp poblano; local artwork on the exposed brick walls
sets a funky, neighborhood tone.

Fluky's S   17 | 10 | 14 | $8

6821 N. Western Ave. (Pratt Blvd.), 773-274-3652 ⊅
The Shops at Northridge, 520 N. Michigan Ave. (bet. Michigan & Ohio Sts.), 312-245-0702
Lincolnwood Town Ctr., 3333 W. Touhy Ave. (McCormick St.), Lincolnwood, 847-677-7726 ⊅
3061 Dundee Rd. (Landwehr Rd.), Northbrook, 847-272-9215 ⊅
☑ Canine critics give "two paws up" to the "hot dogs from
heaven" served at these fast food "fixtures" where faithful
followers "bow [wow] in homage" to a "classic" "dawg"
"done right" as well as "good grilled onions and fries" and "a
not-so-bad chicken-breast sandwich" too; connoisseurs
snarl they're "not real contenders."

Flying Chicken S   – | – | – | I

3811 N. Lincoln Ave. (Wolcott Ave.), 773-477-1090
Though this Lincoln Square Colombian's specialty is
rotisserie chicken, the only flying those birds are doing is
off the plate, as are generous portions of oxtail or hen
soup, empanadas, churrascos and sides of yucca and
plantains; carryout may be your best bet, though, since the
bare-bones ambiance is somewhat lacking.

Fogo de Chão 🖪
_|_|_| E

661 N. LaSalle St. (Erie St.), 312-932-9330

Sword-bearing waiters in gaucho attire slice 15 fire-roasted meats tableside in this clamorous Brazilian churrascaria; one price gets you endless helpings plus side dishes and trips to the cold buffet – until you flip your chip, signaling to the dutiful staff that you're finished; slate, dark wood, amber-tinted glass and a waterfall add to the retro-'70s lodge feel of this international chain outpost in River North.

Follia 🖪
_|_|_| M

953 W. Fulton St. (Morgan St.), 312-243-2888

Foodie fashionistas are mad for this sleek Market District venue attached to (but not affiliated with) the Fulton Lounge, where the front windows sport couture garments direct from the runways of Milan and model-servers proffer a frequently changing menu of Italian dishes including housemade pastas, risottos with saffron or truffles, specialties such as Cotoletta Alla Milanese and crisp individual pizzas from the glittering cobalt-tiled, wood-burning oven.

Fond de la Tour
23 | 23 | 23 | $47

40 N. Tower Rd. (bet. Butterfield & Meyers Rds.), Oak Brook, 630-620-1500

☒ Folks for whom "consistency counts" are fond of the "traditional French" favorites on offer at this "elegant" West Suburban bistro with "nice decor", "one of the few untrendy gems left" where "the food and service remain so special"; though some detractors dismiss it as "overpriced" and "a bit dated", most say it's "an oldie but a goodie."

Fondue Stube 🖪
19 | 12 | 17 | $29

2717 W. Peterson Ave. (Fairfield Ave.), 773-784-2200

☒ People who pine to "play with their food" find "a splendid change of pace from traditional dining" at this "simple treasure" in Rogers Park with "fondue as good as in Switzerland" and "friendly service" in a "quaint, cozy" room; nonetheless, yet-to-be-impressed yodelers yell "you'll need a Swiss bank account for what it charges" and yawn that the decor "could do with an overhaul."

foodlife 🖪
17 | 15 | 14 | $16

Water Tower Pl., 835 N. Michigan Ave., mezzanine level (bet. Chestnut & Pearson Sts.), 312-335-3663

☒ "More intriguing than the usual food court", this "fun" "shopping stop" "at Water Tower" Place is a wonderland of "choices, choices, choices", with 13 kitchens serving everything from Asian to Cajun to Italian to Mexican to Thai to all-American burgers and fries; the "cafeteria"-style setup makes it a "great place for on-the-run eating", though some say the "format is confusing" and "not cheap", warning "watch out for" the "automatic service charge" of 7.5 percent.

Fortunato S — | — | — | E

2005 W. Division St. (Damen Ave.), 773-645-7200
Chef-owner Jennifer Newbury's Ukrainian Village venture
explores an ingredient-driven approach to Italian hearth
cooking, with a seasonal focus on organic vegetables,
fresh-made pasta, and meat and seafood prepared within
her glass-enclosed kitchen's wood-burning oven (and paired
with native vinos); like the cuisine it serves, the stylish
earth-toned dining room conjures the feel of the *campagna*.

Founders Hill Brewing — | 16 | 16 | $20
Co. & Restaurant S
(fka Founders Hill Brewing Co.)
5200 Main St. (Grove St.), Downers Grove, 630-963-2739
■ The "beer's the thing" at this West Suburban "hangout"
"geared to the young drinking crowd" that is known for
creating its own selection of "uniquely flavored" "specialty
brews" on site; nevertheless, suds-swillers "hope" that "a
[post-*Survey*] change in ownership", a new chef (Pete
Kudzin) in the kitchen and a "new" American menu will
"improve" its culinary fortunes.

Four Farthings S 17 | 17 | 17 | $24

*2060 N. Cleveland Ave. (bet. Dickens & Lincoln Aves.),
773-935-2060*
■ "A second kitchen to many" folks in the Lincoln Park
neighborhood, this "local joint" boasts a "comfortable pub
atmosphere" and is "nicer than your typical bar", featuring
"some high-end entrées" such as several "surf 'n' turf"
selections that supplement its Traditional American menu
of "great salads and burgers"; P.S. it's "especially great
outdoors" on the "nice" 75-seat patio that "welcomes
well-behaved dogs."

Fox & Obel Cafe S ∇ 26 | 19 | 21 | $12

401 E. Illinois St. (McClurg Ct.), 312-379-0112
■ The "crowds are starting to show up" at this American
cafe "in the upscale market" of the same name (located at
the corner of McClurg Court in Streeterville) for "excellent
light meals" including "fantastic soups", "great breads" and
"delicious sandwiches prepared with fabulous ingredients",
as well as "good" pastries and coffee; to some, it's the "best
new quick-food" stop around for breakfast, lunch or dinner.

FRANCESCA'S AMICI S 24 | 19 | 20 | $31
174 N. York Rd. (bet. North Ave. & 2nd St.), Elmhurst, 630-279-7970
FRANCESCA'S BRYN MAWR S
1039 W. Bryn Mawr Ave. (Kenmore Ave.), 773-506-9261
FRANCESCA'S BY THE RIVER S
200 S. Second St. (Illinois St.), St. Charles, 630-587-8211
FRANCESCA'S CAMPAGNA S
127 W. Main St. (2nd St.), West Dundee, 847-844-7099
(continued)

(continued)
FRANCESCA'S FIORE 🅂
7407 Madison St. (Des Plaines Ave.), Forest Park, 708-771-3063
FRANCESCA'S INTIMO 🅂
293 E. Illinois St. (bet. Bank Ln. & Western Ave.), Lake Forest, 847-735-9235
FRANCESCA'S NORTH 🅂
Northbrook Shopping Ctr., 1145 Church St. (Shermer St.), Northbrook, 847-559-0260
FRANCESCA'S ON TAYLOR 🅂
1400 W. Taylor St. (Loomis St.), 312-829-2828
FRANCESCA'S TAVOLA 🅂
208 S. Arlington Heights Rd. (NW Hwy.), Arlington Heights, 847-394-3950
LA SORELLA DI FRANCESCA 🅂
18 W. Jefferson Ave. (bet. Main & Washington Sts.), Naperville, 630-961-2706
■ 'Mama' Mia Francesca (Scott Harris' Wrigleyville original) has spread her signature style – "frequently changing" menus of "hearty", "creative" and "reasonably" priced dishes from Rome and the surrounding areas of Tuscany, Umbria and Lazio – throughout Chicagoland with her fast-growing group of "stylish" daughters, "reliable" and "lively" who set a "family-yet-upscale" mood.

Francesco's Hole in the Wall 🅂 | 24 | 16 | 21 | $29
254 Skokie Blvd. (bet. Dundee & Lake Cook Rds.), Northbrook, 847-272-0155
▨ "A sauce slurper's symphony" resounds off the "bare brick" walls of this "ridiculously tiny", "old-style" North Suburban "hangout" serving "fantastic, homemade" Southern Italian fare fans "dream about"; some wallflowers wonder, though, if it's worth the "long wait" for a spot in its "cramped quarters" and suggest you'll either "need to know the owners" or "go at an unpopular hour" "to get seated"; N.B. cash only.

Frankie J's on Broadway 🅂 | – | – | – | M
4437 N. Broadway (Montrose Ave.), 773-769-2959
Local comic-cum-chef Frankie Janisch has found an Uptown home for his two loves: hearty American home cooking from family recipes, served up with a chuckle in the lime-green dining room, and improv comedy at the upstairs MethaDome Theater; N.B. BYO.

Freddy's Ribhouse 🅂 | – | – | – | M
1555 N. Sheffield Ave. (North Ave.), 312-377-7427
Tickling tasters with its "top-tier BBQ at mid-tier prices", including "great babybacks" and "crisp fries", this Lincoln Park rib-wrangler features an early-20th-century look, a "kid-friendly" atmosphere and parent-friendly libations ("try Freddy's lager!") as well as outdoor dining for that true, open-air barbecue experience.

Froggy's French Cafe 24 | 19 | 24 | $36

306 Green Bay Rd. (Highwood Ave.), Highwood, 847-433-7080

■ "Authentic, simple French cooking" with a strong seafood focus from a "friendly and approachable" toque together with "casual but attentive service" from a "knowledgeable staff" and a "comfortable, earthy European" ambiance render this "dependable", "busy" bistro in the North Suburbs an "old favorite" of Francophiles; "try the chef's menu, an ever-changing sampler served in five courses."

FRONTERA GRILL 26 | 22 | 22 | $34

445 N. Clark St. (bet. Hubbard & Illinois Sts.), 312-661-1434

■ "A Chicago legend and deservedly so", this River Norther (the more casual older brother of top-rated Topolobampo) is "the one that started it all", showing "what depth Mexican food can have" with "charming" chef-owner Rick Bayless' "world-class" "died-and-gone-to-heaven" creations; add in "an interesting variety" of "fabulous margaritas" and "great service" from a "professional staff" and it's no wonder "it can be nearly impossible to get in."

Furama [S] ▽ 17 | 10 | 13 | $19

4936 N. Broadway (Argyle St.), 773-271-1161
2828 S. Wentworth Ave. (31st St.), 312-225-6888

◩ "An excellent variety" of "reliable dim sum" is served "from numerous carts" seven days a week at this Uptown and Chinatown duo where a Cantonese-Mandarin "menu is also available"; still, some say the fare is "so-so" and take a dim view of the "slow service" and "old-looking decor."

GABRIEL'S 27 | 24 | 26 | $51

310 Green Bay Rd. (Highwood Ave.), Highwood, 847-433-0031

■ "A most enjoyable evening" awaits at this "classic" New French–Italian on the North Shore where "sincerity is evident" in the "excellent presentation" of "top-notch", "terrific food"; the "creative" kitchen is overseen by "scrupulously attentive" "hands-on chef-owner" Gabriel Viti, and the "elegant but casual" dining room is staffed by "real professionals"; P.S. grape groupies gloat it has "one of the best wine lists" around.

Gale Street Inn [S] 19 | 16 | 18 | $25

4914 N. Milwaukee Ave. (Lawrence Ave.), 773-725-1300
935 Diamond Lake Rd. (bet. Rtes. 45 & 83), Mundelein, 847-566-1090

■ "Everyone makes you feel welcome" at this Suburban Northwest–Northwest Side American duo (unaffiliated for 15 years) known for "tender, tasty ribs" "you can cut with a spoon"; those who "make the trip to Jefferson Park" will find a "traditional" "supper-club" ambiance, while "beautiful views" of Diamond Lake greet guests of the Mundelein sibling, which moved across the street last year.

Gaylord India S

20 | 14 | 19 | $23

678 N. Clark St. (Huron St.), 312-664-1700

Gaylord Fine Indian Cuisine S

555 Mall Dr. (Higgins Rd.), Schaumburg, 847-619-3300

■ Serving an "extensive menu" of "complex, exotic" and "authentic [Northern] Indian food" (and some Southern specialties at the Schaumburg location) like "rich flavorful curries" "as good as on Devon" Street in Chicago's Little India, these "reliable" city and suburban subcontinentals are also prized for "friendly service"; P.S. the "bargain lunch buffets" offer "great choices and good value."

Geja's Cafe S

22 | 22 | 21 | $38

340 W. Armitage Ave. (bet. Clark St. & Lincoln Ave.), 773-281-9101

■ For "something a little different", "take your honey" to this Lincoln Park fondue "favorite", a "rustic", "romantic getaway" where "it's fun to cook your" own "nice, leisurely meal" and sample an "adventurous wine list" while "live guitar music" "adds to the ambiance"; "plan to get your clothes dry-cleaned" afterward, though, as that "hot-oil smell" can cling (don't worry – it's "worth it").

Gene & Georgetti

23 | 16 | 20 | $46

500 N. Franklin St. (Illinois St.), 312-527-3718

☑ "Forget the rest" say fans of River North's "old-time Chicago" "steakhouse saloon", a "famous" "institution" with a "men's club atmosphere" that opened in 1941 and just "gets better with age" thanks to "big slabs" of "great steaks (and they know it)" and "good service (if they know you)"; contrary carnivores claim it's become a "caricature of itself" and slam the "surly" staff and "run-down decor."

Genesee Depot S

21 | 16 | 21 | $26

3736 N. Broadway (bet. Grace St. & Waveland Ave.), 773-528-6990

■ An East Lakeview "BYO bargain", this "unpretentious" Traditional American established in 1974 is still chuggin' along, "nurturing" its regulars with "friendly service" and "yummy", "priced-right" fare that's "like home cooking for a special occasion"; the "rustic" dining room behind its "quaint storefront" may be "unpretentious", but it does offer a "nice", "homey atmosphere."

Giannotti Steak House S

22 | 17 | 20 | $35

17 W. 400 22nd St. (bet. Midwest Rd. & Rte. 83), Oakbrook Terrace, 630-833-2700

☑ "Try the eight-finger cavatelli" (the signature dish) advise aficionados of this "manly" Italian steakhouse situated in a West Suburban strip mall; its traditional menu offers a trip back to a "lost era", when "good food" was "abundant", and its "nice bar" features "good [live] entertainment" most nights; still, faultfinders fret about "heavy" fare that's priced "on the high side for what you get."

GIBSONS STEAKHOUSE ●S   25 | 21 | 23 | $48
1028 N. Rush St. (Bellevue Pl.), 312-266-8999
Doubletree Hotel, 5464 N. River Rd. (bet. Balmoral &
Bryn Mawr Aves.), Rosemont, 847-928-9900
☑ "To see and be seen", a "forty-something crowd" of
"power brokers", "glitterati", "wanna-bes", "pinky ring"-
ers and "major league ballplayers" packs this "exciting",
"testosterone-filled hot spot" and "watering hole", an
"expense-account heaven" for "A-1 martinis" and "obscene
portions" of "excellent" "fresh meat"; those who find it a
"noisy" "Gold Coast cliché" report its offshoot in "Rosemont
is a little quieter."

Gilardi's S   21 | 21 | 21 | $31
23397 N. Rte. 45 (Rte. 21), Vernon Hills, 847-634-1811
■ "Consistently good", "classic Italian home cooking" lures
loyalists to this Suburban Northwest "hidden treasure"; the
"tranquil" and "romantic" setting is reminiscent of "going
to a relative's" "neat old house" with a "great front porch",
and the "friendly host and staff" "make you feel like a part
of the family", helping make this a "nice place to go."

Gino's Steak House S   ▽ 21 | 17 | 20 | $33
16299 S. Wallace Ave. (163rd St.), Harvey, 708-331-4393
☑ Since 1950, this South Suburban steakhouse stalwart (a
senior sibling of the Millennium Steaks & Chops shops)
has been grilling up a "great bone-in steak" and other
"honest, down-to-earth" fare in an "enjoyable" environment
replete with the original stained-glass windows; those
who find it not so genial, however, lament that it's "loud"
and avow the victuals are merely "average."

Gioco S   21 | 21 | 19 | $40
1312 S. Wabash Ave. (13th St.), 312-939-3870
■ "The South Loop comes alive with good Italian food"
proclaim *partisans* of this "pioneer" located "off the beaten
path", where "great chef" Corcoran O'Connor creates
cuisine that's "innovative" and "hearty" (if somewhat
"expensive"), including some "standout specials"; the
"ultra-chic", "inviting" atmosphere of its "fun" former-
speakeasy setting includes a "cool bar" and "great patio
seating in summer."

Giordano's S   18 | 11 | 14 | $17
135 E. Lake St. (bet. Lower Stetson & Upper Michigan Aves.),
312-616-1200
2855 N. Milwaukee Ave. (Wolfram St.), 723-862-4200
730 N. Rush St. (Superior St.), 312-951-0747
5159 S. Pulaski Rd. (bet. Archer & 51st Sts.), 773-582-7676 ●
236 S. Wabash Ave. (Jackson Ave.), 312-939-4646
1040 W. Belmont Ave. (Kenmore Ave.), 773-327-1200
5927 W. Irving Park Rd. (Austin Ave.), 773-736-5553
(continued)

(continued)
Giordano's
223 W. Jackson Blvd. (Franklin St.), 312-583-9400
310 W. Randolph St. (Franklin St.), 312-201-1441
815 W. Van Buren St. (Halsted St.), 312-421-1221
Additional locations throughout the Chicago area
◪ This "casual" chain draws its share of supporters in Chicago's deep-dish derby with "impressive stuffed pizzas" (and "good thin-crust" too, with a "wide spectrum of toppings"); nevertheless, some 'za-lots claim it's "inconsistent" and sneer that service "can be lacking"; N.B. as well as additional city branches, there are dozens of locations in the suburbs and central Florida.

Gladys Luncheonette ◐ [S] 🚫💳 ▽ 26 | 17 | 21 | $16
4527 S. Indiana Ave. (45th St.), 773-548-4566
◪ Since the mid-'40s, this "traditional and homey" Hyde Park institution has been serving "soul food at its best" – from favorites like ham hocks, catfish, collard greens and sweet potato pie to more Yankee-challenging specialties like the curiously complimented "awful good brains 'n' eggs"; N.B. though founder Gladys Holcomb recently passed away, her daughter plans to keep the business going.

Glen Ellyn Sports Brew [S] 16 | 16 | 17 | $24
433 N. Main St. (Duane St.), Glen Ellyn, 630-942-1140
◪ From a "decent menu (for a brewery)", this "pleasant" West Suburban American offers a "simple but dependable" assortment of "hearty food"; those who find the grub "so-so" and the service "spotty" suggest "go for the beer" on tap, a rotating selection of seven proprietary creations by brew-master Mike Engelke.

Glory [S] – | – | – | M
1952 N. Damen Ave. (bet. Armitage Ave. & Homer St.), 773-235-7400
Chef-owner Sharon Cohen presents the bounty of New England in the form of Rhode Island johnnycakes, Maine lobster rolls, Ipswich fried clams, Providence-style grilled pizzas and whoopie pies at this Regional American set in an airy two-story Bucktown bungalow awash in natural light and painted the colors of a Cape Cod summer sky; reasonable prices and a BYO policy for the big folks plus a children's menu for the small fry make a visit a vacation.

Gold Coast Dogs 19 | 8 | 13 | $9
Midway Airport, food court, 773-735-6789 ◐ [S]
2 N. Riverside Dr. (bet. Canal St. & Madison Ave.), 312-879-0447 🚫💳
159 N. Wabash Ave. (bet. Lake & Randolph Sts.), 312-917-1677 [S]
O'Hare Int'l Airport, Terminal 5, 773-462-0125 [S] 🚫💳
O'Hare Int'l Airport, Terminal 3, 773-462-9942 [S]
17 S. Wabash Ave. (Madison St.), 312-578-1133

(continued)
Gold Coast Dogs
Union Station, 225 S. Canal St. (Jackson Blvd.),
312-258-8585 🅂🍴
U Of C Center for Advanced Medicine, 5758 S. Maryland Ave.
(bet. 57th & 58th Sts.), 773-834-7261
Old Orchard Shopping Ctr., 275 Old Orchard Arcade
(bet. Golf Rd. & Skokie Blvd.), Skokie, 847-674-4171 🅂🍴
Additional locations throughout the Chicago area
◪ Though it's "a travesty they closed the original location" on State Street, dogged loyalists who "love that char-broiled taste" still "go out of their way" for the "great grease" at this "classic" chain of "hot doggers" that also serves chicken and "good burgers" (including a "spicy veggie" version); true, there are "no frills", but then again "you're paying for none"; N.B. additional branches are planned for Chicago, Evanston, Glenview, Rosemont and Tinley Park.

Goose Island Brewing Co. 🅂   15 16 16 $19
3535 N. Clark St. (Addison St.), 773-832-9040
1800 N. Clybourn Ave. (Sheffield Ave.), 312-915-0071
◼ Microbrew mavens maintain there's "always a smile" at these "nothing-fancy" brewpubs serving Lincoln Park and Wrigleyville; though "both locations offer" "above-average pub grub" to go with their "awesome selection" of "fresh beer" made "on the premises", some warn "steer clear of anything but" the "good burgers" and "terrific chips."

Grand Lux Café 🅂   – – – E
600 N. Michigan Ave. (Ontario St.), 312-276-2500
The Cheesecake Factory folks spared no amount of gold leaf in opening this extravagantly decorated River North Magnificent Miler whose matching mile-long menu features ample portions of American fare and lots of decadent desserts; glittery frescoes and whimsical velvet upholstery add panache to the spacious dining areas, bar and atrium.

Graziano's Brick Oven Pizza 🅂 ▽ 22 21 21 $22
5960 W. Touhy Ave. (Lehigh Ave.), Niles, 847-647-4096
◼ Northwest Suburbanites credit this "delightful, if noisy, family Italian" for a "steady" kitchen that dishes up "huge portions" of "terrific food" like its signature bowtie pasta with vodka sauce, a "great bottomless salad bowl" and, as the name suggests, pizza; "good service", a "casual" vibe and "comfortable decor" with movie posters on the walls make it a popular "local place."

Greek Islands 🅂   20 18 19 $24
200 S. Halsted St. (Adams St.), 312-782-9855 ●
300 E. 22nd St. (Highland Ave.), Lombard, 630-932-4545
◼ "One of the most consistent in Greektown", the "Halsted location" of this Hellenic pair has been "a favorite for 31

years", and its younger West Suburban sibling has fans too; regulars muse each is "a real value" for "well-executed standards" of "Greek comfort food", "efficiently served" by "sprinting waiters" in a "busy, noisy" "family" setting.

Green Dolphin Street [S] 20 | 21 | 18 | $43

2200 N. Ashland Ave. (Webster Ave.), 773-395-0066

◪ "What more do you need" for nights beyond forgetting ask aficionados of this Lincoln Park New American supper club that supplies the setting with "great food, service and ambiance", as well as "excellent" "live entertainment", "all under one roof"; even so, the jaded aren't jazzed by the "overpriced" and "small portions" or the sometimes "inattentive" staff; N.B. the Food rating may not reflect the post-*Survey* arrival of chef Robert Greene.

Green Door Tavern [S] 15 | 18 | 17 | $19

678 N. Orleans St. (Huron St.), 312-664-5496

■ "Oozing atmosphere that can't be replicated", this "classic" American premiered as a 1921 Prohibition-era speakeasy in a River North structure built just after the Great Chicago Fire of 1871; folks "go to see" its "fun" "paraphernalia" – a "unique" assemblage of fire helmets, political mementos, sports pennants, et al. – more than for its "huge burgers" and other "standard bar food"; N.B. the Decor score may not reflect a post-*Survey* remodeling.

Green Room – | – | – | M

1305 Green St. (bet. Adams & Monroe Sts.), 312-666-9813

Floor-to-ceiling windows and techno tunes provide the counterpoint for an American comfort-food menu at this chic West Loop spot, where local loft-dwellers snack in style as they survey the scene from the backlit vodka bar and the upstairs balcony lounge.

Grill on the Alley, The [S] 19 | 21 | 20 | $41

Westin Hotel, 909 N. Michigan Ave. (Delaware Pl.), 312-255-9009

◪ An offshoot of the Beverly Hills original, this Streeterville steakhouse in the Westin strikes some as a "good place to relax after shopping" or convene for a "power lunch", with "great American cuisine (for a hotel restaurant)" served amid dark oak and "fun art"; critics caution, though, that it "has not lived up to expectations" yet; N.B. the Food rating may not reflect the post-*Survey* arrival of chef Fidel Garcia.

Grillroom, The [S] 19 | 16 | 18 | $34

33 W. Monroe St. (bet. Dearborn & State Sts.), 312-960-0000

◪ Loopsters like the "innovative preparations" of this "classy" "sleeper" of a steak-and-seafood house, especially for a "business lunch", "getting a drink and dinner after work" or "before going to the Shubert Theatre" directly across the street; still, the less impressed say simply that it's a "good" but "not-very-special" "standby."

Grotto S
— — — E

1030 N. State St. (Rush St.), 312-280-1005
Steaking its claim in the Newberry Plaza site vacated by Palette's (and before that, Arnie's), this straightforward Italian steakhouse will appeal to Gold Coast classicists seeking steaks, chops and familiar Italian fare (baked clams, linguine carbonara, chicken Vesuvio); the spacious, handsome dining area done in sage, dark wood and mirrors wraps around an abundant greenhouse atrium inherited from the predecessor.

Hackney's S
18 14 17 $18

733 S. Dearborn St. (Polk St.), 312-461-1116
1514 E. Lake Ave. (bet. Sunset Ridge & Waukegan Rds.), Glenview, 847-724-7171
1241 Harms Rd. (Lake Ave.), Glenview, 847-724-5577
880 N. Old Rand Rd. (Main St.), Lake Zurich, 847-438-2103
9550 W. 123rd St. (La Grange Rd.), Palos Park, 708-448-8300
241 S. Milwaukee Ave. (Dundee Rd.), Wheeling, 847-537-2100
■ "Big burgers are the big draw here" at these "suburban classics" and their newer Downtown sibling where "you always know what you're going to get" with your "thick" patty – their famous "heart-stopping onion loaf" and "average service"; the original Harms Road location has a "dark" "martini-on-the-rocks atmosphere", while the city branch is more "cheerful."

Hai Yen S
▽ 19 11 14 $18

1055 W. Argyle St. (Broadway), 773-561-4077
◪ While this "bright" and "lively" Edgewater eatery's "authentic" Vietnamese cuisine (with some Chinese dishes) is "very good" and the signature Seven Courses of "Beef dinner is wonderful", protesters propose that the "nothing-fancy" decor and "noisy" atmosphere make for an "unappealing room" and say that the "eager-to-please" staff provides somewhat "disorganized service."

Half Shell S⊄
21 10 14 $26

676 W. Diversey Pkwy. (Orchard St.), 773-549-1773
■ "Awesome-shellfish" seekers dig this "delightfully dingy" and "dumpy" "underground dive", a Lakeview "hole in the wall" (or should we say floor?) that's been "going for years" on the strength of some of "the best crab legs in town"; with such "great seafood" "at reasonable prices", "love"-blinded lauders swear that the "service is good – even when they yell at you!"

Happy Chef Dim Sum House ◕ S
▽ 21 6 12 $15

2164 S. Archer Ave. (Cermak Rd.), 312-808-3689
◪ "Even if they don't have carts", this "inexpensive" spot in the Chinatown Square Mall is an "always-busy" "stand-out" thanks to "always-good" "Hong Kong–style dim sum"; still,

the "crowd"-conscious complain it's a "madhouse on weekends", and the style-savvy say that using the plastic tablecloths as "garbage bags is just a bit too pragmatic."

Hard Rock Cafe S
12 | 20 | 15 | $21

63 W. Ontario St. (Clark St.), 312-943-2252

☑ Starstruck surveyors say the chance to "eat in a rock museum" makes this "trendy" River North headbanger "a fun place for all ages" and report that the American eats are "surprisingly good for such a touristy spot"; however, cons criticize the "mediocre food and service" (not to mention all that "noise"), and simply advise "get your T-shirt and go."

Harry Caray's S
20 | 19 | 19 | $32

33 W. Kinzie St. (Dearborn St.), 312-828-0966
Holiday Inn, 10233 W. Higgins Rd. (Mannheim St.), Rosemont, 847-699-1200

Harry Caray's Seventh Inning Stretch S
Midway Airport, 5757 S. Cicero Ave. (55th St.), 773-948-6300

☑ A triple-header of tributes to their late namesake, these Downtown and airport area Italian steakhouses offer "casual dining" "for baseball and steak fans" within "friendly" confines full of "Cubs kitsch" and other "sports memorabilia"; the opposing team, though, curtly counters they're "below par."

Harry's Velvet Room ◑S
▽ 15 | 21 | 15 | $31

56 W. Illinois St. (bet. Clark & Dearborn Sts.), 312-527-5600

☑ "Funky, cool and velvety", this "stylin'", "smoky" River North American "joint just oozes sex", earning it the lounge-lizard vote as the "best late-night fun" spot for after-dinner drinks and people-watching"; those who "have never understood why it offers meals" say stick to the "good appetizers" or "just have the martinis."

Hashalom ⌿
▽ 23 | 10 | 16 | $14

2905 W. Devon Ave. (Francisco Ave.), 773-465-5675

■ For "a real change of pace", Chicagoans visit this "favorite kid-friendly dive" in Rogers Park, a "standby for Middle Eastern food" "at fair prices"; its "innovative menu" of "authentic and well-prepared" "Israeli and Moroccan" dishes – including "special soups", "unusual salads" and "good combo plates" – has some sighing "too bad it's not open on weekends."

Hatsuhana
22 | 16 | 19 | $32

160 E. Ontario St. (bet. Michigan Ave. & St. Clair St.), 312-280-8808

☑ "Bring on the raw fish" cry fans of the "excellent" and "very fresh sushi" at this "small" Streeterville Japanese that's also a "favorite" for "out-of-this-world tempura", despite some protests that it's "pricey" ("you pay for its location" near the Magnificent Mile); also, the "efficient" service strikes some as "surly", and the "modern decor" and "cramped tables" leave others cold.

Heartland Cafe 🅂 | 16 | 15 | 16 | $16 |
7000 N. Glenwood Ave. (Lunt Ave.), 773-465-8005
☑ "Like going back to Woodstock", this Rogers Park "blast from the past" is still golden with groupies for its "good (not great)" "mélange of cooking" – from "healthy, tasty" vegetarian fare to "yummy buffalo"; its "comfortable" digs play host to "great live music" acts and poetry readings for "bohemian people" trying to get their souls free.

Heat | ▽ 22 | 21 | 22 | $60 |
1507 N. Sedgwick St. (North Ave.), 312-397-9818
☑ Raters blow hot and cold over this "trendy" Old Town Japanese whose "gimmick" is tremendous tanks teeming with a quarter ton of swimming soon-to-be-sushi; pros call it "innovative" and "ahead of its time", with an "exquisite menu", "creative maki" and an "excellent sake collection" in a "stark", "elegant" space; detractors who dislike "floppy fish on the plate" dismiss it as an "overpriced novelty."

Heaven on Seven | 20 | 17 | 18 | $23 |
3478 N. Clark St. (Cornelia Ave.), 773-477-7818 🅂
600 N. Michigan Ave., 2nd fl. (bet. Ohio & Ontario Sts.), 312-280-7774 🅂
111 N. Wabash Ave., 7th fl. (Washington Blvd.), 312-263-6443 ⊟
■ Heaven has been easier to get into since this "bustling, harried" original Loop location spun off its Cajun-Creole cousins; though the "good, authentic food" is "spicy", hotheads can "add heat as needed" with a "great collection of sauces", and it's "always Mardi Gras" within the "casual New Orleans"–inspired settings; N.B. menus and hours vary by location.

Hemmingway's Bistro 🅂 | – | – | – | M |
211 N. Oak Park Ave. (Ontario St.), Oak Park, 708-524-0806
In the cozy, lace-curtained basement of the Suburban West Write Inn Hotel (across from Oak Park's Hemingway Museum), this reasonably priced bistro specializes in casual French standards accompanied by folksy service that would have made Ernest himself feel right at home.

Hilary's Urban Eatery 🅂 | 18 | 14 | 18 | $16 |
1500 W. Division St. (Greenview St.), 773-235-4327
■ Urbanites are utterly "glad" this "whimsical" Wicker Park Eclectic eatery is "in the neighborhood"; "unpretentious and relaxing", it's a "colorful" "hangout" where "Gen-Xers" "huddle cozily" over a "good menu" offering "creative and tasty" "twists on normal dishes" (and a "great Sunday brunch"); P.S. folks "love the jelly beans" "on the table."

Hi Ricky 🟦
17 | 13 | 16 | $17

3730 N. Southport Ave. (north of Addison St.), 773-388-0000
1852 W. North Ave. (Wolcott Ave.), 773-276-8300
941 W. Randolph St. (bet. Morgan & Sangamon Sts.),
312-491-9100

☑ Ricky's friends say "it's fun to work your way down the menu" of "interesting concoctions" at this "loud, crowded and entertaining" Asian chain, where the "cheap, tasty and plentiful" noodle dishes are a "cut above fast food"; foes say even if you like the "generally bland", "Americanized fare", "inconsistent" service can "ruin" the experience.

Hong Min 🟦
23 | 6 | 15 | $17

221 W. Cermak Rd. (bet. Archer & Wentworth Aves.),
312-842-5026 ◑
8048 W. 111th St. (Roberts Rd.), Palos Hills, 708-599-8488

☑ This "inexpensive" "favorite" Chinatown "diamond in the rough" and its Southwest Suburban satellite are ranked "best Chinese" in our *Survey*; still, the "huge menu" of "excellent and authentic" Cantonese dishes outclasses the housekeeping-challenged, "old and run-down" settings, so "just close your eyes while you're eating"; N.B. the city location is BYO.

Hot Doug's 🟦
▽ 24 | 16 | 24 | $7

2314 W. Roscoe St. (bet. Clairmont & Oakley Sts.), 773-348-0326

■ "Not your typical hot dog joint", this Roscoe Village wiener wonderland is "a place for sausage lovers to call home"; surveyors crown "creative" chef-owner Doug Sohn "the king of encased meats", giving him an "A for ingenuity" in creating an "awesome variety" of "tasty and cheap" bun embellishers, including a different game version weekly, and for "cooking French fries in duck fat on [Fridays and] Saturdays."

Hot Tamales 🟦
▽ 22 | 15 | 17 | $18

493 Central Ave. (St. John Ave.), Highland Park, 847-433-4070

■ Sombreros off to this "crowded" "neighborhood Mexican" spot in the North Suburbs that may "look ordinary, but is much, much more"; located near Port Clinton Square, it offers "good service" and "unusual, creative and delicious fare" including "wonderful duck tacos", "great tamales" (natch) and "veg options galore", all washed down with "fab margaritas."

House of Blues Back Porch 🟦
15 | 21 | 15 | $27

329 N. Dearborn St. (Kinzie St.), 312-923-2007

☑ With "some of the best music in the city" and "great outsider and folk art", this "fun-and-funky" River North venue (part of a national chain) serving Cajun-Creole and Southern fare has its followers, especially for the "engaging gospel brunch" on Sundays; still, some sigh "if only the food and service were as good as" the "live bands."

HUGO'S FROG BAR & FISH HOUSE ◐ [S] 24 | 20 | 23 | $42

1024 N. Rush St. (bet. Bellevue Pl. & Oak St.), 312-640-0999

■ "Always hopping", this Gold Coaster is a "saner", "not-as-noisy", "easier-to-get-into" but still "clublike" seafood "version of Gibsons" Steakhouse, its beefy, abutting big brother; in addition to the signature frogs' legs and "great" *mer* fare like "crab cakes par excellence" and "fresh", "well-prepared fish", you can also "have them bring you a steak from" next door (they "share a kitchen") – "who could ask for more?"

Iggy's ◐ [S] 18 | 18 | 15 | $24

700 N. Milwaukee Ave. (Huron St.), 312-829-4449

■ Night-owls hoot for this "hip" Near West hangout, a "low-key" lounge/restaurant favored for "really late dining" (the kitchen closes at 3:15 AM most mornings) from an Eclectic menu of "Iggy's eggs", "quality" pastas and "great snacks"; with its "funky" velvet-curtained decor, it's a "dark and mysterious" place where "bikers meets yuppies and they all get along", thanks in part to "killer martinis."

Ina's [S] 21 | 17 | 20 | $22

1235 W. Randolph St. (Elizabeth St.), 312-226-8227

■ With two defunct morning-themed spots under her belt, Chicago's self- and surveyor-proclaimed "breakfast queen" "has done it again" with this "cheery", "warm" Market District sophomore whose "kitschy decor" features a "cute" "salt-and-pepper-shaker collection"; though her "upscale food with homemade flavor" includes lunch and dinner fare, early-birds crow that "nothing could be finer than the pancakes served by Ina."

Incognito [S] – | – | – | M

1 Nippersink Blvd. (Grand Ave.), Fox Lake, 847-587-0360

Refined for the Chain O' Lakes region, Incognito is slyly serving American and Continental fare to an expanding demographic in this Northwest Suburban resort area; servers slink around in fedoras in the former bank building, which is now disguised as an upscale cafe with exposed brick walls, tin ceiling, local artwork and live piano music.

Indian Garden [S] 20 | 14 | 17 | $22

247 E. Ontario St., 2nd fl. (bet. Fairbanks Ct. & Michigan Ave.), 312-280-4910

2546 W. Devon Ave. (Rockwell St.), 773-338-2929

855 E. Schaumburg Rd. (Barrington Rd.), Schaumburg, 847-524-3007

6020 S. Cass Ave. (60th St.), Westmont, 630-769-9662

◪ "Wonderfully flavored" "fiery food" and "plenty of it", as well as some "not-too-spicy" selections, have compatriots crooning kudos to this Northern Indian quartet; "bring friends", as they're "great for vegetarians" and their "buffets are excellent for those interested in trying new food"; service is either "attentive" or "slow", depending on whom you ask, but all agree the "moderate prices" are "bliss."

Inspiration Cafe — | — | — | I

4554 N. Broadway, Ste. 207 (bet. Sunnyside & Wilson Aves.), 773-878-0981

Thursdays and Fridays only, this American cafe serves basic lunches (e.g., spicy catfish, pasta, curried chicken sandwich and peach cobbler, plus weekly specials); as part of its mission of helping Uptown's homeless men and women back to self-sufficiency, it sponsors a job training program in which trainees cook and serve the food; N.B. this is an alcohol-free environment.

Irish Oak Restaurant & Pub [S] ▽ 18 | 20 | 20 | $18

3511 N. Clark St. (Addison St.), 773-935-6669

■ "A super stop" in Wrigleyville for Emerald Islers ("or those wanting to be"), this "real Irish pub" run by a family of Galway natives serves "fresh fish 'n' chips" and "great shepherd's pie" that are washed down with a "wide and lovingly poured selection of draughts"; expats say "the imported bar and other woodwork add authenticity" to the "pleasant" proceedings.

Itto Sushi ◐ 22 | 14 | 18 | $26

2616 N. Halsted St. (Wrightwood Ave.), 773-871-1800

◪ "Grab a quick bite of dependable" and "affordable" "high-quality sushi" at this long-standing "Lincoln Parker", a "casual alternative to the more swanky [Japanese] establishments in town"; though the "friendly", "eager-to-please" staffers "make you feel welcome", detractors declare the "food is good" but "not exceptionally good" and decry the setting as "nothing fancy."

Ixcapuzalco [S] 23 | 19 | 19 | $34

2919 N. Milwaukee Ave. (Diversey Pkwy.), 773-486-7340

■ Even those who "can't say" its "hard-to-pronounce name" ('eeks-ka-poo-sal-ko') love to twist their tongues around this Logan Square Mexican's "absolutely exciting moles", the highpoints of an "imaginative menu" of "regional cuisine" "expertly executed" by "creative" chef-owner Geno Bahena (a Frontera Grill veteran who also helms Chilpancingo) and "nicely presented" by a "helpful staff" "in a surprisingly elegant yet comfortable atmosphere."

Jack's on Halsted [S] 22 | 19 | 22 | $34

3201 N. Halsted St. (Belmont Ave.), 773-244-9191

■ This "stylish" Boys Towner showcases an "inspired menu" by chef-owner Jack Jones (proprietor of Atlantique and Bistro Marbuzet, as well) featuring "innovative takes on American classics" and "fabulous fish" dishes such as the signature ahi tuna; its "wild, contemporary decor" is "comfortably upscale", and its "great location" "on the corner" of Belmont and Halsted makes it a "nice spot" "to watch the area's colorful crowd."

Jacky's Bistro S 24 | 21 | 21 | $40
2545 Prairie Ave. (Central St.), Evanston, 847-733-0899
Supporters of "great chef [-owner] Jacky Pluton's" "sophisticated" North Suburban bistro (a reincarnation of the Winnetka original destroyed by fire in 1999) praise its "terrific" menu of "highly flavored" Regional American and New French "classic dishes" reinterpreted "with modern concepts", as well as its "intimate, inviting surroundings"; the resistance reports "downtown prices" and "some attitude" from a few "inflexible" staffers.

Jake Melnick's Corner Tap ●S – | – | – | M
41 E. Superior St. (Wabash Ave.), 312-266-0400
Levy Restaurants' redo of the Gold Coast's Blackhawk Lodge space verges on an upscale sports bar, offering plentiful baskets of bar food and 16 beers on tap in a masculine, log-cabin atmosphere just off the Mag Mile; a seasonal sidewalk cafe ices the cake.

Jambalaya's S – | – | – | I
1653 N. Damen Ave. (bet. North & Wabansia Aves.), 773-289-3678
The sole embellishments at this Bucktown storefront-cum-po' boy shack are the Tabasco bottles on each table, the painted tin ceiling and a New Orleans street sign, but the straightforward selection of traditional sandwiches, deep-fried seafood and cheap Cajun-Creole specialties plus the lunch-till-late-night hours (11PM weekdays, 2AM weekends) should satisfy hungry neighbors.

Jane's S 21 | 19 | 19 | $28
1655 W. Cortland St. (Paulina St.), 773-862-5263
The "healthy", "fabulous" and "reasonable" Eclectic–New American fare and "cool-but-comfy" "exposed-brick" surroundings of this "funky" "Bucktown hangout" and "date place" have caused cases of Jane's addiction; still, claustrophobes quarrel with "cramped quarters" "too small to handle the weekend crowds", and PETA people are peeved that the "vegetarian choices are becoming fewer" on its "limited menu."

Jang Mo Nim – | – | – | I
6320 N. Lincoln Ave. (Devon Ave.), 773-509-0211
Middle-of-the-night Korean cravers covet this Northsider that offers a broad menu of specialties – fried oysters in pepper sauce, spicy octopus and stewed goat served with beer or sake – until 6 AM; adventurous do-it-yourselfers opt for a table on the perimeter of the room and cook their own *bulgoki* (beef) or *kalbi* (short ribs).

Jia's [S] 19 | 15 | 16 | $22

2545 N. Halsted St. (bet. Fullerton Pkwy. & Wrightwood Ave.), 773-477-6256
2 E. Delaware Pl. (State St.), 312-642-0626

◪ Though no longer affiliated, this "consistent" Lincoln Park original and its Gold Coast spin-off both serve a "nice selection of Asian" dishes from expansive Chinese-Japanese menus ("allow 30 minutes to read" them) and "fresh sushi" bars featuring "some interesting rolls"; though some say their "bland" "atmospheres could use some help", most maintain they offer "excellent food considering the price."

Jilly's Cafe [S] 21 | 19 | 21 | $34

2614 Green Bay Rd. (Central St.), Evanston, 847-869-7636

■ "Fine fare is served with grace" at this "dignified" and "darling" New French–New American cafe, a "romantic place to take your sweetheart" in the North Suburbs; "the jury is still out" on whether chef-owner Brian Newkirk will "keep up" its "reputation" for "terrific food"; P.S. it's not affiliated with the similarly named "supper club" Downtown.

Jin Ju [S] – | – | – | M

5203 N. Clark St. (Foster Ave.), 773-334-6377

A stylish Andersonville spot with a serene, minimalist atmosphere, this Korean offers contemporary, visually appealing versions of authentic dishes – toned down, spice-wise, but still allowing the flavors of the chiles, black beans and kimchi to shine through; alcohol is also served, including martinis made with soju, a sweet-potato liquor.

Joe's Be-Bop Cafe [S] 14 | 16 | 15 | $22

Navy Pier, 600 E. Grand Ave. (bet. Lake Shore Dr. & McClurg Ct.), 312-595-5299

◪ "If you're at Navy Pier" and feeling hungry, this "popular jazz joint" with "pictures of musicians on the walls" and an "outside area for people-watching" is an "adequate" spot for a meal of "good", if somewhat "routine, BBQ" and Southern fare; "the music's the reason to go", though, and foes tune it out altogether as "too touristy" and "noisy."

JOE'S SEAFOOD, PRIME STEAK & STONE CRAB [S] 25 | 22 | 24 | $47

60 E. Grand Ave. (Rush St.), 312-379-5637

■ "Are we in Florida?" ask claw-crackers complimenting this "retro-stylish" Near North "extension of the great Miami flagship", Joe's Stone Crab, which has been serving it up in season since 1913; a "successful Lettuce Entertain You partnership", it brings "big flavors" to Chi-town in "big portions" ("at big prices") of "hands-on seafood grub", as well as steaks "so good" that some can find "no words" to express their feelings.

John Barleycorn ●🅂   14 | 15 | 14 | $18

3524 N. Clark St. (bet. Addison St. & Sheffield Ave.), 773-549-6000
658 W. Belden Ave. (Lincoln Ave.), 773-348-8899

■ These "casual" brothers are American pubs known for "tasty burgers" buoyed by "beer and atmosphere" (the Lincoln Park original has been a tavern since 1890); most say, though, that the "good wings" and other "regular bar food" are "secondary", since "these are drinking joints" first and foremost; P.S. the Belden Barleycorn also has a "great outdoor garden."

Johnny Rockets 🅂   16 | 15 | 15 | $13

901 N. Rush St. (Delaware Pl.), 312-337-3900
405 Stratford Square Mall (Schick Rd.), Bloomingdale, 630-894-0939
Northbrook Court Shopping Ctr., 2338 Northbrook Ct. (Lake Cook Rd.), Northbrook, 847-562-8720
45 Old Orchard Ctr. (Golf Rd.), Skokie, 847-677-6039

◪ Grab a "greasy, guilty pleasure" at this Gold Coast slinging American diner eats while spinning "thick", "old-fashioned milkshakes" in the blender and "nonstop golden oldies" on the jukebox; what's a "retro junk-food heaven" to some, though, strikes others as a "hokey" attempt at "'50s atmosphere without the great '50s food"; N.B. the North and West Suburban branches are unrated.

John's Place 🅂   20 | 16 | 19 | $19

1200 W. Webster Ave. (Racine Ave.), 773-525-6670

■ John Manilow's Lincoln Parker "pleases everyone from vegetarians to the meat-and-potatoes crowd" with its "consistently good" Eclectic homestyle menu; a "brunch favorite", it offers what some call "the best pumpkin pancakes" and "oatmeal better than mom's" – just ask the "mothers with babies", "kids" and "toddlers everywhere" in this "bright, airy", "family-friendly" place.

Joy Yee's Noodle Shop 🅂   ▽ 24 | 17 | 22 | $13

2159 Chinatown Sq. (Archer Ave.), 312-328-0001
521 Davis St. (Chicago Ave.), Evanston, 847-733-1900

■ A "huge selection (and huge portions)" of "great noodles" and other "tasty Thai", Chinese, Korean and Vietnamese dishes keep these "popular" Pan-Asians positively "packed"; though some say the "friendly wait staff" is "fast", a few Siamese cats growl "don't let the secret out – the wait is long enough already"; P.S. the North Suburban is BYO, the Chinatown is alcohol-free.

Julio's Cocina Latina   ▽ 24 | 21 | 20 | $31

(fka Julio's Latin Cafe)
Lakeview Plaza, 95 S. Rand Rd. (Rte. 22), Lake Zurich, 847-438-3484

■ It may be "a surprise to find delicious Latin fare in a strip mall", but that's what surveyors say to expect at this

Northwest Suburban cantina that's generating heat with its "well-prepared", "nontraditional" food – a "creative" mix of South American, Caribbean and Mexican cuisines – and "delightful service"; P.S. live jazz and Brazilian music on weekends provides "great entertainment."

Kabul House [S] — | — | — | I

1629 N. Halsted St. (North Ave.), 312-751-1029
3320 Dempster St. (McCormick Blvd.), Skokie, 847-763-9930
"Authentic Afghan food" comes to the Northern Suburbs courtesy of this "nicer-than-casual" BYO where jaded palates can indulge in "simple, inexpensive fare" that's both "tasty and unusual"; gregarious Abdul Qazi, "the [chef-]owner, exemplifies the warm hospitality" of his native country and has transformed his "small" mini-mall space with photos, posters, costumes, textiles and traditional music from his homeland; N.B. the Lincoln Park branch opened post-*Survey*.

Kamehachi [S] 23 | 19 | 19 | $28

240 E. Ontario St. (Fairbanks St.), 312-587-0600
1400 N. Wells St. (Schiller St.), 312-664-3663 ◐
Westin River North, 320 N. Dearborn St. (Kinzie St.), 312-744-1900
Village Green Shopping Ctr., 1320 Shermer Rd. (Waukegan Rd.), Northbrook, 847-562-0064
■ "Always bustling", this Old Town Japanese can be "tough to get into", but "fresh sushi" from a "diverse menu" of "unique options" makes it worth the effort; the "young, hip crowd" likes its "late hours" and "cool bar upstairs", while purists prefer the more "rigid environment downstairs"; its North Shore sibling also offers "great food" at a "reasonable cost"; N.B. the one-year-old Streeterville location and the new sushi-bar branch in the Westin River North hotel both opened post-*Survey*.

Karma [S] — | — | — | E

Crowne Plaza Hotel, 510 E. Rte. 83 (Rte. 45), Mundelein, 847-970-6900
North Suburban Mundelein's Crowne Plaza Hotel is home to this haute Pan-Asian where an imaginative multi-ethnic menu is paired with a limited wine list and several sake options; the chic, serene decor includes glowing blown-glass bamboo and hydrotherapy in the form of a waterfall and rice paddy–inspired pond; N.B. breakfast, lunch and dinner are served.

Keefer's 22 | 22 | 22 | $44

20 W. Kinzie St. (Dearborn St.), 312-467-9525
■ "Another good" "steak-and-seafood" "joint" (just "how many does Chicago deserve?"), this River North "noteworthy newcomer" serves up "classy comfort food" "with winning service" in an "attractive room"; supporters claim owner "Glenn Keefer is a pro" and say chef John

"Hogan's a hero", crediting the duo for making it not only a "bright new star on the scene" but an "'in'-spot for TV and radio personalities" as well; N.B. its new adjacent 'Kaffe' space offers lower-priced lunch fare to eat in or carry out.

Kevin ∇ 28 | 27 | 26 | $48

9 W. Hubbard St. (State St.), 312-595-0055

■ When "one of Chicago's most creative chefs", Kevin Shikami (ex Jimmy's Place and The Outpost), launched his namesake eatery in River North, he quickly generated interest in his "excellent and adventurous" New French–New American fare (such as wasabi-spiked tuna tartare), which employs "the highest-quality ingredients" and "delivers pure pleasure"; the "stunning" yet "comfortable" storefront echoes the cuisine's Japanese accents.

KIKI'S BISTRO 24 | 22 | 22 | $40

900 N. Franklin St. (Locust St.), 312-335-5454

◪ Tucked into a somewhat "out-of-the-way" section of River North, this "congenial" and "consistently solid" "old favorite" with an "authentic Gallic presence" is prized for "well-prepared, quality bistro food" within a "charming Country French" setting; though generally "professional", the service can "falter when the dining room is too busy"; P.S. there's "nice, free valet parking" (lunch and dinner).

King Crab [S] 17 | 13 | 16 | $29

1816 N. Halsted St. (Willow St.), 312-280-8990

◪ The "good seafood" at this "casual", "low-key" Lincoln Park place make many "glad it's there", such as drama divas who drop by "before the Steppenwolf" or "after the Royal George Theater"; crabs claim its "location brings locals back", not its "ok food", adding that it's "not too busy" for a reason; N.B. now open for lunch seven days a week.

Kinzie Chophouse [S] 20 | 18 | 19 | $37

400 N. Wells St. (Kinzie St.), 312-822-0191

◪ "Mouthwatering steaks" that are "worth the money" draw diners to this "quaint and cozy" River North chophouse, also popular with those "shopping at the Merchandise Mart" for "good salads and pastas at lunch" and for "happy-hour" hanging-out; despite this, a few doubters declare it's "nothing really special", deeming it "disappointing, especially for the price."

Kit Kat Lounge & Supper Club ◐ [S] 18 | 21 | 19 | $32

3700 N. Halsted St. (Waveland Ave.), 773-525-1111

◪ Gender-benders generate "amazing energy" at this "loud" Boys Town venue where "surprisingly good" New American fare is paired with "strong" martinis and a "must-see" revue of "fun female impersonators"; still, peeved patrons pen poisonous proclamations, purporting "they distract you with drag queens" so you won't notice the "unexceptional food" and "arrogant" staff.

Kitsch'n on Roscoe 🅂   16 | 19 | 16 | $16

2005 W. Roscoe St. (Damen Ave.), 773-248-7372

☑ While this "fun retro diner" with "real" "comfort food" and a "good '70s-atmosphere gimmick" "reminds" some of a Roscoe Village "*Leave It to Beaver* with Julia Child as the mom", others call it "one joke taken too far" and complain about "spotty food and service"; still, "where else can you get Tang" martinis and Twinkie tiramisu?

Klay Oven 🅂   20 | 16 | 17 | $27

414 N. Orleans St. (Hubbard St.), 312-527-3999

■ "You'd have to go to Devon" Avenue in Chicago's Little India area, "to find dishes that compare" to the "high-quality food" served at this "cozy" yet "upscale" spot, the "place for Indian in River North"; there are "plenty of choices for the vegetarian and non-vegetarian alike", so many enjoy a "leisurely lunch" making multiple visits to its "great bargain buffet."

Krungthep Thai Cuisine 🅂   _ | _ | _ | I

1512 N. La Salle Dr. (bet. Burton Pl. & North Ave.), 312-274-0909

Aumphai Kusub, owner of Uptown's Thai Pastry, brings her top-notch Siamese cooking to Old Town via this tiny yet comfortably furnished dining room; it's a friendly spot for enjoying inexpensive and authentic chow, though taking *out* is also a popular option; N.B. would-be imbibers be warned, it's BYO.

Kuni's 🅂   23 | 17 | 19 | $28

511 Main St. (bet. Chicago & Hinman Aves.), Evanston, 847-328-2004

■ North Suburban natives say there's "no need to go into the city" in search of "authentic Japanese fare" such as "splendid tempura and great sushi" fashioned from "fish of pristine freshness", since chef-owner Yuji Kunii's creations are so much "the real thing" "you'll feel like you are in Tokyo"; aficionados call him "a prince" and "love" to watch him at work in the "clean but not spartan" surroundings.

Kyoto   ▽ 22 | 12 | 17 | $27

2534 N. Lincoln Ave. (bet. Altgeld St. & Lill Ave.), 773-477-2788 🅂
1408 Butterfield Rd. (bet. Finley Rd. & Highland Ave.), Downers Grove, 630-627-8588
1062 Gage St. (Green Bay Rd.), Winnetka, 847-784-9388 🅂

☑ Belly up to the bar (sushi, that is) for "tasty" Japanese at these "understated" siblings in Lincoln Park and the North and West Suburbs; they may "look like holes in the wall", but with "reasonable prices", "friendly" staffers "without an attitude" and some of "the freshest [fish] in the city", determined diners don't mind that the "decor needs help."

La Bella Winnetka **S**
17 | 17 | 19 | $29

*505 Chestnut St. (bet. Elm & Oak Sts.), Winnetka,
847-441-6002*

Italian fare that's "dependable if not exciting" can be found at this North Suburban stalwart, but it's equally known for its "must-see character" of an owner; most say that from April–December its "great outdoor tent" (illuminated by twinkling lights and heated on chilly nights) "makes for relaxing" and "fun" "outdoor dining worth waiting for", but some judges still find this beauty "past its prime."

La Bocca della Verità **S**
21 | 14 | 19 | $30

*4618 N. Lincoln Ave. (bet. Lawrence & Wilson Aves.),
773-784-6222*

Proponents pronounce this "intimate" Lincoln Square Italian "a storefront treasure" for "always-authentic" and "great food" (like its signature "homemade" "duck ravioli to die for") that's "simply prepared", "outstandingly presented" and offered "at neighborhood prices" that make it a "good value"; the "warm, homey staff" helps compensate for the "unassuming", "dated decor"; N.B. summer sidewalk seating is now available.

La Borsa
▽ 17 | 17 | 15 | $26

375 N. Morgan St. (bet. Carroll Ave. & Kinzie St.), 312-563-1414

Though it's "certainly an odd place", this Near West Northern Italian "well hidden" in an "out-of-the-way industrial district" offers "affordable", "large portions" of "hearty", if "not refined", fare; some quibble with its "offbeat decor", but train-spotters tout its "weird locale" (a converted railway station), saying the "commuter trains racing by the windows" and "spectacular" "skyline views" "make up for what's missing with the food."

La Cantina Enoteca
▽ 20 | 20 | 22 | $29

71 W. Monroe St. (bet. Clark & Dearborn Sts.), 312-332-7005

Though all three of the "Italian Village restaurants" under one Loop roof are convenient "before the theater or a concert", Cantina coveters claim this subterranean sibling is the most "cozy", with "attentive waiters" and "consistently good food"; as its moniker suggests, it also boasts a bevy of bottles, but you won't "find" the "great wine list" on the menu – "ask for" the big, bound book.

La Cazuela Mariscos **S**
– | – | – | I

6922 N. Clark St. (bet. Farwell & Morse Aves.), 773-338-5425

An upbeat apricot-colored room sets the stage for a feast that's anything but your typical Mexican meal at this fresh-not-fancy Rogers Park seafooder where abundant fish stews, tacos and chilled cocktails of octopus, clams, oysters and shrimp are served alongside fried lime-drizzled snapper; with all that bounty from the sea, who needs nachos?; N.B. outdoor dining is also an option.

La Crêperie S
19 15 16 $19

2845 N. Clark St. (bet. Diversey Pkwy. & Surf St.), 773-528-9050
❚ Crêpe crusaders "want to do the cancan" over the "authentic" namesake noshes tucked with "different fillings" at this "unchanged classic" in Lakeview that's "still crêpe-ing [along] after all these years"; though some despair over the "cluttered", "dumpy decor" and service that's "typically French", others say you "can't beat the garden on a warm night."

La Donna ◑ S
20 15 19 $26

5146 N. Clark St. (Foster Ave.), 773-561-9400
❚ "Big portions of authentic Italian" food ferried by "friendly" staffers make regulars "feel at home" in this "romantic" Andersonville "favorite"; still, holdouts who don't hanker for the "predictable" fare harrumph that what some call a "cozy" setting is just "cramped tables in close quarters" that get "too crowded on weekends", causing the otherwise "good service" to be "slow"; N.B. the Decor score may not reflect a post-*Survey* remodeling.

La Fonda Latino S
– – – M

5350 N. Broadway St. (Balmoral Ave.), 773-271-3935
Colombian family fare (and some Cuban and Mexican dishes) is featured at this cozy Uptown cafe reopened in a new spot after fire destroyed the original location in March 2001; generous portions of traditional rice and seafood selections and grilled and roasted meats are served amid exposed brick and charming South American artifacts.

La Gondola S
∇ 22 13 21 $24

Wellington Plaza, 2914 N. Ashland Ave. (Wellington Ave.), 773-248-4433
❚ Gratified gondoliers gloat that "hospitality, warmth" and "wonderful Italian food" (including "great pizza" and some of the "best eggplant parmesan in Chicago") wait within this "affordable" Lincoln Parker despite its "deceptively modest exterior"; still, the "spartan" "strip-mall" setting and "small", "nothing-fancy" "dining room with only a few tables" have some saying it's "best" to phone them up for "delicious" delivery or glide on in for "high-quality carryout."

Lalo's S
– – – M

1960 N. Clybourn Ave. (bet. Clifton Ave. & Cortland St.), 773-880-5256 ⊅
500 N. LaSalle St. (Illinois St.), 312-329-0030
4126 W. 26th St. (Kedvale Ave.), 773-762-1505 ◑
3515 W. 26th St. (bet. Drake & St. Louis Aves.), 773-522-0345 ◑
The original tiny *taqueria* at 3515 W. 26th Street and its family-owned satellite locations raised their profile by taking over the former Michael Jordan's space, bringing this hungry 'hood their signature blend of traditional Mexican

fare (made from family recipes), fruit-flavored margaritas and fair prices; N.B. the Lincoln Park and River North locations feature live entertainment some nights.

La Mora 🆂
– | – | – | M

2132 W. Roscoe St. (Hamilton Ave.), 773-404-4555
Roscoe Village is the setting for this cozy Italian combining original and classic dishes – fillet with garlic-smashed potatoes, Portobello *griglia*, spaghetti carbonara – all complemented by a short wine list and served by a friendly, accommodating staff; the inviting ambiance is abetted by velvet curtains, a fireplace in the center of the room and a lounge in back with comfortable couches and armchairs.

L'anne
– | – | – | E

221 W. Front St. (bet. Hale St. & Wheaton Ave.), Wheaton, 630-260-1234
The Western Suburbs receive an infusion of fusion at this stylish contemporary French-Asian whose name honors owner Lanny Nguyen's two favorite flowers – her daughter, Lynnanne, and the orchid ('lan' in Vietnamese), examples of which abound in the intimate and elegantly exotic room of floor-to-ceiling windows, hand-painted walls, bamboo floors and soft-silk-swathed ceilings.

Lan Sushi & Lobster
∇ 19 | 19 | 17 | $35

(fka Dozu Sushi & Lobster)
100 E. Walton St. (bet. Michigan Ave. & Rush St.), 312-274-1000
■ Fans report that "some amazing food" can be found at this Gold Coast Japanese seafooder, including "fab sushi" that's "fresh (and expensive)" and tanks teeming with lobsters that are so big you'll think they're "on steroids"; also, as the former name suggests, the "elegant decor" and "beautiful" waterfalls are welcoming; N.B. the Food score may not reflect a post-*Survey* chef change.

Lao Sze Chuan Express 🆂⊘
∇ 19 | 8 | 13 | $19

1520 W. Taylor St. (Ashland Ave.), 312-455-0667
Lao Sze Chuan House 🆂
Oak Court Shopping Ctr., 500 E. Ogden Ave. (bet. Cass Ave. & Rte. 83), Westmont, 630-455-4488
Lao Sze Chuan Spicy City ◑🆂
2172 S. Archer Ave. (Fuller St.), 312-326-5040
Szechuan House 🆂
321 E. Northwest Hwy. (Hicks Rd.), Palatine, 847-991-0888
■ "Go with a group and feast" upon "gigantic portions" from the enormous menus of these siblings (the Suburban Northwest outpost premiered post-*Survey*); all serve "good" multi-regional fare, but the Chinatown branch specializes in "authentic Szechuan cooking", including hard-to-find "Chinese hot pots" that may be a "bit too" much of "the real thing" for "the unadventurous eater"; N.B. owner Tony Hu hosts a Channel 13 cooking show.

La Peña S
`– – – M`

4212 N. Milwaukee Ave. (Montrose Ave.), 773-545-7022
The Portage Park neighborhood of the Northwest Side is home to this lively, hospitable Ecuadoran eatery, brightly colored and festooned with tropical bird figurines, where a host of Latin dishes – seviche, *tostones*, yuca, empanadas– is served along with fresh plantain chips and drinks from the full bar; on weekends, its stage hops with live Andean music from a seemingly unending variety of instruments.

la petite folie S
`24 19 21 $40`

Hyde Park Shopping Ctr., 1504 E. 55th St. (Lake Park Blvd.), 773-493-1394
■ "Yes, Virginia, there is fine dining on the South Side", and it can be found in the form of this "little-known", "pleasant French" spot serving a "well-balanced menu" of "simple" yet "consistently superior" cuisine that "selective Hyde Parkers" find both "elegant and satisfying" ("especially the prix-fixe menu", "a bargain"); "perfect for conversations", its "peaceful", "attractive room" is a "lovely place for a quiet, romantic dinner", and "it's handy to the Court Theatre."

La Rosetta
`19 15 17 $27`

3 First National Plaza, 70 W. Madison St. (bet. Clark & Dearborn Sts.), 312-332-9500
◪ Show-goers know this "reliable" and "welcoming" Rosebud-group Italian "in the Loop" is a "great place before the theater", but it's also a triple threat for nose-to-the-grindstoners – it's "popular for business lunches", the "happy hour is worth going for" and stiffs "working late" are "glad it's in the building" for "excellent takeout"; still, what some call "always-tasty" food others opine is a bit "middle-of-the-road"; N.B. now open for breakfast.

La Sardine
`22 20 20 $37`

111 N. Carpenter St. (bet. Randolph St. & Washington Blvd.), 312-421-2800
◪ Despite its name, this "trendy" Market District bistro by "masterful Jean-Claude" Poilevey is a bigger fish than its "tiny sister, Le Bouchon", but its "abundant portions" of "intensely flavored", "plate-licking-good" Gallic food similarly "warms the soul"; still, some panelists are put off by sometimes "indifferent service" and the occasionally "noisy" atmosphere of its formerly industrial space, a "mix of quaint French and hard-edged urban" influences; P.S. "the chocolate soufflé is worth the trip."

Las Bellas Artes S
`▽ 25 21 23 $39`

112 W. Park Ave. (York St.), Elmhurst, 630-530-7725
■ "What a delight" vouch vociferous voters vaunting the "excellent gourmet" fare at chef-owner Gloria Duarte's West Suburban specializing in the cuisine of Mexico City

("not at all what most people think of as Mexican"); "go for the Sunday brunch", "wonderful" afternoon tea or "exciting" dinners, all "graciously served" in a "charming" fine-arts-filled setting.

La Scarola S   23 | 14 | 19 | $30

721 W. Grand Ave. (Milwaukee Ave.), 312-243-1740

☑ With "massive portions" of "wonderful" "old-school" "homemade Italian food at reasonable prices", this "terrific [Near West] hideaway" makes "you feel like grandma is going to walk out of the kitchen and pinch your cheeks"; "now that lots of folks have discovered it", however, rueful regulars report that the "service falters when it gets busy" and claim it can get "close and noisy."

Las Tablas S   24 | 15 | 18 | $20

2965 N. Lincoln Ave. (Wellington Ave.), 773-871-2414
4920 N. Irving Park Rd. (Cicero Ave.), 773-202-0999

■ "A real find", this "charming" and "fun" Lincoln Park BYO churrascaria ("Colombian steakhouse") not only "feels authentic" but is, thanks to chef-owner Jorge Suárez, who hails from south of Bogotá; along with its "excellent grilled meats" and "paella with South American flair", there are "yummy" sides like "delicious plantains with melted cheese" and "Latin root vegetables" like yuca; N.B. the Northwest Side branch opened post-*Survey.*

La Strada Ristorante   19 | 18 | 18 | $37

155 N. Michigan Ave. (Randolph St.), 312-565-2200

■ This "venerable Italian spot" has surveyors standing on opposite sides of the street – some shout that it's an "underappreciated" Loop longtimer that "welcomes you like family", with "high-quality food" and "friendly" service, while others bellow back it's "nothing special", with a "tired menu and decor"; either way, its "location on Michigan Avenue" makes it "convenient to the Art Institute, Grant Park" and "the symphony."

La Tache S   – | – | – | M

1475 W. Balmoral Ave. (bet. Clark St. & Glenwood Ave.), 773-334-7168

Paris comes to Andersonville at this compact spot, styled with tiled floors, brocaded banquettes, dark-wood panels and antique-framed art; prices are neighborhood-friendly, and the menu of tweaked French bistro classics includes the likes of truffled brandade of salt cod and seared duck breast with duck confit, baby turnips and tart cherries.

Lawry's The Prime Rib S   23 | 22 | 22 | $41

100 E. Ontario St. (Rush St.), 312-787-5000

■ "Don't change a thing" implore purists who prize this "wonderfully old-fashioned" Near North "classic" (based on the Beverly Hills original) that's been "keeping it simple and good" since 1974; expect "grand" "mansion decor" and "tableside service", including some of the "best prime rib" around "cut (in front of you)"; P.S. even after the post-*Survey* departure of chef Jackie Shen, her signature Chocolate Bag dessert remains "reason enough to go."

LE BOUCHON 25 | 19 | 20 | $35

1958 N. Damen Ave. (Armitage Ave.), 773-862-6600

◪ It "feels like Paris" has been "teleported to Bucktown" within this diminutive "darling" that devotees declare is "exactly what a bistro should be"; Jean Claude Poilevey's "real home cooking" yields "unbelievably delicious French" fare such as "outstanding duck", but some say it's served up with a side of "authentic snobbery"; the "claustrophobic" complain, as well, of an "uncomfortably" "cramped" setting where "long waits" are de rigueur.

LE COLONIAL [S] 23 | 24 | 21 | $41

937 N. Rush St. (bet. Oak & Walton Sts.), 312-255-0088

■ "Flavors shine at this trendy" Gold Coaster – the Third Coast third of an otherwise bicoastal trio – where the "refined haute Vietnamese cooking" is "delicate and well-seasoned" and the "stunning" French Colonial setting seems so "seductive" and "decadent" you'll "feel like becoming a spy", especially in the "swank" and "exotic upstairs bar"; P.S. "for special occasions", "ask for a balcony seat overlooking the street."

LE FRANÇAIS 28 | 26 | 27 | $75

269 S. Milwaukee Ave. (bet. Dundee Rd. & Strong St.), Wheeling, 847-541-7470

■ Chef Don Yamauchi is "keeping up the great tradition" of founding toque Jean Banchet – so judge jurists two years after a deed juggle jostled Northwest Suburban Wheeling's (once Classic, now New) French standard bearer known for "exceptional cuisine, wine and service"; "holding its own", the "beautifully prepared", "lighter" food remains "picture perfect" and "extremely pricey"; N.B. now serving lunch.

Lem's BBQ ◐ [S] – | – | – | I

311 E. 75th St. (bet. Calumet & Prairie Aves.), 773-994-2428 ⊄

5914 S. State St. (59th St.), 773-684-5007

Open until the wee hours (2:00-3:30 AM depending on day of week and location), these Southside BBQ basics pack 'em in for Southern fried chicken and smoky, hickory-laced ribs and tips; they're pretty much for carryout only, though the State Street location, nearly 50 years old, has three coveted seats; N.B. the 75th Street branch was closed at press time but expected to reopen in 2003.

Leona's [S] 15 | 14 | 15 | $19

1236 E. 53rd St. (Woodlawn Ave.), 773-363-2600

Ford City Mall, 7601 S. Cicero Ave. (76th St.), 773-838-8383

(continued)
Leona's
3877 N. Elston Ave. (bet. Drake & St. Louis Aves.), 773-267-7287
646 N. Franklin St. (bet. Erie & Ontario Sts.), 312-867-0101
3215 N. Sheffield Ave. (Belmont Ave.), 773-327-8861 ◐
6935 N. Sheridan Rd. (Morse Ave.), 773-764-5757
11060 S. Western Ave. (111th St.), 773-881-7700
1936 W. Augusta Blvd. (Damen Ave.), 773-292-4300
1419 W. Taylor St. (bet. Bishop & Loomis Sts.), 312-850-2222
848 W. Madison St. (bet. Grove & Kenilworth Aves.), Oak Park, 708-445-0101
Additional locations throughout the Chicago area
◪ Rater responses to these "down-to-earth" Italian-and-pizza "family restaurants" are all over the map, just like the extensive chain itself; regulars report "you get a lot for your money", namely an "amazing selection" of "dependable and satisfying" chow, but upstarts unleash their umbrage on the "million-item menu of mediocre food", not to mention the "iffy service."

Leo's Lunchroom [S] 🚫💳 | 18 | 12 | 16 | $14
1809 W. Division St. (bet. Ashland & Damen Aves.), 773-276-6509
◪ "Creative, tasty", "cheap grub" makes for "unpretentious dining" at this "funky" Wicker Park "dive" where the "short menu" combines "good, greasy breakfasts", "well-executed diner standards" and "unusual [New American] entrées"; some say "the space is so shabby" "you're overdressed in jeans and a T-shirt", but "one man's dump is another man's treasure" ("stay away – we want it for ourselves").

Le Passage ◐ | 16 | 23 | 18 | $42
1 E. Oak St. (Rush St.), 312-255-0022
◪ Though some say it's "nice for dinner and dancing", the upshot on this "dark", "hip, speakeasy-esque club" beneath the Gold Coast's Le Colonial is that it's "too bad" its "pricey", "ordinary [French] bistro food" "doesn't measure up to" its "beautiful" and "funky" decor or the "eye-candy" offered by the "younger crowd [it] appeals to."

LES DEUX GROS [S] | 27 | 20 | 23 | VE
462 N. Park Blvd. (bet. Hill & Pennsylvania Aves.), Glen Ellyn, 630-469-4002
◪ Brothers Thomas and Michael Lachowicz, the self-proclaimed "two fat guys", "are not afraid of butter", and it shows at their West Suburban French, which is "formal" but "with a sense of humor"; its "well-prepared", "excellent food" is now offered in "thoughtful" prix-fixe menus ranging from five to eight courses ($70-$110), and a post-*Survey* remodeling of the formerly "uninspiring" "strip-mall" setting may outdate the Decor score.

LES NOMADES 28 | 26 | 27 | VE

222 E. Ontario St. (bet. Fairbanks Ct. & St. Clair St.), 312-649-9010

■ A showcase for "talented chef" Roland Liccioni's "exciting", "visually stimulating" and "sensational" New French prix fixe–only menus, this popular spot is revered by well-heeled wanderers as an "oasis of refinement"; though it's no longer a private "club", "you'll feel a little privileged to be seated" within its "formal" yet "lovely Streeterville townhouse" setting where "needs are anticipated" by a "professional" staff; P.S. the wine collection is "stupendous."

LE TITI DE PARIS 28 | 25 | 27 | $55

1015 W. Dundee Rd. (Kennicott Ave.), Arlington Heights, 847-506-0222

■ "They get everything right" at "always-nice owner" Pierre Pollin's haute French – from "imaginative" chef Michael Maddox's "ever-evolving" menu of "excellent", "superbly presented" creations to the "outstanding service" "without snobbery" and the "lovely" surroundings; known as a bastion of "elegance and quality", it's "worth the drive" to the Northwest Suburbs and "the place to go when you want to be spoiled"; N.B. the Decor score may not reflect a post-*Survey* redecoration.

LE VICHYSSOIS [S] 25 | 21 | 23 | $47

220 W. Rte. 120 (bet. Hollywood Terrace & Willow Rd.), Lakemoor, 815-385-8221

■ "Marvelous" chef-owner Bernard Crétier "brings Vichy, France to the [Illinois] countryside", not to mention intrepid Chicagoans who've been braving the "long" journey to this "charming", "intimate" "diamond in an unlikely" Far Northwest Suburban setting for more than 25 years; the draws are "homey but proper French" cooking, "lovely rooms" that afford a "quiet, relaxed" experience and service that's "warm", if "not polished."

Lexi's [S] ▽ 19 | 19 | 20 | $36

1330 W. Madison St. (bet. Ashland & Racine Aves.), 312-829-4600

◪ Once a New American, this West Looper is now a Southern "Italian steak"-house serving "solid fare" that's great for "meat-and-potatoes guys"; those who find the food "unmemorable" and wish the kitchen would "take some risks" may want to sample the new menu introduced after a post-*Survey* change of ownership; P.S. concertgoers appreciate the "free shuttle to the United Center", and there's now live jazz Thursday–Saturday.

Lincoln Noodle House – | – | – | I

5862 N. Lincoln Ave. (Sacramento Ave.), 773-275-8847

Forerunner to some of the better-known noodle chains around town, this modest Northwest Side BYO has for years been quietly putting out miles of its namesake dish in various combinations of hot and cold, mild and spicy – as well as soups, stews and dumplings stuffed with meat or vegetables – all with full flavors, huge portions and low prices; N.B. longtime fans are hopeful that a post-*Survey* change in ownership doesn't result in big changes.

Lindo Mexico S   15 | 15 | 15 | $20

2642 N. Lincoln Ave. (bet. Diversey Pkwy. & Wrightwood Ave.), 773-871-4832

☑ "Tasty, basic Mexican" eats at "fair prices" are the reason to frequent this Lincoln Parker, a "good place to grab" a "fix" of "margaritas and tacos" as long as you're prepared to overlook the "slow service"; still, amigos who aren't in a hurry approve of the patio, saying that it "makes you feel like you're on vacation"; N.B. the former Niles location closed for good in late 2002.

Little Bucharest ◐ S   16 | 13 | 16 | $23

3001 N. Ashland Ave. (Wellington Ave.), 773-929-8640

☑ "Hearty, tasty meals" of "Old European grub" are an "ethnic change of pace" at this rollicking Romanian, a 32-year-old Lakeview veteran now calling itself a 'Euro cafe'; the "fun, crazy owner" and strolling minstrels (on weekends) add to a "festive atmosphere" (Saturday night patrons are even permitted bar-top dancing and dish breaking) and fans also favor the "free limo service"; P.S. the ratings may not reflect a post-*Survey* tweaking of the menu and formerly "dated decor."

Lobby, The S   – | – | – | E

Peninsula Hotel, 108 E. Superior St., 5th fl. (bet. Michigan Ave. & Rush St.), 312-573-6760

Despite its humble name, this posh Near Norther on the Peninsula Hotel's fifth floor is a dining destination in its own right, serving breakfast, lunch, dinner and formal tea (including a new vegan version requiring 24-hours notice); its Eclectic cuisine blends American and Asian influences with a seafood focus, and its sophisticated space boasts gilded ceilings and sweeping floor-to-ceiling windows overlooking tony Boul Mich.

Lou Malnati's Pizzeria S   21 | 12 | 16 | $17

439 N. Wells St. (Hubbard St.), 312-828-9800
3859 W. Ogden Ave. (Cermak Rd.), 773-762-0800
958 W. Wrightwood Ave. (Lincoln Ave.), 773-832-4030
85 S. Buffalo Grove Rd. (Lake Cook Rd.), Buffalo Grove, 847-215-7100
1050 E. Higgins Rd. (bet. Arlington Heights & Busse Rds.), Elk Grove, 847-439-2000
1850 Sherman Ave. (University Pl.), Evanston, 847-328-5400

(continued)

(continued)

Lou Malnati's Pizzeria

6649 N. Lincoln Ave. (bet. Devon & Pratt Aves.), Lincolnwood, 847-673-0800
131 W. Jefferson Ave. (Washington St.), Naperville, 630-717-0700
1 S. Roselle Rd. (Schaumburg Rd.), Schaumburg, 847-985-1525

■ The late Lou Malnati's "very name causes" fans of this "dependable" chain of "old-fashioned pizza parlors" "to start drooling" for his "best-ever" creations, which have earned his heirs bragging rights for the top-rated 'za in our *Survey*; pie-pipers report that "heavenly sauce" and "lots of cheese" and toppings add up to "deep dish that can't get any better", but in-the-know orderers insist that you "be sure to request the butter crust."

Lou Mitchell's [S] ⌀ 20 | 12 | 18 | $14

O'Hare Int'l Airport, Terminal 5 (I-90), 773-601-8989 ◐
565 W. Jackson Blvd. (Jefferson St.), 312-939-3111

■ For a "lip-smacking good" "breakfast dream", wake up to this West Loop "institution", an "old-fashioned diner" where morns commence with "Milk Duds and doughnut holes" (while "waiting in line"), "double-yolk omelets" and "strong coffee", all served with "a blatant disregard for fat and cholesterol"; lament not, late-risers – this "sassy-waitress heaven" serves lunch too; N.B. the O'Hare take-out serves soups, salads and sandwiches.

Lovell's of Lake Forest [S] 21 | 24 | 21 | $46

915 S. Waukegan Rd. (Everett Rd.), Lake Forest, 847-234-8013

◪ "Dine with the blue bloods" at this "classy, pricey" Suburban North New American whose "country-club atmosphere" comes complete with "fireplace and cigar lounge"; "owned by [Apollo 13] Captain James Lovell" and toqued by the "astronaut's son Jay", its "flavorful", "creative food" sends many "to the moon", but cosmo-nots assert it's "unremarkable except for the space memorabilia."

Lovitt [S] – | – | – | M

1466 N. Ashland Ave. (bet. Julian & LeMoyne Sts.), 773-252-1466

This teeny-tiny Wicker Park eatery (formerly Kismet) with a window to the kitchen presents a market-driven menu (including several vegan offerings) in a casual, permanently BYO setting decorated with paintings by local artists; overall, it's like a dinner party at a chef friend's house.

Lucca's [S] 22 | 21 | 21 | $36

2834 N. Southport Ave. (Wolfram St.), 773-477-2565

■ Its name is Lucca's (a hybrid of owners Michael Laconte's and chef Thomas Talucci's appellations), and this "low-key" Mediterranean-Italian "treasure" lives on the first floor of a "romantic" restored building in Lakeview; with "terrific choices" on the "creative menu" (like "heavenly shiitake mushroom pancakes"), a "wonderful, intimate setting" and "warm service", a visit to this "charmer" is "like curling up with a good book."

Lucia Ristorante — | — | — | M

1825 W. North Ave. (Honore St.), 773-292-9700
Diners may be surprised to be greeted by a deli counter, but tucked in back of this corner sandwich shop is a buff-colored dining room embellished with murals; a sparing use of red sauce makes for interesting regional Italian specialties whose low prices should appeal to Wicker Park neighbors; N.B. BYO.

Lucky Platter S 18 | 15 | 17 | $16

514 Main St. (bet. Chicago & Hinman Aves.), Evanston, 847-869-4064
■ "Healthy portions" of "down-to-earth" Eclectic "cheap eats" – from "tasty" tandoori salmon to "excellent pumpkin soup" to one of "the best tuna melts with sweet-potato fries in the city" (and "good vegetarian options" too) – make this "fun, funky", "folksy" and "kid-friendly" North Suburban a popular "hangout", even if it is "no-frills."

Lula S ∇ 22 | 13 | 17 | $19

2537-41 N. Kedzie Blvd. (bet. Fullerton Ave. & Logan Blvd.), 773-489-9554
■ "Please stop telling everyone about" it beg boosters of this "affordable" Logan Square Eclectic-American eatery serving up a "creative" menu of "contagious comfort cuisine", including an "excellent brunch"; it's a "delicious dive" catering to a "cool, funky clientele" of "hepcats", "cute rock girls" and "local artists" (whose work adorns the walls), so don't be surprised if you experience some "weird service"; N.B. the Decor score may not reflect a post-*Survey* expansion.

LuLu's Dim Sum & Then Sum S 17 | — | 17 | $16

804 Davis St. (Sherman Ave.), Evanston, 847-869-4343
☑ LuLu-lovers laud this "funky" and "happening place", an Evanston "original" for "fast, healthy and delicious" Pan-Asian fare that's "great for the price"; still, the jaded judge it "generic"; P.S. a post-*Survey* move to larger digs down the street may have helped the once "mediocre atmosphere."

Lupita's S 21 | 15 | 19 | $19

700 Main St. (Custer Ave.), Evanston, 847-328-2255
■ An "authentic" "favorite", this North Suburban spot overseen by "solicitous and always-present owner Lupita" Carson has "haute" Mexican fare (with a few American dishes as well), "cute decorations" and a "homey feel"; on

"special occasions" such as Valentine's Day, Mexican Independence Day (September 16) and Thanksgiving Eve, it offers a "*Like Water for Chocolate* menu" featuring "wonderful dishes" from Laura Esquivel's novel.

Lutnia ▣
∇ 20 | 20 | 21 | $32

5532 W. Belmont Ave. (Central Ave.), 773-282-5335

▣ "Good" "traditional Polish food", dramatic "tableside cooking", glittering "candles and [live] piano" music make for "a little romance" at this Northwest Side Continental; though most say it's a "one-of-a-kind" "pleasure to visit", the supercilious scoff that "the overdone old-world formality is a hoot", and the "limited wine menu" has quaffers quipping "I guess you're expected to stick to vodka."

Lutz Continental
Café & Pastry Shop ▣
19 | 18 | 18 | $20

2458 W. Montrose Ave. (bet. Rockwell St. & Western Ave.), 773-478-7785

■ A cross between a genuine "German *konditorei*" (confectionery) and an "authentic Viennese cafe", this "restful" Northwest Side Continental classic offers a "slice of Europe" "in Chicago" with "wonderful pastries" that are "just like in the Old Country" and so "delicious" some even "skip the main course"; traditionalists also savor the "enchanting garden" and "step-back-in-time" atmosphere ("my dad took my mom on dates here").

L. Woods Tap & Pine Lodge ▣
18 | 18 | 19 | $25

7110 N. Lincoln Ave. (Kostner Ave.), Lincolnwood, 847-677-3350

▣ Suitable "for all ages", this "casual, crowded" North Suburban "Lettuce Entertain You theme place" serves an "American menu for hungry meat-eaters", as well as a "good kids' menu", in a "folksy" atmosphere "that feels like a Wisconsin lodge"; snipers suggest it "tries to be what it is not" and wryly point out that "after the wait for a table you'll eat just about anything."

Mac's ◕▣
– | – | – | M

1801 W. Division St. (Wood St.), 773-782-4400

Providing something for everyone in diverse Ukrainian Village is a tall order, but Mac's is trying to fill it, blending traditional American comfort food with thoughtful updates on its menu and serving them with cool music in a vintage-pub atmosphere with a prominent bar and plenty of TVs showing sporting events.

MAGGIANO'S LITTLE ITALY ▣
20 | 18 | 19 | $27

516 N. Clark St. (Grand Ave.), 312-644-7700

Oakbrook Center Mall, 240 Oakbrook Ctr. (Rte. 83), Oak Brook, 630-368-0300

1901 E. Woodfield Rd. (Rte. 53), Schaumburg, 847-240-5600

(continued)
MAGGIANO'S LITTLE ITALY
175 Old Orchard Ctr. (bet. Golf & Old Orchard Rds.), Skokie, 847-933-9555

Even if you "come hungry" to any link in this "popular" chain of "boisterous" family spots, "expect" to trundle home toting "big doggy bags" thanks to the "bathtubsful of pasta" and "tremendous portions" of other "tasty" "straight Italian" fare they'll set before you; detractors declare it "noisy" and "hectic", with "inconsistent service" and "long waits" for "Americanized", "cookie-cutter food."

Magnolia Cafe S

			M
–	–	–	

1224 W. Wilson Ave. (Magnolia Ave.), 773-728-8785
Upscale for Uptown, this hip-yet-homey New American raises the bar a bit for its locale, but its fare is nonetheless hearty (the signature dish is braised beef short ribs, though some dishes are more daring) and its prices don't bruise the wallet (generous entrées are under $20); exposed brick, earth tones, candlelight and photographs of magnolia blossoms create a serene setting.

Magnum's Prime Steakhouse

22	20	20	$44

225 W. Ontario St. (Franklin St.), 312-337-8080 S
777 W. Butterfield Rd. (bet. Highland Ave. & Meyers Rd.), Lombard, 630-573-1010 S
1701 W. Golf Rd. (New Wilke Rd.), Rolling Meadows, 847-952-8555

Make your day with "great steaks and cocktails" at these "fancy spots" that a majority of meat-eaters maintain "hold their own with the big steakhouse boys"; the "gaudy atmosphere" makes some "miss Vegas", while others say the "spotty service" is a roll of the dice in its own right; P.S. the city location charges a cover to enter its weekends-only "disco ball and cigars" nightclub.

Maison S

			E
–	–	–	

30 S. La Grange Rd. (Harris Ave.), La Grange, 708-588-9890
"Discriminating palates" report that this still-not-widely-known Contemporary French–Traditional American two-year-old "in the Western Suburbs" "seems up to the challenge"; a husband-and-wife team – private-chefs-gone-public Mary and Christopher Spagnola – offers "excellent seasonal food" from an "inspired" menu that changes every six to eight weeks within a "beautiful, roomy interior."

Mama Desta's Red Sea S

∇ 18	11	13	$18

3216 N. Clark St. (Belmont Ave.), 773-935-7561
For a "unique experience", savvy sybarites stop into this Lakeview spot where the "authentic and inexpensive Ethiopian" eats (including vegetarian choices) are "fun to eat with your hands" and served by a "casual", "friendly staff"; some say "there's not much to" it in terms of design,

calling it a "hole-in-the-wall", but the Decor score may not reflect a renovation in progress at press time.

Mama Thai 🖪   ∇ 20 | 14 | 14 | $18

1112 W. Madison St. (Harlem Ave.), Oak Park, 708-386-0100
■ Oak Parkers say this "good Thai" storefront spot is "better than most local joints", and those from other areas report it's "worth the drive" thanks to "consistently fresh-tasting" Siamese fare including its signature spicy basil chicken stir-fried with garlic, peppers and mushrooms – not to mention some of the "best potstickers around" – all "at great prices"; N.B. beer and wine only.

Mambo Grill   18 | 16 | 17 | $25

412 N. Clark St. (bet. Hubbard & Kinzie Sts.), 312-467-9797
■ "Enjoy the spices" and "different flavors" of this "fun" River North Nuevo Latino's "inventive" and "flavorful dishes", a "surprising blend" of traditional South and Central American cuisines that amounts to "much more than" standard "south-of-the-border" fare; with "mostly hits and infrequent misses" from the kitchen and "interesting drinks" and "great sangria" from the bar, you may find yourself "doing the mambo."

Manny's Café 🖪   23 | 10 | 16 | $14

Midway Int'l Airport, 5700 S. Cicero Ave., Concourse A (55th St.), 773-948-6300
Manny's Coffee Shop ⊘
1141 S. Jefferson St. (Roosevelt Rd.), 312-939-2855
■ "Over 60 years old and going strong", this beloved South Loop "museum of Jewish cooking" is such a "real Chicago" "institution" that some "couldn't live without it"; "even a cardiologist would be tempted" by the "mile-high corned-beef sandwiches", and "you never know who you'll see" – "cops", "politicians", "maybe your lawyer"; N.B. the Decor score may not reflect a press-time remodeling of the original, and the Southwest Side location opened post-*Survey*.

Maple Tree Inn   19 | 16 | 16 | $26

13301 S. Old Western Ave. (Canal St.), Blue Island, 708-388-3461
◪ Crawfish-cravers clash over the Cajun-Creole cookery at this "friendly, hectic" South Suburban spot; some swear by its "good home cooking" like "to-die-for hickory-buttered BBQ shrimp" and "great crawfish pie", but others call the food "inconsistent" and only "fairly authentic", as well as "questioning" the "off-kilter service", saying this "potentially bright star" is performing "below its potential."

Marché 🖪   21 | 23 | 20 | $40

833 W. Randolph St. (Green St.), 312-226-8399
◪ "Take your friends from Kansas" for a "wild" ride at this "still-hip", "circus-like" "winner" in the Market District that lures "ultra-trendy" "pretty people" with "whimsical"

decor and an "exciting" New French–American "menu of temptations"; some say, though, that the "attentive" staff can be as "wacky" as Emerald Cityites and warn that the "loud, loud, loud" scene might have "small-towners" tapping their ruby slippers and hankering for home.

Margie's Candies ●S   23 | 18 | 18 | $10

1960 N. Western Ave. (Armitage Ave.), 773-384-1035
■ "Sentimental" sweet-toothers insist that this "kitschy" and "quirky" "must-try" Bucktown "blast from the past" "becomes a must-return" once you've tried its "homemade candy" and "old-fashioned ice-cream creations" with "butterfat galore" and "hot fudge so thick your spoon stays vertical"; there is an American menu, but most maintain the "great desserts" "are a meal" in themselves.

Marion Street Grille S   ▽ 20 | 18 | 21 | $35

189 N. Marion St. (bet. Lake & Ontario Sts.), Oak Park, 708-383-1551
☑ "Quaint, cozy and romantic", this Suburban West Regional American "find" draws the faithful for "fresh fish" and "worthwhile steak" specialties amid "unique decor" of exposed brick, tin ceilings and vintage advertising posters; the "nice atmosphere" seems especially "quiet" given that the "comfortable" storefront is just a block from bustling Lake Street, but still some scowl that it's "pricey for Oak Park."

Mario's Gold Coast Ristorante   16 | 15 | 20 | $25

21 W. Goethe St. (Dearborn St.), 312-944-0199
☑ "Raving" respondents who "love hanging out" at this "locals' secret" call it "the *Cheers* of the Gold Coast"; even if not "everybody knows your name", count on owner Mario Stefanini (he "truly loves people!") to "treat everyone like an old friend"; with such "warm service", most don't mind that the "inexpensive" Italian "food is only adequate."

Mars S   15 | 16 | 16 | $19

3124 N. Broadway (Belmont Ave.), 773-404-1600
☑ While some say the "interesting food" at this "upbeat" and "upscale" Lakeview Chinese – like orange beef and crispy sesame shrimp – is "proof that quality ingredients don't have to cost an arm and a leg", the less impressed claim the "competent" kitchen is "hit or miss" and the "service leaves something to be desired", adding that "better options abound."

Mar y Sol   – | – | – | M

812-816 W. Randolph St. (Halsted St.), 312-563-1763
Splashy tropical colors set the mood for Cuban-style tapas and Caribbean cocktails at this upscale Latin on the Market District's restaurant row; a sidewalk cafe adds to the see-and-be scene.

Mas 🅂   22 | 19 | 19 | $34

1670 W. Division St. (Paulina St.), 773-276-8700

■ "Reliably awesome", this "energetic" Wicker Park Nuevo Latino has *señoras y caballeros* "crowded" at the bar, consuming "outstanding" caipirinhas and mojitos while eagerly anticipating *más* of chef John Manion's "edgy Latin cuisine" and its "quixotic combos of savory, complex spices"; the "long waits" aren't so "terrible" "now that they take reservations" and there's another one, baby brother Otro Mas in Lakeview.

Masck 🅂   – | – | – | E

Deerfield Commons Shopping Ctr., 730 Waukegan Rd.
(bet. Deerfield Rd. & Osterman Ave.), Deerfield, 847-236-1400
In late 2001, husband-and-wife team Kevin and Michelle Nierman opened this ambitious North Suburban New American in the Deerfield Commons Shopping Center; it features an eclectic seasonal menu ranging from 'floppy cheeseburgers' and thin-crust pizzas to twice-roasted crispy duckling and garlic jumbo prawns (and a fun finish of hot, made-to-order mini-doughnuts), and the stylish dining room is lively, colorful – and often crowded.

Matsuya ●🅂   22 | 13 | 18 | $22

3469 N. Clark St. (Sheffield Ave.), 773-248-2677

■ There's a reason this "solid" "sushi goldmine" in Wrigleyville is "always crowded" (and "deservedly so") "no matter when you go" – they've been serving "fresh, authentic", "consistently good" Japanese fare (including "interesting rolls", "tasty tempura" and "well-flavored teriyaki") "at a great price" "for decades", which packs 'em in despite a near-absence of ambiance.

Max's 🅂   14 | 9 | 13 | $15

Crossroads Shopping Ctr., 191 Skokie Valley Rd. (bet. Clavey &
Lake Cook Rds.), Highland Park, 847-831-0600

☑ Fans of this North Suburban Jewish deli appreciate the "good smoked salmon" and "monster matzo balls", but contrarians claim it's "average", "inconsistent" and "not as good as" its competitors, with some bellicose Big Apple boosters braying that it "can't compare to NYC" and insisting "it's a Chicago deli – in other words, mediocre."

Maza 🅂   ∇ 23 | 17 | 21 | $26

2748 N. Lincoln Ave. (Diversey Pkwy.), 773-929-9600

■ "You can taste the TLC" at this Lincoln Park "gem" specializing in the "Lebanese staple" known as, you guessed it, "maza – small portions" of "a zillion" (well, 20) "tasty" tapas-style treats served "for two"; though you "can definitely make it the main course", "excellent" entrées and "great desserts" are also offered, and a "helpful staff" that makes you "feel at home" warms the "spartan" but "elegant" environment.

McCormick & Schmick's S
21 21 20 $39

41 E. Chestnut St. (Rush St.), 312-397-9500

☑ It's "good to have a seafood place in the middle of beefdom" report red meat–weary regulars who appreciate this Gold Coast national chain outpost's "excellent menu" starring "any fish you can think of" proffered with a plethora of "preparation options" in a "dark", clubby setting with "cozy, semi-private booths"; still, some label it "inconsistent" and a trifle "institutional"; P.S. "the bar hops" "at happy hour."

Menagerie S
– – – M

1232 W. Belmont Ave. (bet. Lakewood & Racine Aves.), 773-404-8333

Chef-owners Craig Fass (ex Bistro 110) and Mandi Franklin (ex Spring) have spruced up the former Lakeview Supper Club space with a fresh coat of pale green paint and added burgundy linens and lots of local art, thus creating a casual eatery with an innovative New American menu and plenty of neighborhood charm; the spacious outdoor deck is sure to be a summer favorite.

Meritage Cafe & Wine Bar S
23 20 21 $40

2118 N. Damen Ave. (bet. Armitage & Webster Aves.), 773-235-6434

■ "Sophisticated cuisine" with "superb seasonings" draws "drools" for this Bucktown New American that purveys provender of the Pacific Northwest; whether you take your meal within the "posh and stylish" interior or "dine under the lights" of its "romantic" "heated patio" ("you can imagine you're in Northern California"), the "warm" ambiance makes it a "mainstay for a night out with a significant other."

Merle's Smokehouse S
20 17 18 $22

1727 Benson Ave. (Church St.), Evanston, 847-475-7766

■ Set in a "historic old bar", this North Suburban BBQ bonanza offers outlaws "awesome pork chops", "yummy brisket" and "amazing ribs" done Memphis-, Texas- and North Carolina–style; it's a "great" place "for guys to pig out" (even if their "girls don't like it" as much) amid "humorous" decorations such as "the sign that says 'cowboys, scrape boots before entering.'"

Merlo Ristorante S
– – – E

2638 N. Lincoln Ave. (Wrightwood Ave.), 773-529-0747

Distinctive Northern Italian fare is fully complemented by tasteful decor and a well-selected wine list (with 15 to 20 by-the-glass pours) at this welcome Lincoln Park spot; try the artichoke tart, lasagna verde and creamy panna cotta with homemade caramel drizzle, but don't try coming here for lunch – they only serve dinner, seven days a week.

Mesón Sabika 🇸   23 | 22 | 21 | $29
1025 Aurora Ave. (bet. Berry Dr. & River Rd.), Naperville,
630-983-3000
Northfield Village Ctr., 310 Happ Rd. (bet. Willow Rd. &
Winnetka Ave.), Northfield, 847-784-9300
■ "Tip-top" for "tempting"-and-"tasty tapas treats" in our
Survey, these North and West Suburban haciendas offer
"a true taste of Spain", with a "wide variety" of "the best"
small plates that are "sublime for sharing" and "beautiful
settings", especially the Naperville original's "historic"
"pillared mansion with veranda"; the "good sangria (in both
red and white)" and "sherry flights" go down smoothly too.

Mia Cucina 🇸   19 | 18 | 17 | $29
56 W. Wilson St. (Brockway St.), Palatine, 847-358-4900
■ "City atmosphere in the suburbs" is among the attractions
at this Northwest Suburban "trendy Italian with upscale
food" such as "good pastas", "terrific breads" and "tasty,
nicely presented specialties from the wood-burning oven";
raters rank it "reliably good, especially for Palatine", and
say the "noisy, happening" atmosphere is enhanced by a
"beautiful bar area with live music on weekends."

MIA FRANCESCA 🇸   24 | 19 | 20 | $31
3311 N. Clark St. (School St.), 773-281-3310
■ "A total favorite", this "buzzworthy" Lakeview original
was the launching pad of Scott Harris' captivating coterie
of contemporary "casual Italians" offering "affordable",
regularly changing menus of "superbly done" dishes from
Rome and the surrounding areas of Tuscany, Umbria and
Lazio; you may have to "enjoy drinks at the bar as you wait"
for a seat in its "crowded" dining room, though.

Midori Japanese 🇸   ▽ 19 | 15 | 18 | $22
3310 W. Bryn Mawr Ave. (bet. Kedzie & Kimball Aves.),
773-267-9733
☑ Below the radar of most Chicago diners, this Northwest
Sider has a cult following for fish that's "always fresh", as
well as "tasty and surprising snacks that come with your
dinner"; some "Japanese-Americans and their visitors go
for sushi" in its cozy tatami rooms and for karaoke and
"bizarre videos" in the bar, but probably not for the service,
which is "sometimes lacking."

Mike Ditka's 🇸   20 | 20 | 19 | $37
Tremont Hotel, 100 E. Chestnut St. (Michigan Ave.), 312-587-8989
☑ "Cigar-smoking jocks" seeking "power pork chops"
head to this "solid", "not-just-for-tourists" Near North
steakhouse with a "heavy-on-meat" menu and a "hall
of fame–like memorabilia" collection; some fans of "da
Bears" who like "da food" but find da dining room "stuffy"
call an audible and head instead for the bar, "where there's
more action" and "more fun."

Milk & Honey S
— | — | — | I

1920 W. Division St. (bet. Winchester & Wolcott Aves.), 773-395-9434

Gallon jars of honey are on display, but the milk stays in the fridge at this airy Wicker Park cafe; novel sandwiches, soups, salads and house-baked breakfast treats are served in the cool green dining room or outdoors on the sunny streetside patio.

Miller's Pub ●S
16 | 14 | 17 | $24

134 S. Wabash Ave. (bet. Adams & Monroe Sts.), 312-263-4988

■A "Loop standard", this "bastion of old Downtown Chicago" "maintains tradition" with "classic" American "grub" ("not haute cuisine"), "early saloon decor" and a staff that "remembers you"; "huge nostalgic value" and a "late-night" kitchen cooking till 1:30 AM have regulars reporting they "hope it never closes."

Mill Race Inn S
18 | 22 | 19 | $29

4 E. State St. (Rte. 25), Geneva, 630-232-2030

☑Five venues in one, this "relaxing" compound "in the Western Suburbs" comprises the Country Inn (a "cultured" dining space) and Mallard Room (for private functions), both with "views of a wooded island park", the Duck Inn (a sports bar), the Grill (a tavern) and the summer-only Gazebo "pleasantly" placed "on the Fox River"; still, most say its "lovely setting" outruns its "conservative" American menus by a mile.

Millrose Restaurant and Brewing Co. S
18 | 20 | 18 | $30

45 S. Barrington Rd. (Central Rd.), Barrington, 847-382-7673

☑ Built from six relocated antique barns, this Northwest Suburban "lodgelike" microbrewery/restaurant/store comes by its "rustic country" feel honestly, and "every" one of its "large rooms" is "a treat"; quaffers claim the "hearty, beef and pork"–heavy menu of "basic American food" that "supports its great beer" list is "a cut above average", but critics caution "expect to wait" for "so-so food and service."

Mimosa S
24 | 19 | 23 | $34

1849 Second St. (bet. Central Ave. & Elm Pl.), Highland Park, 847-432-9770

■ "Constantly innovating chef"-owner Kevin Schrimmer "pleases customers" of this "well-run" North Suburban with an "appealing menu" of "creative" New French–Italian fare that fans feel is "just incredible" and a "good buy", to boot; the atmosphere is "calm" and "uncluttered", maitre d' "Dan [Tarver] and [toque's wife] Karen always make you feel welcome" and the "friendly staff" "gets an A for professional service."

Mirabell
▽ 19 | 17 | 18 | $27

3454 W. Addison St. (bet. Kimball & St. Louis Aves.), 773-463-1962

■ A "wonderful" "neighborhood German", and "one of the few left", this Northwest Sider offers "a night in Bavaria – in a booth!"; "great schnitzel and leberknödel soup" are served in its "rustic" dining rooms and washed down with imported beers on tap from the "convivial bar" where, rumor has it, "chef Werner [Heil] will do shots of Jägermeister on request" (it can't hurt to ask).

Mirai Sushi ⬛
24 | 22 | 19 | $38

2020 W. Division St. (Damen Ave.), 773-862-8500

■ Wicker Park's chart-topping Japanese "screams 'repeat visit'", earning earnest encomiums for the "perfect presentations" of "inventive chef Jun" Ichikawa's "bold" "couture sushi" ("not cheap in either price or quality", it "compares favorably to Tokyo" spots); P.S. the "beautiful people" head upstairs to the "sleek, hip lounge" to partake of the "awesome adult beverages" and "great sake list."

Misto
17 | 16 | 18 | $30

1118 W. Grand Ave. (bet. Halsted St. & Racine Ave.), 312-226-5989

■ A "comfortable" combination of American and Italian cuisines at "reasonable prices" makes this "nice" Near West "find" "a pleasant surprise" for those tired of "the trendy [restaurant] craze", and a sidewalk cafe and "nice hospitality add to the atmosphere"; P.S. "it's worth it just to see [chef] Donny Greco in action" – "go Saturday night when he sings" at 10 PM.

Mity Nice Grill ⬛
18 | 17 | 18 | $25

Water Tower Pl., 835 N. Michigan Ave., mezzanine level (bet. Chestnut & Pearson Sts.), 312-335-4745

■ A "quiet" and "classy yet casual" "oasis in a storm" (namely, the "upscale mall" in Streeterville called Water Tower Place), this Lettuce Entertain You American "really is mity nice" for an "always-satisfying" menu ranging from "down-home comfort-food" "standards" to fancier fare like "great garlic-crusted whitefish"; regulars report it's "the best place to recharge after a heavy day of shopping."

MK ⬛
26 | 24 | 25 | $51

868 N. Franklin St. (bet. Chicago Ave. & Oak St.), 312-482-9179

■ "Terrific food", a "stylish setting" and "expert service" are a "powerful combination" at this River North New American, where "genius" toque-owner Michael Kornick (joined post-*Survey* by chef de cuisine Stephen Dunne) is "at the top of his game"; his "innovative but approachable" food is paired with a "well-crafted and complementary wine list" and followed by "divine desserts", making this "a place to go back to as often as possible."

mk North 23 | 20 | 21 | $42

305 Happ Rd. (Willow Rd.), Northfield, 847-716-6500

◪ "Fresh, understandable Contemporary American fare" that "fits right in" in its affluent North Shore neighborhood makes this "happening" and "family-friendly" "cousin" of Michael Kornick's Downtowner "a welcome newcomer" in town; though doubters don't like the "noise", "high prices" and service that's "not quite there yet", folks report it's "becoming increasingly difficult to get reservations", so plan accordingly.

Mod. [S] 23 | 22 | 20 | $42

1520 N. Damen Ave. (North Ave.), 773-252-1500

◪ A mod nod to New American fare, this "hip" Wicker Parker is "an eye-opener in every sense"; "don't be put off" by the "funky" "*Jetson's* decor" – "the room may be hard"-edged, but the "innovative and electrifying" cuisine is paradoxically "real comfy"; P.S. the Food rating may not reflect the post-*Survey* promotion of Susannah Walker from sous-chef to top toque.

Molive [S] 20 | 20 | 21 | $44

Whitehall Hotel, 107 E. Delaware Pl. (Michigan Ave.), 312-573-6300

■ "Hidden" "in the Whitehall Hotel", in "an out-of-the-way" Near North location "off Michigan Avenuc", this "under-attended treasure" is "sophisticated without snobby excess", pairing "imaginative" New American–Mediterranean cuisine such as "great fish" dishes with "exceptional wine offerings" (including 40 by the glass) in a "stylish", "intimate room" with a "friendly, casual and uplifting atmosphere."

MON AMI GABI [S] 23 | 22 | 22 | $38

2300 N. Lincoln Park W. (Belden Ave.), 773-348-8886

Oakbrook Center Mall, 260 Oakbrook Ctr. (Rte. 83), Oak Brook, 630-472-1900

■ Friends of Gabi (chef-partner Gabino Sotelino) consider "both locations" of this "comfy", "bustling" city-and-suburban bistro brotherhood – "another interesting Lettuce Entertain You" enterprise – to be "spot-on" for "good French favorites" (including "great steak frites") offered by servers with "no affectations"; oenophiles effuse over the "rolling wine cart", and expatriates appreciate the "European feel."

Monsoon [S] – | – | – | E

2813 N. Broadway St. (bet. Clark St. & Diversey Pkwy.), 773-665-9463

Ornate fabrics and shimmering silk curtains add to the exotic atmosphere of this upscale Lakeview newcomer; Shanghai Terrace veteran Sumanth Das takes fusion to a better place with his spice-warmed collection of Indian-inspired Asian dishes.

Montage 🟥
_ | _ | _ | M

3124 S. Rte. 59 (95th St.), Naperville, 630-904-7401
Here's another ambitious New American angling for acceptance in booming Suburban West Naperville; Sean Roe (ex NOLA and Emeril's/Vegas) leaves his N'Awlins roots behind, cooking with a broader, seasonal palette and an urban sensibility; the restaurant serves lunch and dinner seven days a week in a relaxed, modern setting with in-kitchen chef's table, triangular wine room and distinctive patriotic wine list.

Moody's Pub ●🟥⇄
19 | 15 | 16 | $15

5910 N. Broadway St. (Thorndale St.), 773-275-2696
☑ "A real Chicago joint with all the greasy food you love", this place has been serving "cheap eats" in Edgewater since 1959; pleased pub-licans praise the "laid-back" ambiance and "fireplaces that make it a favorite winter-afternoon spot", as well as the "lovely beer garden under the trees" in summer; perturbed ones dub it "dark, dingy and smoky – and that's during the day."

MORTON'S OF CHICAGO 🟥
26 | 21 | 24 | $53

Newberry Plaza, 1050 N. State St., lower level (Maple St.), 312-266-4820
9525 W. Bryn Mawr Ave. (River Rd.), Rosemont, 847-678-5155
1470 McConnor Pkwy. (Meacham Rd.), Schaumburg, 847-413-8771
1 Westbrook Corporate Ctr. (22nd St.), Westchester, 708-562-7000
■ "In the face of tremendous competition", these "clubby" cum lauders continue to claim the coveted steakhouse crown in our *Survey* and have since its inception; the city original and its suburban spin-offs (part of a national chain) each get the meat-eaters seal of approval as a "primo" "red-meat heaven with attentive service" where "the bang lives up to the buck" – though many "thank goodness for expense accounts."

Moti Mahal 🟥
∇ 19 | 9 | 14 | $17

1031-35 W. Belmont Ave. (Kenmore Ave.), 773-348-4392
☑ "Authentic", "inexpensive" and "tasty Indian food" from a "great variety of platters" and a "good buffet" draw bargain-hunters to this "great BYO" in Lakeview, the survivor of an erstwhile duo (the Rogers Park branch has closed), where devoted diners are undaunted by what some call "questionable service"; P.S. the Decor score may not reflect a post-*Survey* redecoration.

Mrs. Levy's Delicatessen
15 | 12 | 15 | $15

Sears Tower, 233 S. Wacker Dr., 2nd level (bet. Adams St. & Jackson Blvd.), 312-993-0530
☑ To some matzo mavens, this "reliable" "standard" in the Sears Tower is "the only place to get good deli in the Loop",

delivering "quick service" and an "extensive menu" of "NY-style" favorites that are "great for the price"; critics, though, contend the "corporate" concept is "getting stale"; N.B. open Monday–Friday.

Mrs. Park's Tavern S   18 | 17 | 18 | $33

Doubletree Guest Suites Hotel, 198 E. Delaware Pl. (Michigan Ave.), 312-280-8882
◪ Run by the Smith & Wollensky Restaurant Group, this Traditional American in the Doubletree Guest Suites Hotel has "offbeat, creative" dishes that are reliably "good" (the "mini-cheeseburgers are a must"); coming here may be "like visiting mom at home."

Mt. Everest Restaurant S   – | – | – | M

618 Church St. (bet. Chicago & Orrington Sts.), Evanston, 847-491-1069
"Besides standard Indian fare" and a "great lunch buffet", adventurous diners will find "good" "Nepalese dishes" to pique their interest at this "interesting" North Suburban where the signature goat dish is "great (for meat eaters)"; the "wonderful cuisine and service" are enjoyed in an "attractive" and colorful dining room dotted with Himalayan paintings and augmented by authentic music.

My Pie Pizza S   20 | 12 | 16 | $15

2417 N. Clark St. (Fullerton Pkwy.), 773-929-3380
2010 N. Damen Ave. (Armitage Ave.), 773-394-6900
■ Fans of "cheap food" who're looking for a "wonderful salad bar" and "great, fresh-tasting deep dish" delight in descending upon this duo of "neighborhood" pie peddlers; loyalists of the Lincoln Park "1970s relic" say "bring a flashlight" to navigate the "dark", "weird, midnight picnic decor" then "snare a seat by the fireplace"; Bucktowners boast their branch's 'za is "just as good."

Myron & Phil's Steakhouse S   22 | 16 | 21 | $35

3900 W. Devon Ave. (bet. Crawford & Lincoln Aves.), Lincolnwood, 847-677-6663
■ "Always a top performer in steaks, chops, seafood and ribs", this "reliable" thirtysomething North Suburban "throwback" meat mecca also satisfies with a "wonderful [complimentary] appetizer tray" (including "cholesterol-bomb chopped liver") and "great green goddess dressing"; it may be "nothing fancy", but it's "pretty darn good", and even detractors who describe it as an "old-school Cadillac" admit the staffers are "reliable pros."

Mysore Woodland S   – | – | – | M

2548 W. Devon Ave. (Rockwell St.), 773-338-8160
6020 S. Cass Ave. (bet. 59th & 63rd Sts.), Westmont, 630-769-9663
Locals line up at this Northwest Side meat-free Southern Indian BYO on the bustling ethnic stretch of Devon Avenue –

home to a vast array of subcontinental markets, boutiques and restaurants – and its banquet-size dining room is frequently full of large families enjoying fare including fried lentil doughnuts, samosas and dosai; N.B. there's also a Suburban West branch.

Nacional 27 22 | 23 | 21 | $37

325 W. Huron St. (Orleans St.), 312-664-2727

■ "Order a mojito and enjoy" the "high-energy fusion" of this "hip Nuevo Latino", a "lively" Lettuce Entertain You River North hot spot where chef Randy Zweiban showcases the "wonderful, bold flavors" of 27 Latin American nations on his "imaginative" menu; "fantastic cocktails" enhance the "glamorous" setting, which is even more "fun when the music starts" and the salsa dancing begins (on weekends).

NAHA 25 | 24 | 23 | $54

500 N. Clark St. (Illinois St.), 312-321-6242

■ A "great addition to the dining scene", this River North spot "works" thanks to "chef Carrie Nahabedian's New American–Mediterranean fusion" featuring "seemingly simple dishes that uncover complex and fresh flavors"; the "polished", "passionate staff" "makes each diner feel special", and the "crisp, clean setting" "feels like a spa"; P.S. since you'll "eat like a king", loyalists laugh you'd better "bring the royal treasury."

Nancy's Original Stuffed Pizza [S] 17 | 10 | 14 | $17

3970 N. Elston Ave. (Irving Park Rd.), 773-267-8182 🚫

2930 N. Broadway St. (Wellington Ave.), 773-883-1977

■ "Artistry with a crust" awaits at this Lakeview deep-disher where the "stuffed giant pizza answers all prayers" and the "chicken cacciatore pie is a can't-miss"; it's "not much to look at", though, pout pie-philes who propose that they "need to renovate"; P.S. plenty are pleased with the pick-up and "prompt delivery" from the smaller Northwest Side branch, which does not offer table service.

Narcisse ◐ [S] ▽ 19 | 23 | 19 | $37

710 N. Clark St. (bet. Huron & Superior Sts.), 312-787-2675

◪ River North locals "love the interior" of this "cozy" lair that's a "great after-dinner spot" and a "nice place for drinks", with "expensive wines" and "cocktails so strong no person could drink one and stay sober"; the "winning staff" and "way-upscale bar food" are a welcome treat to some, though the more down-to-earth deem it a bit self-absorbed and "pretentious"; N.B. the ratings may not reflect a post-*Survey* change in ownership.

New Japan [S] 21 | 17 | 20 | $26

1322 Chicago Ave. (Dempster St.), Evanston, 847-475-5980

■ While this "Evanston mainstay" isn't so new anymore, it continues to boast "superior presentations" of both "inventive" and "traditional Japanese" dishes, including sushi, on its "excellent and varied menu"; though some sigh it's a "jewel with no atmosphere", others say its "setting is serene and peaceful"; P.S. a change in ownership has fans hoping its tradition of "personal service" survives intact.

New Three Happiness S — — — M
(fka Three Happiness)
2130 S. Wentworth Ave. (Cermak Rd.), 312-791-1228
Dim sum seven days a week keeps this sizable Cantonese–Szechuan-Mongolian "classic" in Chinatown busy, if not "frenetic", aided by a prominent corner location near the El stop; "fast service" and "fun people-watching" are additional bonuses, but hecklers hint at "slipping quality" in the kitchen and housekeeping issues; N.B. no longer affiliated with Three Happiness on West Cermak Road.

Next Door Bistro S⊅ 23 17 22 $31
250 Skokie Blvd. (bet. Dundee & Lake Cook Rds.), Northbrook, 847-272-1491
■ You "can't go wrong with any special or menu item" at this "wonderful", "warm" North Suburban Italian-American bistro, kissing cousin to Francesco's Hole in the Wall, where coin counters compliment the "great value" as much as the "excellent" roast chicken; the "funky interior never changes" and neither do the "long waits" (some swear "they seat regulars first"), so "arrive early" and "bring cash."

Nick & Tony's Italian Chophouse S 17 17 18 $30
1 E. Wacker Dr. (bet. State St. & Wabash Ave.), 312-467-9449
Geneva Commons, 1322 Commons Dr. (Randall Rd.), Geneva, 630-845-0025
◪ Some surveyors find that this Italian's "convenient location" in the Loop makes it "great for a business lunch" or "pre-theater" dinner of "large, decently priced portions" (especially when enjoyed "outdoors in summer"); still, others say that, quantity aside, it's just a "so-so" "joint" with "nothing special" going on; N.B. the Suburban West location opened post-*Survey.*

Nick's Fishmarket 24 22 23 $49
Bank One Plaza, 51 S. Clark St. (Monroe St.), 312-621-0200
O'Hare Int'l Ctr., 10275 W. Higgins Rd. (Mannheim Rd.), Rosemont, 847-298-8200 S
■ "A sure catch every time", these "classy", "awesome" Loop and O'Hare seafooders "consistently" net a huge school of fin fans – "even though they hook your wallet along with your palate" – thanks to "elegantly presented" "fine-dining creations" (especially the signature Dover sole and "great lobster bisque") and "dynamite service teams" who "wait on you hand and foot."

Nine   23 | 25 | 20 | $48
440 W. Randolph St. (bet. Canal St. & Wacker Dr.), 312-575-9900
🔳 "If you have something to show, this is the place to go" –
so say the "hip and trendy" about this "big, bold", "see-
and-be-seen hot spot" in the West Loop where the "great"
American steakhouse fare and "champagne-and-caviar
bar" "match the dazzling ambiance"; though scenesters say
the chance to "see someone famous" helps make for "a
great evening out", the jaded just don't get the "pretension"
and "high prices."

Nola's 32nd Ward   – | – | – | M
Seafood House 🅢
1856 W. North Ave. (Wolcott Ave.), 773-395-4300
New Orleans nostalgia now distinguishes Wicker Park's
former Echo space: antique wooden doors, mosaic tiles
and other found objects adorn the bar, walls and tabletops
while a vintage crystal chandelier adds antebellum charm
overhead; a large blue-tinted window provides diners with
a view of the Southern-style crawfish boils and fried oysters
being prepared in the kitchen.

NOMI 🅢   23 | 26 | 23 | $61
Park Hyatt Chicago, 800 N. Michigan Ave. (Chicago Ave.),
312-239-4030
🔳 "You can't beat" the "stunning", "romantic view" at this
"elegant", "sleek" New French set in a "dazzling" room
above the city lights that has the smitten sighing "can I live
here? please?"; while foodies fawn over chef Sandro
Gamba's "adventurous" and "artful" fare, a few frowners
fuss over the "diminutive portions" and "high prices", adding
it's high time for the "arrogant staff" to "lose the attitude";
N.B. terrace seating is available in summer.

Nookies 🅢⊅   17 | 12 | 17 | $14
1746 N. Wells St. (bet. Lincoln & North Aves.), 312-337-2454
Nookies, Too 🅢
2114 N. Halsted St. (bet. Dickens & Webster Aves.), 773-327-1400
Nookies Tree ◖🅢⊅
3334 N. Halsted St. (Buckingham Pl.), 773-248-9888
▪ Native Chicagoans of all persuasions head to this "fun,
fast, cheap" trio of coffee shops for "consistent" American
diner fare and "reliable" breakfasts served "any time of
day" (the Lakeview location is also a great "boy-watching
cafe"); red-eyed partiers hail it for the "best hangover
meal around", but "get there early or you'll wait in line",
especially on weekends; N.B. the Decor score may not
reflect a post-*Survey* remodeling of the Lincoln Park branch.

Noon-O-Kabab 🅢   – | – | – | I
4661 N. Kedzie Ave. (Leland Ave.), 773-279-8899
The main attractions at this tiny family-run Persian BYO on
the Northwest Side are its kebabs of marinated chicken,

filet, salmon or spiced ground beef served atop mounds of fluffy, saffron-flecked basmati rice in portions so large you don't mind sharing; conveniently located right off the brown-line train, it's great for dining in or taking out.

NORTH POND S   24 | 25 | 22 | $43
(fka North Pond Café)
2610 N. Cannon Dr. (bet. Diversey & Fullerton Pkwys.), 773-477-5845
■ You'll feel like you're "dining at Frank Lloyd Wright's home" at this "wonderfully restored" "gem" of an "Arts and Crafts building" "hidden" in Lincoln Park, but the real architect here is "inventive" chef Bruce Sherman, who builds "delicious" New American dishes "using fresh ingredients" from "local organic farms"; P.S. though the "spectacular" "lagoon and skyline view" remain, a post-*Survey* remodeling is not reflected in the Decor score.

Northside Cafe ●S   14 | 14 | 14 | $19
1635 N. Damen Ave. (Milwaukee & North Aves.), 773-384-3555
◪ Biased Bucktowners bill this Traditional American as a "fun burger joint" turning out "reasonably priced", "better-than-average pub grub"; nevertheless, non-locals lambaste its "hit-or-miss entrées" and "surly service", saying they'd sooner set their compasses southward instead.

Noyes Street Café S   – | – | – | M
828 Noyes St. (Sherman St.), Evanston, 847-475-8683
A "dependable" "hidden treasure", this casual and family-friendly North Suburban cafe is "popular" for "large portions" from a varied menu of "good food at fair prices"; not only is it a "neighborhood pasta place" serving Italian classics, but it also proffers "Greek specialties" as well as salads and sandwiches within its cafe setting of booths and original works by local artists; N.B. beer and wine only.

Nuevo Leon S   22 | 13 | 17 | $15
1515 W. 18th St. (bet. Ashland & Blue Island Aves.), 312-421-1517 ●∄
3657 W. 26th St. (bet. Central Park & Lawndale Aves.), 773-522-1515
■ "An anchor of the neighborhood", Pilsen's popular 41-year-old BYO "Mexican diner" on 18th Street offers "dirt-cheap", "delicious, down-home fare" including "classic Mex breakfasts" in a "plain", "homey" space with "no-frills service"; night-crawlers think it nice that it's open till 5 AM on weekends; N.B. the independently operated 26th Street location has a similar menu but serves beer.

Oak Terrace S   ▽ 21 | 21 | 21 | $32
Drake Hotel, 140 E. Walton St. (Michigan Ave.), 312-787-2200
■ "A lunch favorite", this "friendly" Traditional American in the Drake Hotel delivers "delicious food" – including

"really good salads", sandwiches and fresh breads – in a "warm, wonderful room" known for beautiful views of Lake Michigan and its annual Dickens Buffet, a holiday-season highlight; N.B. dinner is served on Fridays and Saturdays.

Oak Tree S   16 | 16 | 16 | $19
Bloomingdale's Bldg., 900 N. Michigan Ave., 6th fl. (bet. Delaware Pl. & Walton St.), 312-751-1988
☑ "On shopping days", Michigan Avenue marauders dodge the "bustling crowds" and drop in to this Traditional American in the Bloomingdale's building "where the Near North crowd meets" for "breakfast or a midday meal"; some browsers beef about "slow service" and claim "it's really a coffee shop", but teetotaling "ladies who lunch" ("no liquor" is served) say it's "ok" by them.

Oceanique   24 | 20 | 22 | $45
505 Main St. (bet. Chicago & Hinman Aves.), Evanston, 847-864-3435
■ An "outstanding selection" of "exquisite" contemporary French–New American "seafood creations" made with "fresh, high-quality ingredients" is paired with the fruits of a "top-notch wine cellar" at this "romantic, comfortable" and "civilized" Evanston eatery; the kitchen's "precise preparation and presentation", as well as the staff's "polished service", make wallet-watchers wistfully "wish they could afford to eat here more often"; N.B. the Decor score may not reflect a post-*Survey* remodeling.

O'Famé S   ▽ 25 | 15 | 24 | $20
750 W. Webster Ave. (Halsted St.), 773-929-5111
■ Famed for its "good food and family atmosphere" for nearly 20 years, this "neighborhood spot" in Lincoln Park prevails with a "great menu" of "inexpensive, basic Italian" including "excellent thin-crust pizza", "consistently fresh pasta" and "delicious salads" as well as "terrific special steak" dishes (it's good "for quick takeout" too); N.B. the Decor score may not reflect a post-*Survey* remodeling.

Ohba S   – | – | – | E
2049 W. Division St. (Damen Ave.), 773-772-2727
Miae Lim (Mirai Sushi) snapped up the former Rambutan space on Wicker Park's hot Division Street restaurant strip to open this modish space serving smart, sexy and pricey plates of chef Gene Kato's Japanese-influenced Eclectic cuisine, paired with a serious selection of sakes; N.B. the fun furnishings include barstools shaped like its namesake – the ohba leaf, a Japanese mint-like herb.

Old Jerusalem S   17 | 8 | 13 | $16
1411 N. Wells St. (bet. North Ave. & Schiller St.), 312-944-0459
☑ An Old Town "standby", this Middle Eastern "takes you back to the Old Country" with "authentic" and "cheap" fare

("ask for their homemade hot sauce"); regulars recommend you ignore that the "staff seems put out by your presence", saying go for a "good, quick bite" and "just eat"; N.B. the Decor score may not reflect a post-*Survey* remodeling of what was a "bare-bones", "grungy" dining space.

O'Neil's S   20 | 17 | 20 | $28

1003 Green Bay Rd. (Scott Ave.), Winnetka, 847-446-7100
◪ Kick back at this "easygoing" and "reliable" Northern Italian seafooder run by a "customer-conscious owner" who offers "upscale fare without breaking the bank" – "a rarity on the North Shore"; although its "no-frills" setting has some patrons perturbed, others call it "comfy" enough "for lunch or a romantic dinner"; besides, "in summer it's nice to sit outside" on the front patio.

One North   – | – | – | E

1 N. Wacker Dr. (Madison St.), 312-750-9700
Across from the Loop's Lyric Opera is this contemporary brasserie from the owners of the Bluepoint Oyster Bar and The Grillroom; the dignified, masculine dining room (featuring soaring ceilings, flagstone walls, leather banquettes) surrounds an open kitchen that turns out a varied list of hearty New American specialties.

ONE SIXTYBLUE   24 | 24 | 22 | $55

1400 W. Randolph St. (Ogden St.), 312-850-0303
■ "This could be the Michael Jordan of restaurants" fawn fans of this "airy" Market District New American, "a class act from start to finish" where "daring" chef Martial Noguier's "stellar", "stylish" French- and Asian-influenced fare is supported by "delicate wines and unobtrusive service" and set against Adam Tihany's "sleek", "chic" backdrop; it's "expensive", but most are happy to "pay for the hipness" and "the hope of seeing [silent partner] MJ"; N.B. chocolate addicts adore its new Cocoa Bar.

120 Ocean Place S   23 | 25 | 23 | $43

120 N. Hale St. (bet. Front & Wesley Sts.), Wheaton, 630-690-2100
■ The "elegant" and "fabulous" environs of this New American in a "beautifully renovated" "former funeral home" may "take your breath away", but it's the "friendly staff" and some of the "freshest seafood in the Western Suburbs" (including the "best calamari and soft-shell crabs") that keep patrons rematerializing; penny-pinchers who consider it "pricey" "go for lunch, when almost the same menu" is available for less.

Opera S   – | – | – | E

1301 S. Wabash Ave. (13th St.), 312-461-0161
Housed in a former Hollywood studio film vault, this pricey but hip South Loop spot features a dramatic setting of upholstered velvet-backed chairs, custom ironwork and

light fixtures, and a section of hidden tables that will make you feel like you're dining in a clandestine urban back alley; noted Thai toque Arun Sampanthavivat consulted with chef Paul Wildermuth (ex Red Light) on the stylish Chinese menu.

Orange 🅂 21 | 16 | 18 | $15

3231 N. Clark St. (Belmont Ave.), 773-549-4400

■ "Too bad everyone knows about it" gripe the Lakeview lunch-and-brunch bunch about this Eclectic BYO they predict "will become a Northside institution" for its "quirky", "inventive" menu including "to-die-for French toast kebabs" and the "must-try 'frushi'" (fruit sushi); "if you don't mind the wait", most say you'll find it "delightful."

Original Gino's East, The 🅂 20 | 12 | 15 | $18

2801 N. Lincoln Ave. (Diversey Pkwy.), 773-327-3737
633 N. Wells St. (Ontario St.), 312-943-1124
2516 Green Bay Rd. (Central St.), Evanston, 847-332-2100
1807 S. Washington St. (south of 75th St.), Naperville, 630-548-9555
6156 W. 95th St. (west of Southwest Hwy.), Oak Lawn, 708-598-5600
15840 S. Harlem Ave. (159th St.), Orland Park, 708-633-1300
1321 W. Golf Rd. (Algonquin Rd.), Rolling Meadows, 847-364-6644
9751 W. Higgins Rd. (bet. Mannheim & River Rds.), Rosemont, 847-698-4949
Tin Cup Pass Shopping Ctr., 1590 E. Main St. (Tyler Rd.), St. Charles, 630-513-1311
315 Front St. (West St.), Wheaton, 630-588-1010

◪ "A Chicago tradition", this veteran pie chain draws droves of deep-dish devotees who line up to devour their "favorite pizza in the whole universe" (it's the "cornmeal crust that makes the difference"); though "graffiti" gurus gleefully "write on the walls and booths to leave their mark" at the Wells Street spot (home of the relocated original Original), others say the sibling sites "miss the boat on atmosphere."

Original Pancake House, The 🅂 22 | 13 | 18 | $14

22 E. Bellevue Pl. (bet. Michigan Ave. & Rush St.), 312-642-7917 ⊄
2020 N. Lincoln Park W. (Clark St.), 773-929-8130 ⊄
10437 S. Western Ave. (104th St.), 773-445-6100
Village Ctr., 1517 E. Hyde Park Blvd. (bet. 51st St. & Lake Park Blvd.), 773-288-2323 ⊄
825 Dundee Rd. (Arlington Heights Rd.), Arlington Heights, 847-392-6600
1615 Waukegan Rd. (Lake Ave.), Glenview, 847-724-0220
200 Marriott Dr. (Milwaukee Ave.), Lincolnshire, 847-634-2220
5148 W. 159th St. (52nd Ave.), Oak Forest, 708-687-8282 ⊄
954 Lake St. (Forest St.), Oak Park, 708-524-0955
106 S. Northwest Hwy. (Touhy Ave.), Park Ridge, 847-696-1381 ◑
Additional locations throughout the Chicago area

■ With "famous eggs" and "killer apple pancakes" "served by happy people", this bevy of breakfast specialists with a flapjack focus is "a great way to start any day" – and "good on the wallet" too; "weekend waits" are the norm ("brutal" ones at the Lincoln Park locale) and it can be "chaos in the dining room", but "you don't go there for atmosphere."

Otro Mas S
21 | 17 | 18 | $32

3651 N. Southport Ave. (bet. Addison St. & Waveland Ave.), 773-348-3200

Surveyors are split on this "cozy" Nuevo Latino Lakeview follow-up that's "a lot like its parent" (Mas, in Wicker Park), reprising John Manion's "*muy bueno*" multi-national cuisine, including "amazing fish tacos" and "wonderful appetizers" (plus the "best caipirinhas in town"); approvers assert it's a "worthy sequel" that's "more intimate", while faultfinders feel that it's "stuffier", the service is spotty and it has the "same noise level" as its progenitor.

Outpost, The S
20 | 16 | 19 | $32

3438 N. Clark St. (Sheffield Ave.), 773-244-1166

"Casual" and "low-key", this Wrigleyville New American is known as an incubator for interesting chefs (e.g. Kevin Shikami of Kevin, Ted Cizma of Elaine) and "creative", "cutting-edge cuisine"; still, some say the "constant kitchen changes make it hard to define", "the decor could use some sprucing up" and service ranges from "attentive" to "slow"; N.B. the Food rating may not reflect the post-*Survey* arrival of chef Chris Darmstaetter.

Oysy S
– | – | – | M

888 S. Michigan Ave. (9th St.), 312-922-1127

South Loop sushi hounds welcome this low-priced slickster (pronounced 'oh-ee-shee', meaning delicious) that offers a broad assortment of traditional and newfangled maki along with a long list of *izakaya* (Japanese bistro) specialties; the coolly lit space lined by Chicago architect Doug Garofalo with bamboo booths and sheer plastic screens creates a hip, contemporary environment.

Palaggi's
▽ 16 | 18 | 19 | $32

10 W. Hubbard St. (bet. Dearborn & State Sts.), 312-527-1010

Proponents praise this "friendly", "family-oriented" River North yearling for its "tasty Italian comfort food" and "romantic" atmosphere created by "candles and draping"; malcontents moan, though, that the "uninspired" fare lacks "brio" and there's "too much confusion" in the service; N.B. live music perks things up on weekends.

Palm, The S
22 | 19 | 20 | $48

Swissôtel, 323 E. Wacker Dr. (bet. Lake Shore Dr. & Michigan Ave.), 312-616-1000

The Loop's Swissôtel is home to Chicago's outpost of this "long-standing" national chain, a "clubby", "old-fashioned" "businessman's place" for "huge" steaks ("don't overlook" the "great big lobsters", though) with "straight-from-the-hip service" and "great caricatures on the walls"; yet some carnivores chew it out as "pricey" and say it's "not as good as" some of the company's other locations.

Pane Caldo S   20 | 18 | 19 | $44
72 E. Walton St. (bet. Michigan Ave. & Rush St.), 312-649-0055
☑ "Authentic Northern Italian food" (such as "fine risottos"), a "friendly, caring staff" and "intimate ambiance" put this "upscale, understated" Near Norther in the pantheon of "Chicago hidden treasures" for many; still, others aren't so warm toward it, painting the kitchen as "inconsistent", the meals as "pricey" (the "bill quickly adds up" to a lot of bread) and the "cramped" digs as in need of "expanding."

Panera Bread S   _ | _ | _ | I
2070 N. Clybourn Ave. (bet. Magnolia & Southport Aves.), 773-325-9035
616 W. Diversey Pkwy. (Clark St.), 773-528-4556
190 Waukegan Rd. (bet. Central Ave. & Kales Rd.), Deerfield, 847-236-1123
108 W. North Ave. (York Rd.), Elmhurst, 630-833-5001
7330 W. North Ave. (Fair Oaks Ave.), Elmwood Park, 708-452-2562
1700 Sherman Ave. (bet. Church & Clark Sts.), Evanston, 847-733-8356
439 N. La Grange Rd. (Homestead Rd.), La Grange Park, 708-482-8070
7023 W. Dempster St. (bet. National & Sayre Aves.), Niles, 847-663-1640
39-41 S. Northwest Hwy. (Touhy Ave.), Park Ridge, 847-696-1880
9611 Skokie Blvd. (Golf Rd.), Skokie, 847-679-9156
Additional locations throughout the Chicago area
Dotting the landscape, these popular bakery/cafe chainsters are considered by some the "best quick stop" "for good food", including "an unusual variety" of "fresh breads", "delectable sandwiches" and "delicious soups and salads", all at a "good value" and served in "cozy" settings.

Papagus Greek Taverna S   20 | 19 | 19 | $28
Embassy Suites Hotel, 620 N. State St. (Ontario St.), 312-642-8450
Oakbrook Center Mall, 272 Oakbrook Ctr. (Rte. 83), Oak Brook, 630-472-9800
☑ "Lettuce Entertain You does it again" with this successful Grecian formula, "charming and fun" River North and Oak Brook sisters that are "good at what they're supposed to be"; while some Hellenes hint the food is "hardly authentic" (i.e. "too American"), the majority is happy with the "consistent", "delicious homestyle meals" and "service with a smile" – all "without the trip to Greektown."

Papajin [S] ▽ 17 | 14 | 17 | $19

1551 N. Milwaukee Ave. (Damen & North Aves.), 773-384-9600

■ Chalk this laid-back Wicker Park Chinese up as a "pleasant" experience thanks to the clean tastes and light sauces of its "nice-looking", "always-good food" (with many choices for vegetarians and vegans) at "great prices" presented within a "quiet atmosphere" of dimly lit "cool decor" featuring a black-tiled bar illuminated by blue neon; N.B. a sushi bar and sidewalk cafe were recently added.

Papa Milano [S] 18 | 12 | 18 | $23

951 N. State St. (Oak St.), 312-787-3710

◪ Die-hard "red-sauce" fans "haunt" this "classic" "hole-in-the-wall" that's passed the half-century mark, hailing its "good basic Italian" – including "great pizza and pasta for pennies" – and "friendly service"; modernists may say it's "so-so", but the nostalgic "hope the wrecking ball never takes it out" of its trendy Gold Coast neighborhood.

Pappadeaux Seafood Kitchen [S] 19 | 18 | 19 | $30

798 W. Algonquin Rd. (Golf Rd.), Arlington Heights, 847-228-9551

921 Pasquinelli Dr. (Oakmont Ln.), Westmont, 630-455-9846

◪ Those who find this "big, busy" Cajun-Creole seafood duo in the West and Northwest Suburbs "a nice change from the usual chains" say its "great Louisiana cooking" "wakes up the buds"; not all are "won over" by this "taste of the bayou", though – some say it's "not so hot", seeing the same scene as "too frenetic, noisy" and "impersonal."

Parkers' Ocean Grill [S] 24 | 23 | 21 | $38

1000 31st St. (Highland Ave.), Downers Grove, 630-960-5701

◪ Some "serious" seafood lovers laud this West Suburban, saying the "delicious" "fine food" (as well as what "may be the best desserts in" Downers Grove), "great presentation", "knowledgeable staff" and "soothing", "quiet" atmosphere "never disappoint"; still, some express concern that it's "a bit expensive for the area" and say that the "room is cold" and a bit "sterile"; N.B. now serving Sunday brunch.

Parthenon ◐ [S] 20 | 16 | 19 | $25

314 S. Halsted St. (bet. Jackson Blvd. & Van Buren St.), 312-726-2407

■ "A genuine Greektown" "rocking good time", this "noisy, bustling" and "family-friendly" "Chicago landmark" circa 1968 is "consistently solid, year in and year out", and "still among the best" for "good portions" of "real food" at "reasonable prices"; the "*saganaki* [flaming Kasseri cheese] is a must", and some say the "wonderful lamb chops" are "the best in the universe" (you'll have to ask the gods on that one).

Pasha ●S
18 | 21 | 16 | $35

642 N. Clark St. (bet. Erie & Ontario Sts.), 312-397-0100

❷ Pasha partisans purport that the "atmosphere and ambiance surpass all others" at this "lively" River North refuge for "nightclub dining" where "the real draw is the deafening but fun music" (live some nights), despite a "good" assortment of New French and Italian dishes from the late-cooking kitchen; bickering buzzkills bemoan that it "doesn't live up to the hype" and whine about "weird service" from "snobby staffers."

Pasta Palazzo S∅
▽ 18 | 14 | 18 | $17

1966 N. Halsted St. (Armitage Ave.), 773-248-1400

■ A "friendly, fast, low-budget" option in Lincoln Park, this "quaint Italian" is "reliably good" for "great pasta" and "daily specials", plus a "reasonably priced wine list" and "unpretentious service"; its intimate interior with a colorful mosaic may not be palatial (perhaps contributing to its popularity as a take-out spot), but it's "one of the best values on North Halsted."

Pasteur S
23 | 23 | 20 | $34

5525 N. Broadway St. (bet. Bryn Mawr & Catalpa Aves.), 773-878-1061

❷ A "pleasant" meal is in store at this "elegant, seductive" "oasis in Edgewater" where the "exciting taste treats" – "refined Vietnamese with French influences" – showcase "extremely fresh ingredients"; some surveyors say the staff is "unobtrusive" and the environment "relaxing", while others "would go more often if the service were as good as the food" and it weren't so "noisy."

Pauline's S∅
_ | _ | _ | I

1754 W. Balmoral Ave. (Ravenswood Ave.), 773-561-8573

A "kitschy" and "eclectic" "favorite" for all-American "omelets and burgers in Andersonville", this "nice place for a casual meal" (breakfast and lunch only) has "all sorts of retro things on the walls to look at"; even though food-wise, some say, "you could do as well at home, it's the place and the people" that keep regulars returning.

Pegasus ●S
20 | 19 | 20 | $27

130 S. Halsted St. (bet. Adams & Monroe Sts.), 312-226-4666

Pegasus on the Fly S
Midway Int'l Airport, 5700 S. Cicero Ave., Concourse A (55th St.), 773-581-1522

■ "Great Greek grub" is the ongoing tradition at this "solid Greektown establishment", a "classic" with a "good menu", a "friendly" and "courteous" staff that "makes you feel like part of the family" and an "amazing rooftop deck" that's the "perfect" place "for nibbling and drinking" – "there's no place like it with its views of the city and live" "band on summer" weeknights; N.B. the Southwest Side branch, which opened post-*Survey*, offers a limited takeout menu.

Penang ●🄢   19 | 14 | 15 | $20

2201 S. Wentworth Ave. (Cermak Rd.), 312-326-6888

☑ You don't hear someone say "great Malaysian" every day, but you might if you frequented this "cheap" Chinatown nonconformist known for an "interesting, eclectic" and "broad menu" with "a little of everything" Asian ("they even have a sushi bar" and "well-done Thai" dishes); still, you might also hear someone say it's "not much to look at" and the "service declines when it's crowded."

Penny's Noodle Shop 🄢   21 | 13 | 17 | $14

1542 N. Damen Ave. (North Ave.), 773-394-0100
3400 N. Sheffield Ave. (Roscoe St.), 773-281-8222
950 W. Diversey Pkwy. (Sheffield Ave.), 773-281-8448

■ "Fast and filling", these "reliable" and "affordable [Pan-] Asian" "staples" (including the "newest location in Wicker Park") have become "city favorites" for "oodles of noodles", "great gyoza", "flavorful" Vietnamese spring rolls, "tasty" "Thai ravioli" and "to-die-for Tom Yum soup" that "helps you through the Chicago winter", all dished up "for just pennies" in "spartan but clean" spaces.

Pepper Lounge ●🄢   ▽ 20 | 20 | 18 | $28

3441 N. Sheffield Ave. (Clark St.), 773-665-7377

■ "An outpost of good food in the Wrigleyville wasteland", this "loungey" New American draws an "eclectic crowd" lured by a kitchen that turns out an "inventive menu" until 1 AM most nights, barkeeps who "whip up a mean martini" (including the chocolate house specialty) and "friendly, interesting servers"; the "dark", "trendy decor is great for late-night dining" – complete with "too much smoke."

Pete Miller's Seafood &   21 | 19 | 20 | $38
Prime Steak ●🄢

(fka Pete Miller's Steakhouse)

1557 Sherman Ave. (bet. Davis & Grove Sts.), Evanston, 847-328-0399

■ A "one-stop fun night out", this "clubby", "noisy and busy" "Evanston hangout" features "fine", "upper-end steaks", "great chops" and (as the post-*Survey* name change suggests) seafood selections, plus "the best garlic mashed potatoes in town", an "excellent liquor selection" and "good" "live jazz" that "adds a nice touch" six times a week; N.B. a Wheeling branch is slated to open in 2003.

Petterino's   18 | 20 | 20 | $37

Goodman Theatre Bldg., 150 N. Dearborn St. (Randolph St.), 312-422-0150

☑ Stage buffs and business types cast this "classy joint" in the Goodman Theatre building as the "place to go before the show" and a "blessing in the Loop" for its "nice" Traditional American fare, "polished" staffers and "throwback" "'40s-supper-club" setting; still, critics are less impressed by what they call an "expensive", "mundane" menu and dismiss the production as a "Sardi's wanna-be."

P.F. Chang's China Bistro S — 19 | 20 | 18 | $25
530 N. Wabash Ave. (Grand Ave.), 312-828-9977
2361 Fountain Square Dr. (Butterfield & Meyers Rds.), Lombard, 630-652-9977
1819 Lake Cook Rd. (east of I-94), Northbrook, 847-509-8844
☑ Fans "can't get enough of the eclectic", "tasty and adventurous" Chinese cuisine (lots of "hoorays" for the "amazing" lettuce wraps) at these "upscale" outposts of the "novel" national Sino chain; although purists pan the "gimmicky", "Americanized" cooking as "not authentic" and truly "average", these "trendy" spots are for many a "dependable" option offering "good value."

Philander's Oak Park S — – | – | – | M
Carleton Hotel, 1120 Pleasant St. (bet. Maple Ave. & Marion St.), Oak Park, 708-848-4250
A clubby, dark-wood haven in Oak Park's Carleton Hotel, Philander's is named for (and decorated with photos of) the village historian, not for straying West Suburban husbands; the American fare is modern but not manipulated beyond recognition, and top-notch live jazz emanates nightly from the vicinity of the vintage octagonal oak-and-marble bar; N.B. check out the winning wine list.

Phil & Lou's ● S — – | – | – | M
1104 W. Madison St. (Aberdeen St.), 312-455-0070
Elevated comfort food – think lobster mac 'n' cheese or seared scallops – fills out the menu of this West Loop New American named by owner Nick Andrews (ex Lexi) in honor of his two canine companions; the spare but agreeable space features Kraft-paper topped tables, exposed brick, and rust-colored duct work.

Phil Stefani's 437 Rush — 20 | 20 | 19 | $38
437 N. Rush St. (Hubbard St.), 312-222-0101
☑ "It's fun to be a grown-up" at this Near North Italian steakhouse, a "favorite local after-work" "watering hole" and "biz-lunch" destination whose "handsome", "clubby decor" pays homage to the heyday of its applauded predecessor, penman-popular Riccardo's; fans find the "consistently good food" "flavorful", but the lukewarm lament it's "not Stefani's best."

Phlair — – | – | – | M
1935 N. Damen Ave. (Homer St.), 773-772-3719
Serving up small wonders in the form of tapas-style plates (and a fun selection of "martinys", or petite martinis) as well

as entrée-size plates (including the signature smokin' beef, cooked at the table on a sizzling river rock), contemporary American Phlair has an artsy ambiance that's vintage Bucktown; N.B. neighborhood nightowls note that food is served 'til midnight on weekends.

Phoenix S
22 | 12 | 16 | $23

2131 S. Archer Ave., 2nd fl. (Wentworth Ave.), 312-328-0848

☑ Champions of this Chinatown choice say its "fresh, creative" daily dim sum is "to die for", which helps explain why the "bright, airy" space is always "bustling"; "slow service" prompts pleas to "get more carts on the floor", but aficionados agree the "great selection" of "delightful delicacies" is "worth the wait"; N.B. Chinese dishes are served at lunch and dinner.

Piazza Bella S
▽ 21 | 19 | 20 | $26

Roscoe Village, 2116 W. Roscoe St. (bet. Damen & Western Aves.), 773-477-7330

■ Locals "love this little place" tucked away in Roscoe Village for its "true Italian-style" cooking, i.e. "simple dishes made with excellent ingredients" and served by a "friendly staff" that "makes you feel like you're visiting their home for dinner"; the setting is "festive" yet "cozy", prompting devotees to declare "we need more like this."

Piece S
18 | 16 | 15 | $18

1927 W. North Ave. (bet. Damen & Wolcott Aves.), 773-772-4422

☑ "Homemade pizza, homemade beer – what could be better?" say a slice of surveyors about this Wicker Park sophomore's "unique", New Haven–style thin-crust pies "done right", "many choices" of house microbrews and "cool" "hangout" setting (once featured on MTV's *The Real World*); crusty contrarians "don't get" the "East Coast" allure, judging them "overrated."

Pie Hole ●S
– | – | – | I

606 N. Racine Ave. (Ogden Ave.), 312-666-6767
739 W. Roscoe St. (Halsted St.), 773-525-8888

Who wants pie? – premium thin-crust pizza pie, that is, topped with pile-ons such as house-smoked bacon, meatballs or capers and served up with the sort of attitude you'd expect of this Near West spin-off from the Twisted Spoke folks; though formerly offering phone-in delivery only, this 'hole' in the backside of Bone Daddy now boasts a handful of tables, including some outside; N.B. the Lakeview branch opened post-*Survey*.

Pierrot Gourmet S
– | – | – | M

Peninsula Hotel, 108 E. Superior St. (Rush St.), 312-573-6749

A rustic Euro-style retreat in the Near North's Peninsula Hotel, this combination cafe/bakery/wine bar is a casually chic setting for sipping from an extensive wine list and snacking from a limited menu of hearty housemade sourdough tartines, fresh-baked goods and artisanal cheeses; there's even a communal table for gregarious guests, as well as a wine retail area.

Pili.Pili S — — — M
230 W. Kinzie St. (Franklin St.), 312-464-9988
Simple, savory Provençal fare is proffered at this bistro-style boîte in River North, brought to you by a Coco Pazzo alum and chef Francois de Melogue (who trained under such luminaries as Joel Robuchon and Louis Szathmary); in addition to fresh takes on hearty French cooking, there are also some dishes exhibiting Med influences (after all, the restaurant is named for an African hot pepper), all served in either the fine dining room, informal cafe or seasonal outdoor patio.

Pine Yard Restaurant S ▽ 25 18 21 $19
1033 Davis St. (Oak St.), Evanston, 847-475-4940
■ Though "relocated" in the fall of 2000, this 30-year-old "Chinese oasis" in the Northern Suburbs remains a "classic" "local institution" that's still "always packed" with fans of its "distinctive flavors" and "great, inexpensive lunch specials"; some Evanstonians effuse that with Sino fare this good so close at hand, there's "no need to go to Chinatown"; N.B. beer and wine only.

Ping Pong ◑S — — — M
3322 N. Broadway St. (bet. Aldine Ave. & Buckingham Pl.), 773-281-7575
A hipster haunt with minimal decor and clubby music, this fast-track Lakeview BYO proffers moderately-priced Pan-Asian with a preponderance of Chinese dishes to a high-energy crowd as diverse as the menu; N.B. the tiny space is expanded to sidewalk seating in summer.

Pizza Capri S 16 13 14 $18
1501 E. 53rd St. (Harper Ave.), 773-324-7777
1733 N. Halsted St. (Willow St.), 312-280-5700
962 W. Belmont Ave. (Sheffield Ave.), 773-296-6000
☑ Usually "mobbed", these "bustling joints" dish out "tasty" "pizzas a cut above the ordinary" (in both "crispy thin-crust" and "deep-dish" varieties) and "at reasonable prices", as well as "interesting" salads and "a somewhat" "limited entrée menu"; homebodies hail them the "takeout-and-delivery champions" of the city and suburbs, but that could be because the "service is lacking."

Pizza D.O.C. S 21 14 16 $22
2251 W. Lawrence Ave. (Western Ave.), 773-784-8777
☑ Fans of this Lincoln Square pizzeria attest that the "paper-thin", "seriously authentic Italian" pies from its wood-burning oven are the "next best thing to being in the Piazza

Navona"; few would mention the decor and Bernini in the same breath, though, and the service can be "uneven", but there's always "carryout"; P.S. "the name is misleading – they have great pastas too."

Pizzeria Uno ◐🅂   21 14 16 $19
29 E. Ohio St. (Wabash Ave.), 312-321-1000
Pizzeria Due ◐🅂
619 N. Wabash Ave. (Ontario St.), 312-943-2400
Pizzeria Uno Chicago Bar & Grill 🅂
O'Hare Int'l Airport, 773-894-8667
986 N. Rte. 59 (Liberty Ave.), Aurora, 630-585-8075
4901 Cal-Sag Rd. (Cicero Ave.), Crestwood, 708-824-0700
6593 Grand Ave. (Hunt Club Rd.), Gurnee, 847-856-0000
Sportmart Plaza, 275 W. Roosevelt Rd. (Surrey Dr.), Lombard, 630-792-1400 ◐
1160 Plaza Dr. (Golf Rd.), Schaumburg, 847-413-0200
■ "Sentimental favorites" "savored time and again", these Near North "classics" are "musts" for "terrific deep-dish pizzas"; be "prepared to wait" for "hours", however, in a "dark, noisy" and "touristy" setting, unless weather permits sitting outside where you can "eat and watch the street"; N.B. numero Uno has spun off an international chain with links in the suburbs.

P.J. Clarke's ◐🅂   18 15 17 $21
1204 N. State Pkwy. (Division St.), 312-664-1650
Embassy Suites Hotel, 302 E. Illinois St. (Columbus Dr.), 312-670-7500
■ This "local hangout" for a "mature" Gold Coast crowd serves a "great variety" of "solid", Traditional American "tavern fare" (from "awesome mini-burgers" to "tasty meatloaf") in a "dark", "pub-style" setting that's "always busy"; it's "not fancy", but it's a "good value" and its "late-night" kitchen cooks until 1:30 AM; N.B. the Near North branch opened post-*Survey*.

Platiyo 🅂   – – – M
3313 N. Clark St. (bet. Aldine Ave. & Buckingham Pl.), 773-477-6700
Brightly colored folk art, a curved bank of windows and an ample selection of margaritas and tequilas set the mood in this Lakeview Nuevo Latino storefront where oversized plates carry artfully prepared upscale Mexican cuisine; expect more Platiyos to pop up near other Mia Francesca's soon, as both concepts share the same owner.

Pompei Bakery 🅂   ▽ 25 17 21 $16
2955 N. Sheffield Ave. (Wellington St.), 773-325-1900
1531 W. Taylor St. (Ashland Ave.), 312-421-5179
17 W. 744 22nd St. (S. Summit Ave.), Oakbrook Terrace, 630-620-0600
■ Descendents of a Taylor Street bakery opened in 1909, this family-owned triumvirate of "kid-friendly" Italian spots

offers a "wide selection" of "quick and consistently good"
fare at an "exceptional value"; the "cafeteria-style"
presentation with "great counter service" makes it easy
"to eat in or take out" "casual lunches or dinners."

Potbelly Sandwich Works 19 | 13 | 15 | $9
508 N. Clark St. (bet. Grand & Illinois Aves.), 312-644-9131 S
*2264 N. Lincoln Ave. (bet. Belden & Webster Aves.),
773-528-1405* S
3424 N. Southport Ave. (Roscoe St.), 773-289-1807 S
190 N. State St. (Lake St.), 312-683-1234 S
*One Illinois Center, 111 E. Wacker Dr. (Michigan Ave.),
312-861-0013*
*The Shops at North Bridge, 520 N. Michigan Ave. (Grand Ave.),
312-644-1008* S
175 W. Jackson Blvd. (bet. Financial Pl. & Wells St.), 312-588-1150
303 W. Madison St. (Franklin St.), 312-346-1234
55 W. Monroe St. (Dearborn St.), 312-577-0070
1422 W. Webster Ave. (Clybourn Ave.), 773-755-1234 S
Additional locations throughout the Chicago area
■ "There's always a line, but it moves fast" at this chain
where you can "choose your own ingredients" to create
"tasty, custom-made subs and toasted sandwiches" and
chase them with "old-fashioned milkshakes"; it's an
"absolute staple" for sammy savants "on the run" thanks
to the staff's "ridiculous efficiency" and the "cheap prices."

Prairie S 22 | 22 | 22 | $41
*Hyatt on Printer's Row, 500 S. Dearborn St. (Congress Pkwy.),
312-663-1143*
■ "First-rate without pretension", this "solid" Regional
American, housed in Hyatt on Printer's Row in the South
Loop, is known for its "creative seasonal menus" of
"Midwestern food with a gourmet twist" (including game
in season); name notwithstanding, the "beautiful Arts and
Crafts–style ambiance" of its Frank Lloyd Wright–inspired
dining room is anything but plain.

Prairie Moon S – | – | – | M
1502 Sherman Ave. (Lake St.), Evanston, 847-864-8328
Americana prevails in this spacious tavern in North
Suburban Evanston where the menu offers traditional
dishes from around the country, supplemented by a strong
selection of microbrews; tin road signs and other found
objects add atmosphere to the airy decor, while the taproom
in back provides a more intimate setting for locals and
students; look for outdoor patio dining come summer.

Prego S ∇ 19 | 15 | 19 | $26
*2901 N. Ashland Ave. (bet. Diversey Pkwy. & Wellington Ave.),
773-472-9190*
■ This "small and quaint" Lakeview sophmore serves a
"wonderful selection" of "lovely and simple Italian" "taste

treats" (including "great risottos and tortellini"); while boosters hail it as a "gem that's just being discovered", some anxious amici are praying that "it doesn't get overrun."

PRINTER'S ROW 25 | 21 | 23 | $46

550 S. Dearborn St. (bet. Congress Pkwy. & Harrison St.), 312-461-0780

■ Offering "innovative" New American fare in a "traditional setting", Michael Foley's South Loop production makes an indelible impression with its "creative menu", which takes advantage of the "freshest local ingredients", and its "knowledgeable" staff; cronies crow that its "unfailing commitment to food, wine and service" and its "quiet excellence" make for "quality dining."

Privata Café [S] 🚫 – | – | – | I

1938 W. Chicago Ave. (Damen Ave.), 773-394-0662

Mexican meets Italian in a funky fusion (including create-your-own pasta combinations) that manages to work at this Eclectic Wicker Park eatery, a relocated version of the original; the youthful crowd appreciates the bargain prices, BYO policy and bodacious Sunday brunch buffet.

P.S. Bangkok [S] 18 | 13 | 16 | $18

3345 N. Clark St. (bet. Addison St. & Belmont Ave.), 773-871-7777
2521 N. Halsted St. (bet. Fullerton Pkwy. & Wrightwood Ave.), 773-348-0072

◪ These separated Siamese twins in Wrigleyville and DePaul offer "huge menus" of "consistent" native fare including "fabulous curries" and "great crunchy pad Thai", and early-birds sing the praises of the Clark Street location's "wonderful Sunday brunch" ("worth getting up" for); cynics, though, sniff at the "predictable" eats and "so-so service"; N.B. the North Halsted branch is BYO.

Public Landing [S] ▽ 23 | 22 | 22 | $34

200 W. Eighth St. (bet. Canal & State Sts.), Lockport, 815-838-6500

■ A "charming oasis in a historic location" in the Southwest Suburbs, this "excellent" American tempers the "traditional with a taste of inspiration"; with its "picturesque room" and "personable service", it continues to be many a fan's choice as "best meal for the price in the suburbs."

Puck's at the MCA [S] 20 | 19 | 17 | $23

Museum of Contemporary Art, 220 E. Chicago Ave. (Mies van der Rohe Way), 312-397-4034

◪ "You can't beat the views in this jewel" pronounce peckish patrons of Wolfgang Puck's "hidden", "upscale" lunch-only spot installed in the Museum of Contemporary Art in Streeterville, where a "limited but well-prepared" New American menu is displayed in a "chic, arty setting" with "wonderful outdoor seating"; critics cavil that it's "understaffed", resulting in "iffy" service; N.B. now serving afternoon tea 5-8 PM, with live jazz on Tuesdays.

Pump Room, The S　　21　25　21　$49
Omni Ambassador East Hotel, 1301 N. State St. (Goethe St.), 312-266-0360

◤ "The grand queen of the old dinner houses" continues to hold court at the Gold Coast's Omni Ambassador East Hotel, offering a "memorable" "dress-up" experience that includes "excellent" New French cuisine, "attentive, detail-oriented" service, "romantic dancing" and live jazz on Fridays and Saturdays; detractors, however, lament that it's merely "resting on its laurels" and say "the glamour is sadly gone, though Booth One remains."

Rainforest Cafe S　　12　21　15　$21
605 N. Clark St. (bet. Ohio & Ontario Sts.), 312-787-1501
Gurnee Mills Mall, 6170 W. Grand Ave. (bet. I-94 & Hunt Club Rd.), Gurnee, 847-855-7800
Woodfield Mall, 121 Woodfield Mall (bet. Golf & Higgins Rds.), Schaumburg, 847-619-1900

◤ This trio of city and suburban links in a "novelty" chain are popular more for their "jungle" settings, complete with "thunder, lightning" and "moving animals", than their "average, overpriced" American eats, "long waits and poor service", but defenders declare it's "great for kids."

Ranalli's S　　16　13　14　$17
2301 N. Clark St. (Belden Ave.), 773-244-2300 ●
1925 N. Lincoln Ave. (bet. Armitage Ave. & Clark St.), 312-642-4700 ●
1522 W. Montrose Ave. (Ashland Ave.), 773-506-8800

■ "Nothing spectacular" – just "good-quality" pizza and other "basic" eats with "a great selection of beers" – awaits at this "casual" "brew-and-a-bite" pizzeria chain; the Lincoln Avenue site has a "nice outdoor area", while the Montrose location is mainly takeout and serves no alcohol.

Rancho Luna del Caribe S　　– – – M
2554 W. Diversey Ave. (California St.), 773-772-9333
Authentic and ample Cuban and Puerto Rican platters are the rule at this approachable Northwest Side supper club complete with white tablecloths, woven ceiling fans, live palm trees and a bar full of beguiling tropical drinks; weekend nights feature dancing and salsa bands, and live Latin jazz accompanies the Sunday brunch buffet.

Ravinia Bistro S　　21　17　20　$31
581 Roger Williams Ave. (bet. Green Bay Rd. & St. Johns Ave.), Highland Park, 847-432-1033

■ "Small but elegant", this "solid bistro" in the Northern Suburbs "tries hard to please" and succeeds with "quality French cooking", "personal service" and "warm" ambiance;

music lovers sing its praises as the "best place to go before concerts" at the annual Ravinia Festival; N.B. its wine list offers 35 by-the-glass selections.

Raw Bar & Grill ◐ [S] — | — | — | M

3720 N. Clark St. (bet. Grace St. & Waveland Ave.), 773-348-7291

More than its name implies, this funky Wrigleyville all-American serves a sizable, frequently changing menu of seafood, plus prime rib, smothered alligator and, of course, a raw bar; the casual, Deco-tavern space is home to live entertainment on weekends, and the kitchen is open 'til 1:00 AM; N.B. pucker up for a pomegranate martini.

Redfish [S] 16 | 16 | 17 | $26

400 N. State St. (Kinzie St.), 312-467-1600

◪ "Damn good" gumbo, jambalaya and "anything blackened (yum!)" highlight the seafood-focused Cajun-Creole menu at this "casual" River North "homage" to the Big Easy; foes, however, malign the "New Orleans–style" fare as a "poor try" "without any soul" served in a setting that's more "Disneyland" than bayou.

Red Light [S] 21 | 23 | 19 | $36

820 W. Randolph St. (Green St.), 312-733-8880

◪ Asiaphiles file into this "racy" purveyor of Pan-Asian fare in the Market District for its "excellent", "innovative" "fusion" featuring "incredible flavor combinations", while trendoids go for the "dramatic" decor and "hip", "bustling" setting that looks like an "*Alice in Wonderland* for beautiful people"; the "overpowering" decibel level and "pricey" tabs, though, give detractors pause; N.B. the Food rating may not reflect the post-*Survey* arrival of chef Jackie Shen (ex Lawry's The Prime Rib).

Red Lion Pub [S] 15 | 18 | 18 | $19

2446 N. Lincoln Ave. (Fullerton Pkwy.), 773-348-2695

■ Britain boosters applaud this "dark", "charming" Lincoln Park taproom that "really evokes the atmosphere of a London pub", with "ghosts upstairs" and "typical English" grub such as "fish 'n' chips" and "Welsh rarebit and pasty"; noticeably (and blessedly) absent is the "Bud-guzzling, football-brained crowd."

Red Star Tavern [S] — | — | — | M

Deerfield Commons, 695 Deerfield Rd. (Waukegan Rd.), Deerfield, 847-948-9700

Geneva Commons, 1602 Commons Dr. (bet. Bricher & Randall Sts.), Geneva, 630-845-0845

Another contagious concept from the Bar Louie boys, these North and West Suburban updates on the classic American tavern bring home the BLT (with a layer of grilled salmon added), and other upscale comfort food like pot roast and whole spit-roasted chicken; mondo martinis and other cool cocktails help you slip further into the buttery leather booths; N.B. both locations offer outdoor dining.

Red Tomato 🟦   18 | 16 | 17 | $23

3417 N. Southport Ave. (Roscoe St.), 773-472-5300

☑ Some paesani plug this "convenient", "local Italian eatery" they say "serves a purpose" – providing Lakeview with "dependable" pastas, "a good variety of salads" and "delicious thin-crust pizzas" at "modest prices", as well as "family-style" service; naysayers sniff that it's "getting tired" and may have "lost its edge", dishing out eats that are "nothing innovative" and merely "adequate."

Restaurant on the Park   ∇ 19 | 18 | 18 | $29

The Art Institute of Chicago, 111 S. Michigan Ave. (Monroe St.), 312-443-3543

■ A "touch of tranquility in the Loop", this "civilized" Continental is an "Art Institute masterpiece" exhibiting "artistically presented entrées" and "great service" in a "quiet" setting with "beautiful views" of Grant Park; patrons paint it as a "great little place" that's one of the neighborhood's "best spots for lunch", which just happens to be the only meal it serves.

RETRO BISTRO   26 | 19 | 23 | $35

Mt. Prospect Commons, 1746 W. Golf Rd. (Busse Rd.), Mt. Prospect, 847-439-2424

■ Mt. Prospect-ors panning for "excellent" French bistro fare that's a "good value" strike it rich at this "small", "intimate" spot, an "oasis" in a Northwest Suburban strip-mall "wasteland" that edges out its sibling, D & J Bistro, with the top-rated food for its category in our *Survey*; "happy, friendly service" and the transporting "feeling of being in Europe" round out the "memorable dining experience."

Reza's 🌑🟦   19 | 15 | 17 | $22

5255 N. Clark St. (Berwyn Ave.), 773-561-1898
432 W. Ontario St. (Orleans St.), 312-664-4500

■ Partisans promise "you'll leave full" from these River North and Andersonville Middle Eastern–Med stalwarts prized for their "fairly priced" and "large portions" of "consistently good", "healthy" choices from a "huge menu that aims to please", including "many vegetarian choices"; those who have trouble "getting the attention" of the "distracted" staff will be pleased to know they're "reliable for takeout too."

Rhapsody 🟦   22 | 22 | 21 | $41

Symphony Ctr., 65 E. Adams St. (bet. Michigan & Wabash Aves.), 312-786-9911

☑ Working its way through a repertoire of chefs, this sophisticated New American in the Loop's Symphony

Center has changed its tune again with the transfer of the
baton from former chef Romuald Jung to Patrick Crane,
whose post-*Survey* arrival may not be reflected in the Food
rating; the "stunning" decor scores well, though some say
"spotty" service sounds a sour note.

Rinconcito Sudamericano 🖪   ▽ 21 | 11 | 18 | $22

1954 W. Armitage Ave. (Damen Ave.), 773-489-3126
■ The "wonderful opportunity" to savor the "delicious",
"out-of-the-ordinary flavors" of "real food from the Andes"
gives Lake-level locals a natural mountain high at this
"fabulous" Peruvian in Bucktown; regulars recommend
you "get a Pisco sour" (a brandy-and-lime concoction)
and "try" the national potato dish, "*papas huancaina* – a
must"; given "bountiful portions" at "fair prices", few mind
that the "storefront" space is "not very exciting."

Ringo 🖪   ▽ 24 | 17 | 21 | $21

*2507 N. Lincoln Ave. (bet. Fullerton Pkwy. & Wrightwood Ave.),
773-248-5788*
■ It's not a monument to the funny Beatle, but rather a
"small" Lincoln Park Japanese BYO that gets by with a
little help from "outstanding" sushi and other "unusual"
fare served within a "simple" ocher interior that's bedecked
with colorful kites.

Rise 🖪   ▽ 21 | 20 | 15 | $26

3401 N. Southport Ave. (Roscoe St.), 773-525-3535
■ While most folks Rise *then* Shine, the Zhang family did it
the other way around, opening this "hip" new Wrigleyville
Japanese and sake lounge after their Lincoln Park Asian
hybrid was well established; its "yummy, different sushi
rolls" are "priced right" and "don't disappoint", making it
a "terrific new addition to Southport Avenue", though some
find the "techno dance music" "annoying."

RITZ-CARLTON CAFÉ 🖪   24 | 24 | 24 | $36

*Ritz-Carlton Hotel, 160 E. Pearson St. (Michigan Ave.),
312-573-5160*
■ "You'll feel like a pampered tourist" at this "pleasant"
cafe "overlooking a waterfall fountain" in the Streeterville
hotel's lobby; "still beautiful" after more than 25 years, its
"quiet-but-not-stuffy" room is the setting for meals marked
by "consistently high-quality" American fare and "upscale
service", making it a "great breakfast, luncheon or supper
venue" and a "nice stopover from shopping"; yes, it's
"pricey, but it's the Ritz."

RITZ-CARLTON DINING ROOM 🖪   28 | 27 | 28 | $68

*Ritz-Carlton Hotel, 160 E. Pearson St. (Michigan Ave.),
312-573-5223*
■ A "top dining experience" awaits at this "refined" New
French in the Ritz-Carlton, a Four Seasons hotel; chef "Sarah

Stegner is a treasure", and her "fantastic" food matches the "posh" yet "understated" surroundings; add in an "epic wine list", "absolutely fabulous cheese cart" and Sunday brunch that's a "food orgy with piano" and this is "the place to splurge" "when elegance, not money, is the object."

Riva S
20 | 22 | 18 | $42

Navy Pier, 700 E. Grand Ave. (Lake Shore Dr.), 312-644-7482

One school of respondents rates Phil Stefani's "beautiful" American-Italian "fish specialist" as "the best on the Navy Pier", with "a great lake view" and "good seafood" that add up to "a delightful dinner before the Shakespeare Theatre" nearly "next door"; a rival retinue reacts reproachfully to what it calls "unenthusiastic service" and hints they hit a "captive audience with high prices."

Rivers
19 | 18 | 18 | $33

Mercantile Bldg., 30 S. Wacker Dr. (bet. Madison & Monroe Sts.), 312-559-1515

In the ebb and flow of Chicago's fine-dining scene, this Loop New American has established itself as "the place for [Civic] Opera–goers", as well as a "great client-lunch spot" or "after-work stop" "for socializing", with "good fare" and a "serene view of the Chicago River" (you "can't beat the patio"); some, however, like the "location, not the food", which they say "misses the boat."

R.J. Grunts S
18 | 16 | 18 | $19

2056 N. Lincoln Park W. (Dickens Ave.), 773-929-5363

"Thirty-plus years of greatness" mark Rich Melman's "legendary" first Lettuce Entertain You enterprise, a Lincoln Park "so-old-it's-new-again" "nostalgic treat" that's "stuck in the '70s and proud of it"; "bountiful burgers", a "gold-standard salad bar" and "humorous" decor (including the "wall of waitresses'" photos) make folks so "glad it hasn't closed" they don't even grunt that it's "small and crowded."

RL S
21 | 26 | 22 | $44

115 E. Chicago Ave. (Michigan Ave.), 312-475-1100

Adjacent to his Michigan Avenue flagship, Ralph Lauren's maiden voyage into the victuals biz is now under the management of the Gibsons folks, who've morphed this Near North changeling's menu from Italian to American 'club cuisine' more befitting the "terrific" "old-school decor", "a fashion statement all its own" with "lots of leather" and "impressive artwork."

Robinson's No. 1 Ribs S
20 | 11 | 15 | $18

225 S. Canal St. (Adams St.), 312-258-8477
655 W. Armitage Ave. (Orchard St.), 312-337-1399
940 W. Madison St. (Clinton St.), Oak Park, 708-383-8452

The secret to these city and suburban BBQs' success "is in the sauce" ("if you like sweet") that makes its "great ribs" "finger-lickin' good"; several suggest, though, that they're best "for takeout, not eat-in", due in part to "spotty service" and decor that "leaves something to be desired."

Rock Bottom Brewery **S** | 15 | 15 | 15 | $21
1 W. Grand Ave. (State St.), 312-755-9339
28256 Diehl Rd. (Winfield Rd.), Warrenville, 630-836-1380
◪ "The beer is the reason to go" to any outpost of this "casual" chain serving "mainstream" American fare; some suds-lovers say they're "good for work gatherings" or to "catch a game", but uncharitable chuggers chide that they're "aptly named"; N.B. the River North location boasts a rooftop beer garden in summer.

Roditys ●**S** | 19 | 16 | 19 | $24
222 S. Halsted St. (bet. Adams St. & Jackson Blvd.), 312-454-0800
■ Since 1973, "good Greek hospitality" and an "extensive menu" of "standard", "old-fashioned food" that's "hot, fresh and well presented" – especially "great lamb dishes" "done exactly as you order" them – have kept constituents of this Greektown classic happy; "reasonable prices" and a "clean" environment add to its "fun, festive atmosphere."

Ron of Japan **S** | 20 | 18 | 20 | $33
230 E. Ontario St. (bet. Fairbanks Ct. & St. Clair St.), 312-644-6500
633 Skokie Blvd. (Dundee Rd.), Northbrook, 847-564-5900
◪ "Great for a large group", this "classic" Downtown and Northbrook Japanese teppanyaki duo features "cook-at-the-table" chefs whose "showmanship at the grill" while slicing and dicing "excellent" chicken, lobster, shrimp and steak dishes makes for an "entertaining and tasty" evening; those who "love the preparation" say it "beats Benihana any day", but holdouts hint "the years are beginning to show" and hope for "better ventilation."

Room, The **S** | 23 | 20 | 21 | $35
5900 N. Broadway St. (Rosedale Ave.), 773-989-7666
■ Room-mates regard this Edgewater Eclectic–New American as "the best high-end BYO" around, with "good food" and a "hip", "homey" and gay-friendly atmosphere within a "spacious" "exposed brick" space; the menu may be "limited", but "fair prices" and "fun service" have fans saying owner "Jody [Andre] has done it again"; N.B. the Food score may not reflect the post-*Survey* arrival of chef Linda Raydl (ex Tomboy).

Roong **S** | – | – | – | M
1633 N. Milwaukee Ave. (bet. Damen & North Aves.), 773-252-3488
Roong Petch
1828 W. Montrose Ave. (bet. Ashland & Damen Aves.), 773-989-0818
The long-standing, more downscale Roong Petch storefront standard in Lakeview has given birth to Roong, whose Thai

dining room brings *lad nar, pad woon sen* and *satays* – as well as the clever signature "007 secret stir-fry" and sticky rice with mango dessert – to Wicker Park, along with stylish decor well suited to the trendy neighborhood.

RoSal's Italian Kitchen ◐   ▽ 21 | 17 | 22 | $27
1154 W. Taylor St. (Racine Ave.), 312-243-2357
■ A "classic gem on Taylor Street", this "friendly and filling" Southern Italian in the heart of Little Italy is a "throwback" with "excellent home-cooked" Sicilian fare (and "shopping bags of leftovers"), "real charm" and an "adorable", "homey atmosphere"; on the last Tuesday of the month, its upstairs dining room hosts prix fixe *Big Night* dinners for 15 or more that pay homage to the Stanley Tucci movie.

Rose Angelis S   23 | 20 | 21 | $26
1314 W. Wrightwood Ave. (bet. Racine & Southport Aves.), 773-296-0081
■ Legions of Lincoln Parkers are loyal to this "charming" "favorite" "date place" "cozily set" within the "meandering rooms" of "a great brownstone", insisting it's "always worth the wait" for its "mouthwatering", "rich" Italian fare smothered in "divine sauces" and delivered with "down-to-earth service" in "portions large enough for a linebacker" ("get ready for" "the inevitable doggy bag").

Rosebud, The S   21 | 18 | 19 | $33
1500 W. Taylor St. (Laflin St.), 312-942-1117
Rosebud on Rush S
720 N. Rush St. (Superior St.), 312-266-6444
Rosebud of Highland Park S
1850 Second St. (Central Ave.), Highland Park, 847-926-4800
Rosebud of Naperville S
48 W. Chicago Ave. (Washington St.), Naperville, 630-548-9800
◪ Alex Dana's group of "real Chicago Italians" furthers the "formula" of his "crowded" Taylor Street original, "a favorite" for "ridiculously large portions" of "honest, old-fashioned food" from a "consistent" kitchen, consumed "under the watchful eye of the Frank Sinatra portrait"; not everyone agrees "these roses have no thorns", though, with protesters pointing to "predictable food", "spotty service" and "too much noise."

Rosebud Steakhouse S   23 | 21 | 20 | $45
192 E. Walton St. (Mies van der Rohe Way), 312-397-1000
◪ "They snuck a great little steakhouse east of Michigan Avenue" – so say supporters of this "excellent" example of "Alex Dana branching out" from his Italian roots; a "sophisticated crowd" considers it "a keeper" for its "classy", "clublike" "neighborhood feel", its "juicy steaks" and its "very good wine list", and even adversaries who say the "price is high" admit it's "one to watch."

Roy's 🅂 — | — | — | E
720 N. State St. (Superior St.), 312-787-7599
"You can almost feel the tropical breezes" at this River North branch of Roy Yamaguchi's national haute Hawaiian chain, "a winner from the start" thanks to an exhibition kitchen turning out "exceptionally tasty food" "you don't see everywhere" ("mostly seafood with unexpected flair") served amid "sophisticated" decor – not a tiki torch in sight.

Ruby of Siam 🅂 — | — | — | M
1125 Emerson St. (Ridge Ave.), Evanston, 847-492-1008
Skokie Fashion Sq., 9420 Skokie Blvd. (Foster Ave.), Skokie, 847-675-7008
Sizzling rice soups, brightly flavored glass-noodle salads, chicken and pork satay and a variety of curry dishes make these Suburban North Thais popular for both dine-in and takeout (or a bargain buffet lunch); both are family-friendly and tastefully decorated with Siamese artifacts, but the Evanston strip-mall location serves beer and wine, whereas the Skokie storefront BYO offers no alcohol.

Rumba 🅂 — | — | — | M
351 W. Hubbard St. (Orleans St.), 312-222-1226
From the mojitos to the Nuevo Latino cuisine, it's like a trip to the Tropicana at this River North supper club that's transformed the old Hubbard Street Grill space into a vibrant and capacious room (seating more than 250) where light-up mahogany-hued conga drums separate elevated, cushy, high-backed banquettes, live mambo or Afro-Cuban music pulsates Wednesday–Saturday nights and *I Love Lucy* reruns flicker on TV screens above the oval bar.

Rushmore 23 | 19 | 20 | $43
1023 W. Lake St. (Carpenter St.), 312-421-8845
⚑ "A fantastic find" in a "quirky location" ("under the El" in the Market District), this "hip" New American boasts an "exciting menu", a "mix of haute cuisine and comfort food" ("try the lobster pot pie" on Saturdays), served with "lots of attitude" in an "austere but romantic" space; most say it's "so good you forget the sound" of the "train overhead"; N.B. the Food score may not reflect the post-*Survey* arrival of chef Gilbert Langlois (ex The Room).

Russell's Barbecue 🅂 18 | 11 | 14 | $14
1621 N. Thatcher Ave. (North Ave.), Elmwood Park, 708-453-7065
■ "It's not BBQ – it's a religion" posit parishioners of this West Suburban "institution" packing the pews since 1930 thanks to "old-time" stuff like "tasty beef sandwiches" and "fall-off-the-bone ribs" slathered in "sauce you could drink from the bottle"; though a "sentimental favorite" of the "over-60" set, it's also a "great place for kids" to "be noisy and messy" while making "lots of memories" of their own.

Russian Tea Time [S] 20 | 20 | 20 | $32

77 E. Adams St. (bet. Michigan & Wabash Aves.), 312-360-0000

■ For a "nice change of pace", fans of "Eastern European food" "love the samovars" full of "strong tea", "great" "flavored vodkas" and "authentic" "Russian specialties" (including "lots of vegetarian choices") at this "civilized" Loop "treasure" "convenient to the Art Institute and Symphony Center"; with its "quiet, intimate", "old-world" air, it strikes lovers as "the place to have a passionate affair."

RUTH'S CHRIS STEAK HOUSE [S] 24 | 20 | 22 | $45

431 N. Dearborn St. (Hubbard St.), 312-321-2725
933 Skokie Blvd. (Dundee Rd.), Northbrook, 847-498-6889

■ "Beef with butter . . . I love America!" belt out boosters of these "comfortable and consistent" chophouses, saying they're "always a good choice" (albeit an "expensive" one) and a "favorite place to escalate the cholesterol level" via "tender fillets you can cut with a fork"; even those who prefer to "support local" "hometown steakhouses" admit they're "excellent, despite being part of a chain."

Sabatino's ◐ [S] 22 | 17 | 21 | $28

4441 W. Irving Park Rd. (bet. Cicero & Kostner Aves.), 773-283-8331

■ "Old-fashioned Italian – and proud of it!" characterizes the bill of fare at this "dependable" Northwest Side "Chicago classic" that "hasn't changed in years (and that's good)"; "you get a lot" of "delicious food" "for a little", and strolling musicians every night (and a piano player on weekends) add to its "dark, crowded", "romantic" atmosphere.

Sabor [S] – | – | – | M

Schaumburg's Town Square Ctr., 160E S. Roselle Rd. (Schaumburg Rd.), Schaumburg, 847-301-1470

Young chef-owner Christina Hernandez's innovative use of Nuevo Latino flavors from Caribbean, Spanish and South American sources – as evidenced in her signature plantain-crusted mahi-mahi with mango-pepper salsa – does her proud at this vibrant, casually upscale two-year-old in the Northwest Suburbs, with a colorful South Beach deco ambiance and complementary wine list; N.B. patio seating is now available.

Sai Café [S] 23 | 15 | 18 | $29

2010 N. Sheffield Ave. (Armitage Ave.), 773-472-8080

■ "When good fish die, they don't go to heaven – they go to" this "noisy and busy" Lincoln Park Japanese "favorite" to be turned into "fresh, generous portions" of "consistent-quality" sushi; its "homey" setting may be a bit "lacking" in the decor department, but "interesting specials" and "helpful", "smiling" servers make it "a must" for novices and a "mainstay" for "experts."

Sal & Carvao Churrascaria ⓢ   _ | _ | _ | E

801 E. Algonquin Rd. (Roselle Rd.), Schaumburg, 847-925-0061
Meat is on the menu at this white-tablecloth Brazilian
steakhouse (the name translates as 'salt and charcoal') in
the Northwest Suburbs, home of huge hunks of sizzling,
slow-roasted flesh-fare on skewers (sliced tableside by
costumed servers), an eye-popping salad buffet, and
caipirinha cocktails; the all-you-can-eat, fixed-price lunch
and dinner service includes salads, sides and 14 varieties
of animal protein – and is cheaper for kids.

SALBUTE   25 | 17 | 20 | $30

*20 E. First St. (bet. Garfield & Washington Sts.), Hinsdale,
630-920-8077*
■ "Worth the wait at twice the drive", this West Suburban
Hinsdale haven "deserves its raves" for the "wonderful
flavors" of "inventive" chef-owner Edgar Rodriguez's
"thrilling, complex, delicious" "gourmet Mexican cuisine"
and its "knowledgeable" staff; remember, "reservations
are a must", especially since the "wait" for "the long-
promised liquor license" has ended – now "all it needs
is more space."

Saloon Steakhouse, The ⓢ   21 | 18 | 21 | $41

*Seneca Hotel, 200 E. Chestnut St. (bet. Lake Shore Dr. &
Michigan Ave.), 312-280-5454*
■ Pardners praise this "solid" Streeterville "hideaway from
Michigan Avenue" for rustlin' up "excellent" cuts of beef,
"great fish" dishes and "perfect cocktails" "without all the
fuss of the better-known joints in town"; still "something
of a secret", it's "a manly place" with "personable and
friendly service" and a "comfortable", "stylish setting" that
can get "smoky and noisy" at times.

Salpicón ⓢ   22 | 18 | 20 | $36

1252 N. Wells St. (bet. Goethe & Scott Sts.), 312-988-7811
■ Mexican-lovers say *muy bueno* about this "loud,
happy" and "crowded" Old Towner and the "innovative",
"intriguing options" on chef-owner-"magician" Priscila
Satkoff's menu of "authentic regional" dishes coupled
with a "superior wine list" (overseen by her husband,
sommelier-proprietor Vincent) and an "amazing selection"
of "top-shelf tequilas", all served in a "brightly colored
room" that "accentuates the brightly flavored food."

Salt & Pepper Diner ⓢ⌿   16 | 15 | 16 | $12

2575 N. Lincoln Ave. (Sheffield Ave.), 773-525-8788
3537 N. Clark St. (Addison St.), 773-883-9800
■ You "get what you expect" at this Wrigleyville and Lincoln
Park paired set that seasons "cheap", "classic diner food"
"with '50s decor", "blaring" jukeboxes and some of the
"best milkshakes in Chicago"; rock-around-the-clockers
also report it's "fun" "to roll out of bed and into S&P on

Saturday mornings" (or afternoons), since breakfasts here are "good for a hangover."

Salvatore's Ristorante S | 19 | 22 | 19 | $31 |
525 W. Arlington Pl. (Clark St.), 773-528-1200
■ "Tucked" into "a vintage building" in Lincoln Park, this "timeless" "gem" boasts a "dark, elegant", "old-world" "supper-club setting" (plus a "wonderful outdoor garden" for "alfresco summertime" dining) and "quality" Northern Italian cooking; the "romantic atmosphere" of this "big date spot" is further enhanced on weekends by a professional ivory tickler; P.S. since it sometimes "closes for private parties, call ahead."

Samba Room S   ▽ | 20 | 20 | 18 | $32 |
22 E. Chicago Ave. (Washington St.), Naperville, 630-753-0985
◪ It's "never boring" at this "trendy" cafe (with six siblings in several states) that locals laud as "a good reason to stay in Naperville" thanks to "tasty food" showcasing "creative" "combinations" of "great Cuban" classics with "wonderful *nuevo* Latin" influences; "don't plan on having much conversation", though, as the "fun", "festive" setting can get "so noisy you can't even talk."

San Soo Gab San ◐S | – | – | – | M |
5247 N. Western Ave. (Foster Ave.), 773-334-1589
It's always packed at this Uptown Korean BBQ eatery – sometimes even at its ungodly 6 AM closing time – and the harried staff is always hustling out heavy platters holding a vast array of specialties, including tabletop-grilled octopus and seafood, marinated skirt steak and spicy hot pots of tofu and vegetables with noodles; N.B. now also serving sushi.

Santorini ◐S | 20 | 19 | 19 | $31 |
800 W. Adams St. (Halsted St.), 312-829-8820
■ "Be transported to a Greek village" via this "beautiful taverna", an "island namesake" "in the heart of Greektown" specializing in "excellent seafood" such as "great whole" red "snapper or [black] sea bass" "from the grill"; "more subdued than some" of its counterparts, it has "charming", "cozy decor", a "lovely fireplace" and a new patio, but remember your options – "go early, have reservations or wait a long time!"

Sarkis Grill S⊘ | 18 | 9 | 19 | $12 |
2632 Gross Point Rd. (Crawford St.), Evanston, 847-328-9703
◪ "A North Shore relic" circa 1965, this "classic" "hole-in-the-wall" serves up "eggs with an attitude" as well as other "old-fashioned diner" fare; "regulars ranging from denim-clad kids to businessmen" report that though founder Sarkis Tashjian "sold his grill", this "joy of a man" known for his "welcoming personality" "still comes in every day" and remains "the main attraction."

Saussy
▽ 21 | 18 | 19 | $39

1156 W. Grand Ave. (Racine Ave.), 312-491-1122

■ "Well-presented" and "good American" cuisine "with inventive touches" and a "tasting menu [that's] a bargain" satisfy supporters of this "conversation-friendly" Near North eatery; "great service" from a "friendly, reliable" staff and a "sleek", "romantic" atmosphere round out its appeal; N.B. the Food score may not reflect the post-*Survey* arrival of chef Lionel Ramos (ex The Outpost).

Sayat Nova **S**
– | – | – | M

157 E. Ohio St. (bet. Michigan Ave. & St. Clair St.), 312-644-9159

Since 1969, this family-owned restaurant in River North has been serving its uncommon, low-budget Armenian fare (kebabs, couscous and lamb dishes) to the faithful; now a new attitude has bi-monthly themed DJ nights drawing a hip, diverse crowd, turning the restaurant into a club later in the evening; N.B. patrons can 'puff, puff, pass' on fruit-flavored tobaccos in the house hookahs.

Scoozi! **S**
20 | 20 | 19 | $30

410 W. Huron St. (bet. Kingsbury & Orleans Sts.), 312-943-5900

■ Striking "a balance between food and fun", Lettuce Entertain You's "informal", "loftlike" River North Italian is a "dependable" choice for "affordable, good" fare (folks "love the butternut squash ravioli" and "crispy, paper-thin pizza"); the "lively", "casual" atmosphere is "good for singles and families" alike, helping make this a "favorite" for "happy hour" and "celebrations"; in short, young and old agree "Scoozi! is a doozi!"

SEASONS **S**
28 | 27 | 27 | $65

Four Seasons Hotel, 120 E. Delaware Pl., 7th fl. (bet. Michigan Ave. & Rush St.), 312-649-2349

■ Clients coo over this "crème-de-la-crème" New American whose "classic yet contemporary" "creations" are top-rated for Food among Chicago restaurants (the "lunch buffet is wonderful" and the "Sunday brunch is spectacular") and covet being "coddled by the loving staff" for whom "the customer is king" within the cosseting confines of its "classy" accommodations; N.B. the Food score may not reflect the post-*Survey* transfer of the toque from Mark Baker to Robert Sulatycky (ex Four Seasons Hotel Toronto).

SEASONS CAFÉ ●**S**
24 | 26 | 25 | $38

Four Seasons Hotel, 120 E. Delaware Pl., 7th fl. (bet. Michigan Ave. & Rush St.), 312-649-2349

■ Cafe society settles into this "intimate" "treat" on the Four Seasons Hotel's seventh floor then tucks into "wonderful" Traditional American dishes offered with "the same great service" as at its superior sibling and "at reasonable rates" (considering it's like "dining in a millionaire's home"); it's "the perfect antidote to shopping-weary feet" and "great for a pre-theater" repast, too.

Settimana Café [S] 20 | 17 | 19 | $31

2056 W. Divison St. (Hoyne Ave.), 773-394-1629

◪ When it comes to this Wicker Park two-year-old, the ayes appreciate its "very good" "authentic [Northern] Italian dishes" served by a "friendly" staff "in a festive" and "comfortable" "city atmosphere" (including "excellent patios") "without the city prices"; the nays nonetheless knock it as "noisy" and having "hit-or-miss" service and food, saying "it seems they still have kinks to work out."

1776 ▽ 23 | 15 | 22 | $32

397 Virginia St. (bet. Dole & McHenry Aves.), Crystal Lake, 815-356-1776

■ There's "always a little something unusual" at this "innovative", independent New American in the Northwest Suburbs, where the "seasonal cuisine" is "a treat" for "wild-game" lovers and the "excellent planked" salmon is cooked like it was in 1776; owner "Andy [Andresky]'s hospitality" warms the "homey" space, but it's his "great wine knowledge" – and "huge" 550-label, 7,200-bottle collection – that really gets revolutionaries fired up.

Shabu-ya [S] – | – | – | M

3475 N. Clark St. (bet. Cornelia & Newport Aves.), 773-388-9203

Those who like to work for their supper will love the healthful if high-maintenance shabu-shabu at this small, laid-back Japanese BYO yearling in Wrigleyville; various meats, seafood and vegetables are cooked in broth bubbling on built-in hot plates (forgoing any oil or MSG in the process); special sauces complete the savory, self-cheffed results, and the broth is then eaten with rice or noodles.

Shallots [S] 22 | 19 | 21 | $44

2324 N. Clark St. (bet. Belden Ave. & Fullerton Pkwy.), 773-755-5205

◪ Lincoln Park is home to this "first [of its kind] in Chicago" – an "upscale", "top-notch restaurant that just happens to be kosher" (and "could succeed even if it weren't"), turning out "creative", "gourmet" Mediterranean fare the faithful feel is "well-done" and "luscious"; other kashruth-keeping critics concede it "fills a niche" but caution that its "small portions" are "not equal to" its "golden-calf prices."

Shanghai Terrace ◐ [S] ▽ 26 | 25 | 26 | $51

Peninsula Hotel, 108 E. Superior St., 4th fl. (bet. Michigan Ave. & Rush St.), 312-573-6744

■ Pamper yourself with some posh Pan-Asian in this "beautiful and blessedly quiet" refuge on the fourth floor of the Near North's Peninsula Hotel; you may "pay big for the upscale room" reminiscent of 1930s Shanghai and the "attentive service", but the "gourmet" cuisine is "excellent", and the "five-spice duck will blow your mind"; N.B. outdoor terrace seating is available in warm weather.

Shark Bar, The **S**   – | – | – | **M**
212 N. Canal St. (bet. Fulton & Lake Sts.), 312-627-0800
Southern/Soul food is on the menu at this revived West Loop spot with siblings in New York and Atlanta; high beamed ceilings, exposed-brick walls and red velvet curtains lend an R&B vibe to its dining room, where visitors groove on the likes of smothered pork chops and blackened catfish; afterward, many go upstairs to enjoy the 212 Lounge and a stunning roof deck offering a sparkling city panorama.

Shaw's Crab House & Blue Crab Lounge **S**   22 | 19 | 20 | $38
21 E. Hubbard St. (bet. State St. & Wabash Ave.), 312-527-2722
Shaw's Crab House & Red Shell Lounge **S**
1900 E. Higgins Rd. (Rte. 53), Schaumburg, 847-517-2722
■ Bringing "the Atlantic shore to the Midwest", these "great Lettuce Entertain You" "steakhouse-style seafooders" supplement "classy" main dining rooms with "more casual" lounges (the River North's Blue Crab "is the place to go" for "fresh oysters", and the Suburban Northwest's Red Shell is shrimp-centric); N.B. the Food score may not reflect the post-*Survey* arrival of chef Tony Fraski (ex Mity Nice Grill) at the Schaumburg branch.

She She   21 | 17 | 20 | $35
4539 N. Lincoln Ave. (bet. Sunnyside & Wilson Aves.), 773-293-3690
◪ "Flamboyant servers" in "leopard-print pants" present plates of "diverse and creative" Eclectic New American fare at this "adorable, tiny" Lincoln Square spot (owned by Dana Hechtman and chef Nicole Parthemore – she and she, respectively) with a "loud, hip, gay-dominated" scene and "a pretty back-garden area"; a few she-devils declare the kitchen "uneven", but most maintain its "sometimes surprising combinations usually work."

Shine & Morida **S**   20 | 17 | 19 | $24
901 W. Armitage Ave. (Fremont St.), 773-296-0101
■ Fans of these fraternal Lincoln Parkers tout the "trendy" twin-set as a "don't-miss" treat, saying "what a great idea" – "good Chinese and Japanese" in one stop; Shine serves "fresh" Hunan, Mandarin and Szechuan dishes "in a pleasant and serene" setting while next-door Morida slices "yummy sushi" in a "hip", "clubby atmosphere" with "pretty lighting"; N.B. you can order either cuisine on either side.

Shiroi Hana **S**   ▽ 21 | 11 | 16 | $19
3242 N. Clark St. (Belmont Ave.), 773-477-1652
■ "An extensive, well-executed Japanese menu" including "tasty" "sushi without the attitude" tempts the crowds into

the "tight seating" of this "small, friendly" Lakeview "standby"; true, it's also "without all the glitz of some newer spots", but it's "good for carryout", the "great lunch specials" are a "fantastic bargain" and "you can't beat the party trays"; N.B. wine and beer only.

Shula's Steakhouse S   18 | 18 | 18 | $48

Sheraton Chicago, 301 E. North Water St. (Columbus Dr.), 312-670-0788
Wyndham Northwest Chicago, 400 Park Blvd. (Thorndale Ave.), Itasca, 630-775-1499

☑ Not surprising, these "workhorse steakhouse joints" in Streeterville and the Northwest Suburbs (part of a national chain owned by legendary NFL coach Don Shula) serve "mammoth-size steaks" that fans say are not only "big enough for a football player" but "good too"; still, some spoilsports are stymied by the "strange contrast" of a "sports-bar feel" and a "pricey", "upscale setting."

SIGNATURE ROOM   18 | 26 | 19 | $45
AT THE 95TH S

John Hancock Center, 875 N. Michigan Ave., 95th fl. (bet. Chestnut St. & Delaware Ave.), 312-787-9596

☑ Like the song says, "on a clear day you can see forever" from this "romantic" New American perched high atop the John Hancock Center, a "memorable" "must for visitors" with a "great, economical lunchtime buffet"; loyalists are "never disappointed", but others opine it's "overpriced" and note that while "you can't beat the view", you also "can't eat the view"; N.B. the Food score may not reflect the post-*Survey* arrival of chef Michael Pivoney (ex Carlucci).

Silver Cloud Bar & Grill S   18 | 15 | 17 | $19

1700 N. Damen Ave. (Wabansia Ave.), 773-489-6212

■ "Just-plain-good" American "comfort-food favorites" – from "amazing sloppy joes" and "delicious pot roast" to "the mother of all grilled-cheese" sandwiches – as well as "lots of good beer on tap" (all of them microbrews) are the prizes that lure the "young and old alike" to this "cozy" "neighborhood sit-down" establishment with a "fun, funky" atmosphere (complete with "rotating art exhibitions") that simply "screams Bucktown."

Silver Palm ◑   – | – | – | M

768 N. Milwaukee Ave. (Ogden Ave.), 312-666-9322

Owner David Gevercer opened this dinner-only American eatery right next door to his Near West standby, the much-loved Matchbox bar; installed in a restored vintage-1947 railroad dining car, it boasts renowned cocktails and a train-themed menu of American-with-a-twist cuisine such as Southern Pacific Railways double-ginger duck and a deep-fried shrimp-and-scallop po' boy with pickled green tomatoes and Cajun remoulade.

Silver Seafood ●🄢   – – – I
4829 N. Broadway St. (Lawrence Ave.), 773-784-0668
A seafood sleeper in Uptown, this colorfully decorated
Chinese will steam you a fish that may have been swimming
(in a small tank in the rear) when you walked in the door;
fin fare aside, roasted birds such as pigeon, duck and quail
are a specialty; insiders bypass the Americanized menu for
the Sino version with loose translations and more interesting
offerings, including bubble teas and fruit shakes.

Sinibar ●🄢   ▽ 15 21 17 $29
1540 N. Milwaukee Ave. (North Ave.), 773-278-7797
🖿 A light Eclectic menu of spring rolls, quesadillas, satays,
panini, pastas and desserts is designed to appeal to the
"see-and-be-seen" crowd that loves to lounge at this
"too-cool" Moroccan-accented Wicker Park spot with a
"snazzy downstairs for drinks" and DJ-driven grooving;
the jury is still out, though, on the revamped menu, which
now includes entrées.

Sixty-Five 🄢   15 8 11 $16
336 N. Michigan Ave. (Wacker Dr.), 312-372-0306
Union Station, 225 S. Canal St. (bet. Adams St. & Jackson Blvd.),
312-474-0065 ⊟
201 W. Madison St. (bet. Franklin & Wells Sts.), 312-782-6565
🖿 The "good reputation" of this once-venerated group of
Chinese fish specialists seems to be "on the way down";
while hopefuls still like the "large portions", "fast service"
and "cheap prices", almost all concede that the "good
seafood" is "not what it used to be" while the "dumpy
atmosphere", unfortunately, is.

Slice of Life/Hy Life Bistro 🄢⊟   14 12 15 $23
4120 W. Dempster St. (bet. Crawford Ave. & Keeler St.),
Skokie, 847-674-2021
🖿 Set in the North Suburbs, this "interesting place" is
actually two kosher restaurants with "separate dining
rooms" and kitchens under one roof – one a "casual"
"vegetarian" (Slice of Life), the other serving meat (Hy Life
Bistro) and both "family-friendly"; but what strikes some
as "cheerful service" and "orthodox Jewish soul food"
"leaves something to be desired" according to others.

Smith & Wollensky 🄢   21 20 20 $46
318 N. State St. (bet. Kinzie St. & Wacker Dr.), 312-670-9900
🖿 A "New York steakhouse tradition brought to Chicago",
this River Norther in a "romantic riverfront location" is
"always jumping with an after-work crowd" that gathers in
its "great watering hole downstairs" or one of its handsome
dining rooms for "beautiful steaks"; not surprisingly, some
say it's not quite "up to the standards of" "its namesake"
in Manhattan despite its "NYC prices"; N.B. the smaller
Wollensky's Grill on premises offers a more casual menu.

Smoke Daddy ◐ [S] 20 | 14 | 16 | $18

1804 W. Division St. (bet. Ashland & Damen Aves.), 773-772-6656

■ 'Cue cravers queue up for the "melt-in-your-mouth ribs", "fabulous pulled-pork and brisket" sandwiches and "amazing" "greasy fries" at this "offbeat", "no-frills roadhouse" in Wicker Park, the "perfect neighborhood dive" where the "cool vibe" from a "laid-back" staff and "fun" crowd enjoying "great live music" (blues and jazz nightly excluding Wednesdays, rockabilly on Sundays) more than makes up for the "hole-in-the-wall decor."

Soju – | – | – | M

1745 W. North Ave. (bet. Hermitage Ave. & Wood St.), 773-782-9000

Upscale urban decor is a hallmark of this hip *bulgoki* headquarters offering a menu of tasty Korean (and some Japanese) dishes; also aiding in accessibility is its Wicker Park location, much closer to most city-dwellers than Lawrence Avenue; N.B. the unusual namesake liquor (a sweet-potato vodka) makes for a different sort of cocktailing.

Sorriso ▽ 16 | 21 | 18 | $32

321 N. Clark St. (Kinzie St.), 312-644-0283

◪ For those who see "the Chicago River as the Grand Canal in Venice", the chance to "eat right on it is the real draw" of this River North Italian with "nice views" from both its dining room and large outdoor seating area; "an awesome summer place" and "great lunch spot", it offers fare that some find "solid", others "uninteresting", and service that's "ok"; N.B. the ratings may not reflect a post-*Survey* change of ownership.

Souk ◐ [S] 18 | 20 | 18 | $34

1552 N. Milwaukee Ave. (bet. Damen & North Aves.), 773-227-1818

◪ Adventurous diners "love the decor and spices" at this "funky" spot "in the heart of Wicker Park" serving "good Middle Eastern" and Med fare in an "exotic" environment complete with bands and belly-dancing on Wednesdays and Saturdays – "they even provide the pipes" (hookah, that is, filled with fruit-flavored tobaccos); still, for some the "novelty-act aspects overshadow the food"; N.B. the Decor score may not reflect a post-*Survey* remodeling.

Soul Kitchen [S] 21 | 20 | 19 | $31

1576 N. Milwaukee Ave. (bet. Damen & North Aves.), 773-342-9742

■ An "original" "interpretation of soul food" featuring "fascinating flavors" and "awesome spices" combines with "colorful decor" and an "offbeat", "upbeat scene" that's "great for people-watching" to make this Regional American a Wicker Park "favorite" of a "painfully hip, attractive clientele" (folks "wait a long time" for the "great weekend brunch"); N.B. now serving lunch.

South Gate Cafe S
17 | 18 | 18 | $28

655 Forest Ave. (Deerpath Ave.), Lake Forest, 847-234-8800
◼ Fresh-air fiends favor this Lake Forest "standby" as much for its "lovely, scenic outdoor patio" with "pretty views of the market square" as its "basic", "consistently good" Traditional American fare; grouchy gate-crashers grouse that it's only "busy because it's convenient", though, grumbling that it "needs improvement"; N.B. the Food rating may not reflect a post-*Survey* chef change.

Southport City Saloon S
14 | 14 | 16 | $21

2548 N. Southport Ave. (bet. Lill St. & Wrightwood Ave.), 773-975-6110
◼ "Great burgers" stand out on an otherwise "average" menu of Traditional American fare at this local "staple" in Lincoln Park where a "fun", "clublike" ambiance pervades; the enclosed patio is not only "great in summer" but is heated by a fireplace in the winter.

South Water Kitchen S
- | - | - | M

Hotel Monaco, 225 N. Wabash Ave. (Upper Wacker Dr.), 312-236-9300
Hats off to the Loop's Hotel Monaco, which has transformed its former French bistro, Mossant, into this spacious venue specializing in Traditional American home cooking with some Contemporary accents; highlights such as hearty blue-plate specials from the vast exhibition kitchen, grinders from the brick oven and a clutch of clever cocktails make it a fine spot for a business lunch in the Loop or a pre-theater meal.

Spago
22 | 22 | 21 | $47

520 N. Dearborn St. (Grand Ave.), 312-527-3700
◼ "Chicago goes Hollywood" at River North's "trendy", "noisy" satellite of the LA original, where "beautiful people eat beautiful [New American] food"; aficionados applaud the menu's "wonderful eclecticism" – "pizzas, Wiener schnitzel" – and the room's "warm look", but critics slam it as "overpriced", "overrated" and "losing its edge."

Sparacino Ristorante
- | - | - | M

6966 W. North Ave. (bet. Harlem & Oak Park Aves.), 773-836-2089
A sophisticated slant on Italian cuisine comes to the Far West side via this one-year-old run by brother and sister Mark and Stefania Sparacino; its intimate coffee-and-cream-colored dining room is set in a space that it shares with its sibling, a catering concern called Traveling Fare.

SPIAGGIA S
27 | 27 | 26 | $62

One Magnificent Mile Bldg., 980 N. Michigan Ave., 2nd fl. (Oak St.), 312-280-2750
◼ "You know you've arrived when you enter the gorgeous dining room" of this "wildly expensive" "romantic splurge spot" in the Gold Coast, ranked No. 1 for Decor by surveyors

who also laud "talented chef" Tony Mantuano's "refined", Italian fare as the "best [of its kind] in the city"; "attentive" service and "awesome views" of Lake Michigan from its "grand" setting add to a "special" experience; P.S. its nearby "cafe is wonderful and less" costly too.

SPRING S | 26 | 25 | 25 | $53 |

2039 W. North Ave. (Damen Ave.), 773-395-7100
■ A "favorite" of the "chic" set, this "hot", "hip" New American in Wicker Park "lives up to its hype" on the strength of "magnificent" chef-owner Shawn McClain (ex Trio) and his "gorgeous", "sublime" "Asian-influenced" cuisine, which includes "swimmingly fresh seafood", "professionally" served in a "stark", "stylish", "tranquil" space graced with a Zen garden; it's "pricey" but "worth springing for"; N.B. now offering a tasting menu.

Stained Glass Wine Bar Bistro S | 24 | 20 | 23 | $40 |

1735 Benson Ave. (bet. Church & Clark Sts.), Evanston, 847-864-8600
■ "A sparkling treasure" to bacchic boosters, this Evanston *enoteca*/bistro entices oenophiles with its "fun, flight-oriented approach" and "terrific selection", but many who first "go for the wine" later "come back for" the Eclectic-American food, which supporters describe as "top-notch", "complex" and "fabulously creative"; "enjoyable service" helps make this "a welcome addition to Chicago's limited wine bar scene"; N.B. outdoor seating is now available.

Standard India S | ∇ 21 | 11 | 17 | $18 |

917 W. Belmont Ave. (Clark St.), 773-929-1123
◪ Supporters of this Lakeview Indian counsel "go on an empty stomach", for "you'll be tempted to try every dish" on the "superb buffet" that's a "must" for its "excellent value"; cynics, however, find "no charm" in fare they feel is, well, "standard"; N.B. the Decor score may not reflect a post-*Survey* remodeling.

Stanley's Kitchen & Tap S | 18 | 14 | 16 | $18 |

1970 N. Lincoln Ave. (Armitage Ave.), 312-642-0007
■ "Tasty homestyle cooking" and "family atmosphere" make this Traditional American eatery in Lincoln Park "good" for a "casual brunch on Sundays" "with the kids", but it's also nice for a "bar buddies'" or "girls' night out"; just remember you may "need a wheelbarrow to get" yourself home; P.S. "they've got Tater Tots!"

Starfish S | – | – | – | M |

804 W. Randolph St. (Halsted St.), 312-997-2433
Beautiful people meet beautiful fish at the latest hipster sushi-lounge hangout to hit the Market District's Randolph Street restaurant row; cool greens and seaweed shapes set an ultra-modern, aquatic mood, perfect for indulging in

creative, colorful, dramatically-presented Japanese fare, paired with a good selection of sake.

Star of Siam [S]   19 | 15 | 17 | $18

11 E. Illinois St. (State St.), 312-670-0100

■ "Amazing value", "consistent" cooking and a "comfy atmosphere" keep 'em coming to this 20-year-"old Thai favorite" in River North offering "plenty of variety" at "reasonable prices in an area where everything else is expensive"; some find the "fast service" "mind-blowing" (in a good way), while others say it's "too quick", but most agree the place is "great for eat-in or takeaway."

Stefani's [S]   20 | 16 | 20 | $29

1418 W. Fullerton Ave. (Southport Ave.), 773-348-0111

■ Amici of Phil Stefani's "reliable" DePaul-area Northern Italian (including the husband of NY's Chicago-born junior senator) appreciate the "huge portions" of "consistently good", "basic" fare ("plentiful pasta, no paltry poultry") at "reasonable prices"; the decor may need "sprucing up", but the "nice outdoor area" offers "alfresco in the summer."

Stevie B's [S]   ▽ 19 | 8 | 14 | $19

1401 N. Ashland Ave. (Blackhawk St.), 773-486-7427

■ "Good ribs fast – 'nuff said" gush grandiloquent groupies of this casual Wicker Park BBQ, who also pen poems to its "great sandwiches", compose arias in honor of its "fine chicken" and give glory to its "good sides"; as reflected by the single-digit Decor score, "no atmosphere" might help explain why insiders rely on it "strictly for takeout."

Stir Crazy [S]   19 | 17 | 17 | $20

1186 N. Northbrook Court Mall (bet. Skokie Blvd. & Waukegan Rd.), Northbrook, 847-562-4800
Oakbrook Center Mall, 105 Oakbrook Ctr. (Rte. 83), Oak Brook, 630-575-0155
Woodfield Mall, 5 Woodfield Mall (Perimeter Dr.), Schaumburg, 847-330-1200

■ "Eating by the numbers has never been so fun" exclaim fans of these "attractive", mall-based "build-your-own" Asian stir-fry spots that are "good places to experiment"; "delicious, fresh ingredients" including "a large selection of vegetables and sauces" are "cooked fast" by a "friendly staff" that "handles crowds well" – it has to, as the "always-busy" scene is no wok in the park.

Strega Nona [S]   17 | 17 | 17 | $29

3747 N. Southport Ave. (bet. Grace St. & Waveland Ave.), 773-244-0990

◩ A "solid performer in the crowded Italian scene" is how pros portray this Lakeview spot offering "dependable" *paesano* cooking (as well as some American fare) and a "comfortable, low-lit setting" (with "nice outdoor seating") that's handy for pre- or post- "movie or theater" dining; cons contend that it "manages to lower the bar" with "so-so" eats and "spotty service", opting for it "only when in a hurry."

Su Casa 🆂 | 16 | 16 | 16 | $24 |

49 E. Ontario St. (bet. Rush St. & Wabash Ave.), 312-943-4041
❚ Friends of this "well-located" Near North Mexican vet say *si* to its "ample portions" of "authentic", "basic" south-of-the-border fare, "great margaritas" and "cute" environs, but enemigos insist that the "average" eats "fill the stomach but leave something to be desired", saying this old-timer "needs upgrading" across the board.

Sugar: A Dessert Bar ●🆂 | - | - | - | M |

108 W. Kinzie St. (bet. Clark St. & La Salle Blvd.), 312-822-9999
Sweet tooths unite at Jerry Suqi's candy-colored River North dessert mecca (which doubles as a nightclub after 11 PM); former Charlie Trotter's pastry whiz Christine McCabe Tentori sends out plate after wicked plate to a champagne-sipping, go-go-booted crowd perched on slick lollipop stools while spun-sugar neon buzzes overhead.

Sullivan's Steakhouse 🆂 | 21 | 20 | 20 | $43 |

415 N. Dearborn St. (Hubbard St.), 312-527-3510
244 S. Main St. (bet. Jackson & Jefferson Aves.),
Naperville, 630-305-0230
❚ It takes a lot to "survive in this steak town", and these links of a national chophouse chain "stand tall" ("yes, sir!") with "consistently" "great steaks" accompanied by "quality sides" such as "mushrooms to die for" served by "enthusiastic" staffers in a "dark", "clubby" setting brightened by the strains of "live jazz"; they're "pricey", but they "don't disappoint."

Suparossa 🆂 | 17 | 14 | 16 | $22 |

4256 N. Central Ave. (Cullom Ave.), 773-736-5828
7319 W. Lawrence Ave. (bet. Harlem & Oketo Aves.),
Harwood Heights, 708-867-4641 ●
6301 Purchase Dr. (Rte. 53), Woodridge, 630-852-1000
❚ Although it's a chain, this city and suburban Italian duo of "friendly and casual" "neighborhood" spots earns props as "favorite stops" serving "good pizzas" (both thick and thin) and other "standards"; "excellent delivery" is another plus; N.B. the Harwood Heights location only offers takeout under the Suparossa name.

Superdawg Drive-In ●🆂⇗ | 22 | 18 | 18 | $9 |

6363 N. Milwaukee Ave. (Devon Ave.), 773-763-0660
❚ "As much a part of Chicago as the Bears and the Daleys", this "kitschy, retro" Northwest Side "top dawg" is the No. 1 Bang for the Buck in our *Survey* and "has been there forever [actually, since 1948] for a reason": "the Rolls-Royce of hot dogs" is "hung on your window" by carhops (so "the decor

depends on your car"); P.S. loyalists love the "dancing mascots on the roof."

Sushi Naniwa S 23 | 15 | 20 | $28
607 N. Wells St. (bet. Ohio & Ontario Sts.), 312-255-8555
■ "No nonsense", "no attitude" – "just excellent", "creative and colorful" raw fish in "generous portions"; that's what keeps this River North Japanese joint jumping and makes "sitting at the sushi bar" with the "hip crowd" "a joy" (by the way, the "great specials" and "friendly service" don't hurt either); N.B. outdoor seating is now available.

Sushi Wabi S 24 | 19 | 18 | $33
842 W. Randolph St. (bet. Green & Peoria Sts.), 312-563-1224
☑ A "real scene" awaits at this "so-cool-even-the-fish-wear-black" West Loop raw-fin-fare affair where "fresh, high-end" seafood that's "a cut above" is sliced by knife-wielding "artists" then served in a "loud", "industrial" setting resembling "an after-hours club" – "complete with DJ"; if you can "ignore the attitude" from the "know-it-all staff", this place will "make you fall in love with sushi again."

Takkatsu S – | – | – | M
45 Green Bay Rd. (Scott Ave.), Winnetka, 847-784-9031
Distinguishing itself from the tidal wave of sushi spots, this North Shore sophomore specializes in tonkatsu, a breaded pork cutlet popular in its native Japan but less-known stateside, as well as beef, chicken, shrimp and cheese versions of its signature dish, curried pork and pork skewers, and more recognizable Japanese fare such as, yes, the ubiquitous raw fish.

TALLGRASS S 27 | 25 | 27 | $63
1006 S. State St. (10th St.), Lockport, 815-838-5566
■ Diners deem it "worth the trip" to this "small", "romantic" Southwest Suburban New French in the "lovely canal town" of Lockport, where chef Robert Burcenski "continues to amaze" with his prix fixe menus of "creative", "serious" fare highlighted by "innovative pairings" and "gorgeous presentations"; the "reserved and understated space" as well as "excellent" service contribute to the "world-class" experience; N.B. jacket and reservations required.

Tango Sur S 20 | 14 | 17 | $24
3763 N. Southport Ave. (Grace St.), 773-477-5466
■ "In a city known for great steakhouses", the "excellent Argentinean beef" served at this "Lakeview hideaway" BYO cow palace is "something different" that "aims to please" with "cattle-ranch-size portions" of "awesome" meat, "don't-miss empanadas and flan"; "friendly, helpful" service and "great prices" are added bonuses and help excuse the "intimate" digs (read: "close quarters") and "long waits"; N.B. live tango music on Wednesdays.

Tapas Barcelona 🆂
19 | 18 | 17 | $26

1615 Chicago Ave. (bet. Church & Davis Sts.), Evanston, 847-866-9900

■ "So many choices" of "good cheap eats" are a "fun way to try new things" at Evanston's "authentically Spanish" tapas "hot spot" and "great date place"; though sometimes a bit "noisy", its transporting Iberian ambiance nevertheless provides a "relaxing atmosphere in which to enjoy your meal", whether inside or out in the "wonderful garden."

Tarantino's 🆂
20 | 19 | 20 | $32

1112 W. Armitage Ave. (Seminary St.), 773-871-2929

■ Hitting the Lincoln Park "trifecta of food, atmosphere and service", this "classy" "joint" wins praise from loyal locals for its "light", "flavorful" Italian fare, "knowledgeable" staff and "cozy", "romantic" ambiance that makes it a popular "date place"; N.B. outdoor seating is now available.

Tasting Room, The ●
▽ 19 | 22 | 21 | $28

1415 W. Randolph St. (Ogden Ave.), 312-942-1212

■ Aficionados aver "you can't beat" this Market District wine bar for an "impressive list" of vintages (including 110 by-the-glass pours) complemented by "great cheese and charcuterie plates" and a "limited menu" of New American appetizers and desserts; the "comfortable", "loftlike" setting ("love the sofas") offers "romantic skyline views", creating a "cozy environment."

Tavern
▽ 20 | 22 | 23 | $40

(fka Tavern in the Town)
519 N. Milwaukee Ave. (bet. Cook Ave. & Lake St.), Libertyville, 847-367-5755

■ "A little gem of a place on a busy street" in Northwest Suburban Libertyville, this "lovely", "popular" Contemporary American "continues to please consistently" with "excellent food" and a "good selection of wines by the glass" in a "gorgeous room" with "wonderful atmosphere"; N.B. next door, the casual, unrated Firkin offers a more Eclectic menu.

Tavern on Rush ●🆂
19 | 20 | 18 | $41

1031 N. Rush St. (Bellevue Pl.), 312-664-9600

🗷 A popular "people-watching" "meet market", this Gold Coast steakhouse has a "happening bar" and a "busy outdoor cafe" that tend to upstage the "lovely" upstairs dining room, as well as its "friendly" service and signature steaks, which garner only mixed reviews ("great" vs. "just ok"); detractors dismiss it as a "noisy tourist trap."

Tecalitlan ●🆂
19 | 14 | 16 | $18

1814 W. Chicago Ave. (Wood St.), 773-384-4285

■ "Consistently good" "down-home, authentic" Mexican cooking "you can't get anywhere else" — including "burritos as big as your head" and "high-quality steaks" — and "dangerous margaritas" help explain why this Ukrainian Village Mexican is "always busy"; while a few banditos bellyache that it's "cheap, and you get what you pay for", defenders counter "value, value, value."

Tempo ◐🅂⌿   18 12 16 $15
6 E. Chestnut St. (State St.), 312-943-4373
■ "Everyone goes" to this Gold Coast "Greek coffee shop" for breakfast at "any time of day", so "be prepared to wait in line" for "excellent omelets", "huevos rancheros that rock" and other "good, basic, cheap eats"; its "trendy location" and 24/7 hours make it "a great place to refuel after clubbing", though hopeful hangover healers won't hit upon hair-of-the-dog here – no liquor is served.

Thai Classic 🅂   ∇ 21 15 20 $18
3332 N. Clark St. (bet. Belmont Ave. & Roscoe St.), 773-404-2000
■ "The name says it all" crow cronies who clamor for the "consistently reliable", "moderately priced" fare on offer at this Thai pad in the heart of Lakeview, including "fabulous curries" and one of the "best buffets [at lunch on Saturdays and all day Sunday] in Chicago"; "kind, relaxed service" complements the "cozy atmosphere", which jurists gingerly suggest "could be slightly enhanced by better decor"; N.B. it's BYO.

Thai Little Home Café 🅂   ∇ 22 12 19 $18
4747 N. Kedzie Ave. (Lawrence Ave.), 773-478-3944
■ A "dependable" "favorite" on the Northwest Side, this "consistent" BYO performer offers "wonderful", inexpensive Thai dishes, and regulars recommend the "lunch buffet feast" (which doubles as weekend brunch) as a "great way to taste different dishes"; it may not be much in the looks department, but "friendly service" makes it feel like a little home of your own.

Thai Pastry 🅂   22 13 18 $17
4925 N. Broadway St. (bet. Argyle St. & Lawrence Ave.), 773-784-5399
■ "Top-notch", "authentic and fresh" Thai dishes exhibiting "flavor and creativity" are the draw at this "friendly", "delightful", "inexpensive little gem" in Uptown; some say "the name is deceiving" (though there is a pastry case, "they are not known for it"), others that the "storefront" setting and "bright dining room" are "bleak", but advocates argue "what it lacks in ambiance it more than makes up for in the kitchen"; N.B. sidewalk seating is now available.

Thai Star Cafe 🅂   17 9 14 $17
660 N. State St. (Erie St.), 312-951-1196
◪ Star-gazers who favor this River North "hole-in-the-wall" say they "don't go for" the venue but for the "good-value", "reliable Thai" cooking; foes, however, can't "ignore" the

"drab exterior", "cramped", "tired-looking" and even housekeeping-challenged interior, "unbearably slow service" and "unappetizingly served" "boring fare."

Three Happiness ◐ S — | — | — | M
209 W. Cermak Rd. (Wentworth Ave.), 312-842-1964
"Adventurous offerings" of dim sum from the "rolling tables" are a daily draw at this small Chinatown storefront, as well as "very good", "cheap" Szechuan seafood; cognoscenti counsel "disregard the decor" – or "take it to go"; N.B. no relation to New Three Happiness (its former sibling) on South Wentworth Avenue.

302 WEST 25 | 25 | 24 | $49
302 W. State St. (3rd St.), Geneva, 630-232-9302
■ "If this place were on the Near North Side, you wouldn't be able to get in" boast boosters of Joel Findlay's "first-class" Contemporary American in the Western Suburbs, a "longtime favorite" for its "wonderful, inventive, always-changing menu" and "great selection of small-provider wines" "served with care" in a "beautiful, gracious dining room" set in a former bank; P.S. "they understand that desserts are supposed to be fun."

312 Chicago S 20 | 18 | 19 | $36
Hotel Allegro, 136 N. La Salle St. (Randolph St.), 312-696-2420
◪ Named after the city's area code, this "jewel" in the Loop's Hotel Allegro connects with many surveyors thanks to chef Dean Zanella's "damn good", "interesting" Italian-inspired American cuisine, served in a "pleasant" setting suitable for "power breakfasts", "business lunches" or "pre-theater dining"; critics, however, are hung up on the "inattentive" service and "noisy, frenetic" scene.

Thyme S 22 | 21 | 20 | $42
464 N. Halsted St. (Grand Ave.), 312-226-4300
◪ Fans rave over this "trendy", "out-of-the-way" Near West French–New American production thanks to chef-owner John Bubala's "creative" and "consistent" cooking seasoned with "subtle and sensuous flavor infusions", as well as its "lovely" interior and "romantic courtyard" that's "fabulous" in the summer; foes, however, have no time for the "noisy" scene and "overpriced" menu.

Tiffin S 22 | 17 | 18 | $23
2536 W. Devon Ave. (Maplewood Ave.), 773-338-2143
■ It's "Indian at its best" declare devotees describing this "elegant" establishment on the Northwest Side, where an "abundant" selection of "authentic", "flavorful" dishes is served in "classy", "fancy" digs; the "attentive and friendly" owner Jagbish Khatwani's "pride in his restaurant is a joy for patrons" and a big reason why many say it's the "clearly superior choice on the Devon strip."

Tilli's S
16 | 19 | 17 | $22

1952 N. Halsted St. (bet. Armitage Ave. & Willow St.),
773-325-0044

◪ It gets "loud and crowded" at this "friendly, casual"
Lincoln Park "after-work" spot that's "great for drinks" and
"people-watching", sporting a "cozy" setting, complete
with fireplace, patio and window seats that are "ideal
for couples"; the "diverse" Eclectic menu elicits mixed
responses ("decent", "different", "blah"), which is why
some skeptics just "get drinks and skip the food."

Tin Fish S
– | – | – | M

Cornerston Ctr., 18201 S. Harlem Ave. (183rd St.), Tinley Park,
708-532-0200

They're serious about their seafood at this comfy Southwest
Suburban spot, where a lip-smacking list of fresh shellfish
and fin-fare preparations (you can build your own entrée
by selecting a species, a treatment, and a cooking style) is
paired with a reasonably-priced wine list in an atmosphere
of underwater whimsy (the space is festooned with colorful
tin fish); N.B. the selection of landlubber items is limited.

Tizi Melloul S
21 | 25 | 21 | $35

531 N. Wells St. (Grand Ave.), 312-670-4338

■ You "feel like you've stepped into another world" upon
entering this "sultry", "spectacular" River North Med
specialist (don't miss the "round room" with "pillow seating"
that's "wonderful for groups of friends"); after a gradual
cuisine shift, the menu still shows signs of its original
Moroccan influences, offering "distinctive flavors" that
are "a playground for your taste buds"; N.B. the Sunday-
night belly dancer survived the concept change.

Toast S
20 | 15 | 15 | $15

2046 N. Damen Ave. (Dickens Ave.), 773-772-5600
746 W. Webster Ave. (Halsted St.), 773-935-5600

◪ The toast of the town for its "large portions and crazy
combinations", including the "don't-miss mascarpone-
stuffed French toast" and "mouthwatering 'crabby eggs
Benedict'", this "funky" duo of "urban" "breakfast and
lunch joints" is "worth getting up and standing in line" for
declare diurnal devotees; "hour-long waits" and "cranky
service", though, burn crusty critics.

Tokyo Marina S
∇ 22 | 12 | 16 | $21

5058 N. Clark St. (Carmen Ave.), 773-878-2900

■ There's "never a wait" for a slip at the dock of this
Andersonville "sushi dive" where finatics moor themselves
at the bar then plunge into "fresh, yummy" fish, as well as
other "reliable and tasty" Japanese dishes on the menu;
"the price is right", with "generous portions" ensuring "good
value", and the "chefs will accommodate fussy diners",
which is typical of the "friendly service."

Tombo Kitchen S
– – – M
3244 N. Lincoln Ave. (Melrose St.), 773-244-9885
Bringing trendy sushi to Lakeview, this hip spot is a lively setting for reasonably-priced creations by some serious sushi chefs (especially informative if you sit at the hammered copper sushi bar); the raw and the cooked Japanese fare are presented with panache in a modern atmosphere dominated by a padded orange wall, colorful artwork and TVs replaying the house action; N.B. they plan to keep their BYO policy after they receive their impending liquor license.

Tomboy S
20 18 18 $32
5402 N. Clark St. (bet. Balmoral Ave. & Clark St.), 773-907-0636
■ "Interesting" Eclectic fare, "pleasant decor" and "fun", "accommodating" service draw a "hip crowd" to this "urban", "gay-friendly" spot in Andersonville; while critics throw up their hands at some "hit-or-miss" cooking and a "crowded" dining room that "offers charm but is noisy", stalwarts hang in there for the ambiance and "great value"; N.B. the ratings may not reflect a post-*Survey* change in ownership.

Tommy Nevin's Pub ●S
17 16 17 $21
1450 Sherman Ave. (Lake St.), Evanston, 847-869-0450
■ "Northwestern students and locals" alike hie to this "casual" Evanston pub whenever "they're feeling Irish" or just in the mood for "beers by the pint and bar food"; still, the "authenticity" of this Gaelic-American spot is questioned by purists who would prefer "a little more [of the former] and a little less [of the latter]; N.B. a change in ownership was planned at press time.

Topo Gigio Ristorante S
21 18 19 $31
1516 N. Wells St. (bet. Division St. & North Ave.), 312-266-9355
■ Advocates avow there's nothing mousy about this "tried and true" Old Town "Chicago tradition", a "cozy" yet "high-energy" stop for "satisfying, good Italian food" ("splendid osso buco", "yummy pastas"), served in a "busy and boisterous room" and a "great outdoor area" that's a "must in summer"; while most approve of the "no-nonsense" service, a few find it borderline "rude."

TOPOLOBAMPO
27 24 25 $50
445 N. Clark St. (bet. Hubbard & Illinois Sts.), 312-661-1434
■ A "real star in a big food town", this River North Mexican (Frontera Grill's "upscale cousin") "continues to shine" thanks to "serious", "daring" cuisine admirers insist is "better than any in Mexico"; chef Rick Bayless dazzles fans with his "exciting treatment" of "the best ingredients", while "professional service", "beautifully artistic decor" and a "good tequila selection and wine list" contribute to an "all-around outstanding" experience.

Tournesol 🟦   – | – | – | M
4343 N. Lincoln Ave. (bet. Cullom & Montrose Aves.), 773-477-8820
Now in its second year, this storefront bistro in Lincoln Square boasts a menu in keeping with its casual yet traditional decor, emphasizing classic dishes at moderate prices, such as *salade lyonnaise*, steak frites and braised rabbit; as befits a restaurant named for the sunflowers that dot the Gallic countryside, its accessible wine list focuses on French country vintages.

Trader Vic's   17 | 20 | 18 | $33
Palmer House Hilton, 17 E. Monroe St. (bet. State St. & Wabash Ave.), 312-917-7317
☑ "Where's the Rat Pack?" wonder wags about this "retro-funk" Polynesian in the Loop's Palmer House Hilton, where the "hokey '50s decor and drinks" are "so unhip they're hip"; while pros protest "don't pupu" the "unappreciated fantasy food" that's "much better than its reputation", hecklers hiss at the "hodgepodge" of "hotel-ish fare."

Trattoria Gianni 🟦   20 | 16 | 21 | $32
1711 N. Halsted St. (bet. North Ave. & Willow St.), 312-266-1976
■ "Never a disappointment", this "unassuming" Lincoln Park "sleeper" reminds regulars of "a lovely little trattoria in Rome" with its "fresh, simple, unpretentious Italian fare"; "convenient to the North Side theater row", it's a natural for "pre-Steppenwolf" dining, and though it offers a "fabulous brunch" on Sundays, some pastaphiles "wish it were open for lunch" during the week.

Trattoria No. 10   22 | 20 | 21 | $36
10 N. Dearborn St. (bet. Madison St. & Washington Blvd.), 312-984-1718
■ Surveyors say this "basement beauty" of an "efficient trattoria" is "a staple in the Loop business and theater district" for "tasty" "classic Italian, done well" and served in a "comfortable cave atmosphere" that's "a refuge for romance and rotini" ("try the homemade butternut squash ravioli" or the "bargain bar buffet"); N.B. the Food rating may not reflect a post-*Survey* chef change.

Trattoria Roma 🟦   ▽ 20 | 16 | 20 | $29
1535 N. Wells St. (bet. North Ave. & Schiller St.), 312-664-7907
■ This "quaint", time-honored Old Town Italian serves up "quality", "delicious" fare with "classic flavors", as well as "down-home feel" and "informal" service; it's "not pretentious or overpriced", which is why it's been a "favorite" "through the years."

Trattoria Trullo 🟦   – | – | – | M
1700 Central St. (Eastwood Ave.), Evanston, 847-570-0093
Named for the conical limestone houses of Puglia, this popular Southern Italian in the Northern Suburbs focuses on

refined renditions of the region's hearty cuisine paired with a Boot-centric wine list that features several varieties from that area; the atmosphere of romantic rusticity carries throughout, from the interior frescoes to the stucco facade and sidewalk cafe.

Tre Kronor S

23 17 21 $18

3258 W. Foster Ave. (bet. Kedzie & Kimball Aves.), 773-267-9888

■ "You'll think you're in Sweden" at this "bright, sunny" storefront BYO spot on the Northwest Side serving "a variety of Scandinavian specialties" at "reasonable prices"; admirers muse "this is what they mean when they say 'a cozy little place'", with "homestyle" "comfort food", a "family atmosphere" and "wonderful service"; P.S. "the trolls dancing on the walls are not to be missed."

TRIO S

28 25 28 $74

Homestead Hotel, 1625 Hinman Ave. (Davis St.), Evanston, 847-733-8746

■ "The French Laundry comes to Evanston" in the esteemed personage of toque Grant Achatz (ex Thomas Keller's California legend), whose "finesse, bravado and quality" make him "as original a [chef] as you'll ever find"; satisfied supplicants say his "exceptional cuisine" is "as serious as the setting" of this "true foodies' restaurant", while "inspired wine pairings" and "knowledgeable service" add to the "near-perfect experience", after which "all you can think about is doing it again."

TRU

27 27 27 VE

676 N. St. Clair St. (bet. Erie & Huron Sts.), 312-202-0001

■ Rick Tramonto and Gale Gand "add humor and surprise to elegant cuisine" in their Streeterville Lettuce Entertain You partnership, a haven "for serious foodies" voted No. 1 for Popularity in our *Survey* where "splendid [New French] food and synchronized service" are showcased in a "spartan setting" and at a "leisurely pace" (with "dinner lasting two to four hours", depending on your choice of prix-fixe or "collection" menus); even "demanding diners" concede its "excellence" is "worth the astronomical price."

Tsunami S

20 18 18 $33

1160 N. Dearborn St. (Division St.), 312-642-9911

◪ Bucking the tide of "average Japanese restaurants", this "classy" Gold Coaster does "sexy sushi" served in a "dark", "clublike" setting with a "swanky sake lounge" upstairs; champions praise the "consistently good" seafood that "can make anyone a [raw-fish] eater", but boat-rockers retort it's really "for those looking to be seen", and wallet-watchers are wiped out by tabs that are "way too high"; N.B. the Food score may not reflect the post-*Survey* arrival of chef Kenju Horikoshi.

Tucci Benucch [S] 17 | 18 | 18 | $26

900 N. Michigan Ave., 5th fl. (Walton St.), 312-266-2500

◪ In the Bloomie's building, this "cute", "rustic" Gold Coast Italian eatery serves "consistent" "standard Italian fare" that's "better than average mall food"; although the digs look a bit "tired" and are often "crowded", the "casual" vibe and "fast" service make it an attractive stop "after a movie or shopping" to "escape the Michigan Avenue madness."

Tufano's Vernon Park Tap [S]💳̸ 21 | 15 | 19 | $23

1073 W. Vernon Park Pl. (bet. Harrison & Racine Sts.), 312-733-3393

■ "Hidden" away in Tri-Taylor, this timeless "favorite of locals and politicians" is a "fun, raucous, truly family-style" Southern Italian "joint" serving "inexpensive, no-frills" red-sauce fare "as old-school as can be" in a "noisy" room adorned with "celebrity pictures"; "brisk service" and "low prices" enhance the classic "Chicago atmosphere."

Tuscany [S] 21 | 19 | 20 | $33

3700 N. Clark St. (Waveland Ave.), 773-404-7700
1014 W. Taylor St. (Morgan St.), 312-829-1990
1415 W. 22nd St. (Rte. 83), Oak Brook, 630-990-1993
550 S. Milwaukee Ave. (bet. Dundee & Hintz Rds.), Wheeling, 847-465-9988

Tuscany Café [S]

Shops at North Bridge, 520 N. Michigan Ave. (bet. Grand Ave. & Ohio St.), 312-595-9090

◪ Phil Stefani's "tried-and-true" Little Italy original and its spin-offs "consistently" deliver "robust dining" and "a good variety" of Northern Italian fare that's "not fancy but reliable"; the convivial proceedings can get "noisy" when the room gets "crowded", and some penne-pinchers pan the "pricey" tabs; P.S. the cafe's "fast-food" offerings "don't reflect the full-scale restaurant."

Twin Anchors [S] 21 | 14 | 17 | $25

1655 N. Sedgwick St. (bet. Eugenie St. & North Ave.), 312-266-1616

■ "Chicago's best ribs" ("huge, tender slabs" with "zesty sauce") continue to make this "fun, retro" stalwart in Old Town a "family tradition" ("my parents went there as kids"); the "homey", "classic tavern setting" is "quintessentially 'local'", and while there's "always a wait", service that's "surprisingly good, given the crowds", keeps things on an even keel; still, cagey connoisseurs prefer to "take out."

Twist [S] ▽ 22 | 19 | 18 | $25

3412 N. Sheffield Ave. (Clark St.), 773-388-2727

■ "Killer tapas" and "tasty sangria" make this "cute" Lakeview two-year-old a "new favorite" of in-the-know worshipers who warrant "everything on the [Spanish-Eclectic] menu is great" and wonder "why everyone doesn't know about this place"; still, they advise "getting there early", as the space is "tight" and "there's no waiting area"; N.B. outdoor seating is an added twist.

Twisted Lizard, The S 17 15 16 $19
1964 N. Sheffield Ave. (Armitage Ave.), 773-929-1414
◪ Fans flock to this "noisy", "local" Lincoln Park "basement" (with tables outside too) for "fresh, fun Mexican" eats, including "holy *mole*" and "righteous margaritas" (try the "worthwhile cranberry version"); cynics snipe at the "so-so" sustenance, however, and sneer "go for the drinks and the scene" then "leave when you want to eat"; N.B. the Decor score may not reflect a post-*Survey* remodeling.

Twisted Spoke ◐S 18 16 16 $16
501 N. Ogden Ave. (Grand Ave.), 312-666-1500
■ For "yuppies who like to live dangerously", this "safe" but "grungy" Near West hog heaven with a "biker-bar motif", "rooftop picnic tables" and an American pub-grub menu "reflects a sassy attitude"; while some warn it's "not for the faint of heart", a few wild ones dismiss the "faux" scene with "stick-on tattoos in a vending machine" as "'trendy meets Harley'"; N.B. a Wrigleyville branch is slated to open in 2003.

Udupi Palace S ▽ 25 11 18 $16
2543 W. Devon Ave. (bet. Maplewood Ave. & Rockwell St.), 773-338-2152
■ "Dive" digs on Devon don't deter diehards from delighting in the "delicious Indian vegetarian fare" that's "cheap and really great" at this "no-frills" storefront sibling of the more elegant top-rated Tiffin; the mostly "conventional" cuisine contains "a few innovations", and the kitchen is accommodating to spice girls and boys – "if you ask for it hot, they provide"; N.B. a Schaumburg branch is slated to open in 2003.

Uncle Julio's Hacienda S 17 16 15 $21
855 W. North Ave. (Clybourn Ave.), 312-266-4222
◪ "Big portions" of "cheap", "consistently good" Mexican fare served in a "loud, fun atmosphere" have supporters saying this Lincoln Park link in a national chain is "great for kids" and big folks alike; still, snipers snort it's "*nada especial*", sneering at what they say is "Americanized food" "for the undiscriminating", while the impatient cry uncle over the "long waits."

Uncommon Ground S ▽ 17 16 16 $14
1214 W. Grace St. (Clark St.), 773-929-3680
■ With its "good, healthy" Eclectic menu full of "vegetarian options", this "cool, casual" Wrigleyville local has grown beyond its coffeehouse roots into a "perfect hangout" for the "granola crowd" (though java junkies advise "don't

pass up the bowl of latte"); "great live musicians" add allure to the "fantastic, warm atmosphere", and there's outdoor seating in summer; N.B. the Decor score may not reflect an expansion in progress at press time.

Va Pensiero [S] 24 | 22 | 23 | $44

Margarita Inn, 1566 Oak Ave. (Davis St.), Evanston, 847-475-7779

■ A "special place" in Evanston's Margarita Inn, this "relaxing" "elegant eatery" pairs "outstanding", "creative", "contemporary fare" from The Boot with a "top-notch" "all-Italian wine list", "sophisticated decor" and "impeccable service"; better still, despite the somewhat "formal" feel there's "virtually no snob factor"; P.S. "don't miss" the "terrific monthly wine dinners."

Via Carducci [S] 23 | 18 | 20 | $25

1419 W. Fullerton Ave. (Southport Ave.), 773-665-1981

■ A "great Italian" in Lincoln Park, this "casual dining favorite" "keeps getting better" at serving "big portions" of "fresh", "good, basic" fare such as "wonderful pastas" and "gnocchi like silk" that taste like they were made from someone's "mother's recipes"; the prices are "reasonable", and the setting is as "romantic" as a "hole-in-the-wall" can be (it's handy for takeout too).

Via Emilia Ristorante [S] ▽ 20 | 18 | 18 | $31

2119 N. Clark St. (bet. Dickens & Webster Aves.), 773-248-6283

◪ Specializing in the cuisine of the under-exposed Emilia-Romagna region, this "cozy" Lincoln Park Italian offers "tasty, affordable" fare, including "excellent pastas" and "wonderful salads", with an emphasis on seafood (both in its specials and its risottos); the "enthusiastic" staff of native *paesani* enhances the "authentic" ambiance, but opinions of the service range from "ok" to "spotty."

Via Veneto [S] 20 | – | 20 | $29

6340 N. Lincoln Ave. (Drake St.), 773-267-0888

■ "Big portions" of "consistently good", "well-prepared" "classic Italian" dishes (including "outstanding pastas" and "great risottos") are offered with "warm service" from an "attentive" staff at this "authentic" "favorite" on the Northwest Side; P.S. those who complained of "tight seating" and a "small dining room" "needing work" may be pleased by its post-*Survey* move to new digs.

Viceroy of India [S] 20 | 15 | 17 | $22

2520 W. Devon Ave. (bet. Campbell & Maplewood Aves.), 773-743-4100

555 Roosevelt Rd. (Highland Ave.), Lombard, 630-627-4411

■ "Delicious Indian" dishes delight diners at these "great" Northwest Side and West Suburban "standbys" that stand out with their "authentic" "tandoori cooking", "superb vindaloos made to order" and "fast, bountiful lunch buffets";

though a trifle dated, the city location's decor is slightly more "upscale" than the Devon Avenue standard, and insiders warn that both can "get crowded on weekends."

Victory's Banner **S** ▽ 19 | 13 | 17 | $13
2100 W. Roscoe St. (Hoyne Ave.), 773-665-0227
■ "Don't let the Midwestern waitresses in saris scare you away from" this "soulful" Roscoe Village vegetarian advise advocates; while the "meditative atmosphere" can be "annoying" to the unconverted, "pure, tasty, healthful fare that's served with spirit" (though not with spirits – there's no alcohol or BYO) makes this "crazy little place" a winner in the eyes of many.

Village, The ● **S** 20 | 20 | 20 | $28
71 W. Monroe St., 2nd fl. (bet. Clark & Dearborn Sts.), 312-332-7005
■ A "vintage Chicago" landmark, this namesake located on the second floor of the Loop's venerable Italian Village (with Vivere at ground level and La Cantina Enoteca underneath) is "still an old favorite" for "solid, traditional" Northern cuisine and "professional", "take-the-shirt-off-my-back service"; also, the "cozy", "quirky decor is always a hit with first-timers."

Vinci **S** 22 | 21 | 20 | $36
1732 N. Halsted St. (Willow St.), 312-266-1199
■ "A longtime, reliable pre- or post-theater" spot in Lincoln Park's Halsted corridor, this "quiet" Italian from chef Paul LoDuca (who also helms Adobo Grill) is "romantic and refined", with "delicious" and "unadorned food" that's "not overly expensive"; "Royal George and Steppenwolf" mavens recommend you "request a coveted window table" for its "great, uncrowded brunch" on Sundays.

Vinh Phat BBQ **S**⊄ – | – | – | I
4940 N. Sheridan Rd. (bet. Ainslie & Argyle Sts.), 773-878-8688
Mahogany-hued crisp-roasted ducks, quail and chickens hang in the window of this casual Uptown Chinese where a bountiful steam table features trays of duck feet, pig intestines and other stewed-until-ultra-tender vittles; there are only a few tables within its small space, so it's most popular as a place to pick up provender for a picnic or outdoor concert in the park.

Vive La Crepe **S** – | – | – | I
1565 Sherman Ave. (bet. Davis & Grove Sts.), Evanston, 847-570-0600
North Suburban Evanston's new crêperie poses the pertinent question 'if fondue is back, why not crêpes?', and answers it with a menu of 20-plus creations for lunch, dinner, dessert and weekend breakfast, plus updated bistro fare for the in-crêpe-ulous, all served in a cozy little storefront with an oh-so-French striped awning.

Vivere
23 | 23 | 22 | $43

71 W. Monroe St. (bet. Clark & Dearborn Sts.), 312-332-4040
■ The more contemporary counterpart of the Italian Village's old-guard dining duo (The Village above and La Cantina Enoteca below), this "wine lover's paradise" combines an "exceptional" 1,000-bottle list with "playful and tantalizing food" served by "knowledgeable" staffers amid "beautiful" "cosmic-trip decor" courtesy of Jordan Mozer; N.B. the Food score may not reflect the post-*Survey* arrival of chef Drue Kennedy (ex Meritage).

Vivo 🖪
20 | 20 | 19 | $36

838 W. Randolph St. (bet. Green & Peoria Sts.), 312-733-3379
◪ A pioneer of "the Randolph Street restaurant row", this "trendy" "hipsters' Italian" serves "good", "straightforward food" amid a "dark and mysterious" "scene"; it's "a great place to be alone with the one you love (or like)", unless you agree with those who find its fare "uninteresting" and its "crammed" room "too noisy"; P.S. the "outdoor summer seating offers a great view of the city."

Volare 🖪
22 | 17 | 21 | $32

201 E. Grand Ave. (St. Clair St.), 312-410-9900
■ The "reasonably priced", "solid offerings" of "classic" Italian fare at this "wonderful neighborhood restaurant" in Streeterville may be "nothing novel", but they are "hearty and tasty"; in fact, testifiers tout them as "red-sauce and garlic done with flair and sophistication" (and the "creamy pasta dishes are cholesterol heaven!"); it's considered a "good date place" even though it "gets loud and crowded."

Vong's Thai Kitchen 🖪
21 | 22 | 20 | $40

(fka Vong)
6 W. Hubbard St. (State St.), 312-644-8664
◪ The "reinterpretation" of this River North Lettuce Entertain You import, originally a spin-off of Jean-Georges Vongerichten's New York Vong, has surveyors seesawing: some "love the revamp", praising the "more accessible prices" of its still–"exotic and imaginative" Thai–New French fusion menu and the "great makeover" of its "dramatic" but now "cozier setting"; fans of the first version feel "disappointed", though, and wonder "why does everything have to be dumbed down?"

Walker Bros.
Original Pancake House 🖪
23 | 18 | 19 | $15

825 W. Dundee Rd. (bet. Arlington Hts. Rd. & Rte. 53), Arlington Heights, 847-392-6600
1615 Waukegan Rd. (bet. Chestnut & Lake Aves.), Glenview, 847-724-0220
620 Central Ave. (bet. Green Bay Rd. & 2nd St.), Highland Park, 847-432-0660

(continued)

(continued)
Walker Bros.
Original Pancake House
Lake Zurich Theatre Development, 767 S. Rand Rd. (Rte. 22),
Lake Zurich, 847-550-0006
200 Marriott Dr. (Milwaukee Ave.), Lincolnshire, 847-634-2220
153 Green Bay Rd. (bet. Central & Lake Aves.), Wilmette,
847-251-6000
■ For a "great breakfast any time of day", these North and Northwest Suburban "family"-"favorite" "institutions" "never disappoint", with "wonderful, filling and inexpensive treats" that are "worth the wait"; not only does their "legendary apple pancake live up to its rep" – "calling it a 'pancake' is like calling champagne a 'drink'" – but "there's real cream" for "your always-full cup" of "heavenly coffee."

Walter's 🅂   – | – | – | M
28 Main St. (Prairie Ave.), Park Ridge, 847-696-2992
A New American, this Northwest Suburban spot lists black bean soup, salmon in garlic-mashed potato crust, and chocolate chess tart among its house specialties; Decor highlights include a skylight, a stone balustrade and a spacious indoor garden; N.B. Sunday brunch is offered, and its market offers fine cheeses and other delectables.

Watusi ◑🅂   21 | 20 | 20 | $34
1540 W. North Ave. (Ashland Ave.), 773-862-1540
☒ The "high-design" home of a "hipster crowd", this Bucktowner puts "a creative, crazy mix" of "Caribbean flavors" into its New American cuisine; fans say the "daring menu works surprisingly well", but those who "can't comprehend the approach" propose that the "pricey" and "overly bizarre drinks" "are better than" the "too-inventive" food; N.B. name and DJs aside, there's no dance floor.

Wave ◑🅂   ▽ 20 | 22 | 17 | $41
W Chicago Lakeshore, 644 N. Lake Shore Dr. (Ontario St.),
312-255-4460
☒ Streeterville's "vibrant", "loud" "hot spot" in the W Chicago Lakeshore is a "way-cool scene with lots of beautiful people" in "terrific booths" surrounded by "hip", "modern decor" and eating "beautiful food" – namely, mod Med cuisine (some surfers say it's "wonderful", some suggest it "sounds better than it is"); for others, pluses are wiped out by a wave of service minuses; N.B. the Food score may not reflect a post-*Survey* chef change.

Weber Grill 🅂   18 | 16 | 17 | $30
Hilton Garden Inn, 539 N. State St. (Grand Ave.), 312-467-9696
2331 Fountain Sq. Dr. (Meyers Rd.), Lombard, 630-953-8880
920 N. Milwaukee Ave. (Lake Cook Rd.), Wheeling, 847-215-0996
☒ It's "fun to watch the chefs at work on the giant Webers" at these "relaxed" city and Suburban bastions of barbecuing

backed by the business behind those ubiquitous backyard bowl-bottomed briquette-burning braziers; still, many meat mavens maintain you might "do better" to "stay home and grill" such "standard fare" "yourself"; N.B. the Near North location opened post-*Survey*.

Webster's Wine Bar ●S   18 | 20 | 19 | $24

1480 W. Webster Ave. (bet. Ashland Ave. & Clybourn St.), 773-868-0608

■ A "sexy, cozy" haven in Lincoln Park's Clybourn corridor, this "unpretentious", "wonderful wine bar" is a "great date place" and a "favorite" "choice for meeting with friends"; "knowledgeable staffers" serve an "expanded appetizer menu" of "good" Eclectic fare "complementing" "fun flights" from the cellar; P.S. night-owls should note that both its dining room and patio are "open late."

West Town Tavern   – | – | – | M

1329 W. Chicago Ave. (Throop St.), 312-666-6175

Drew and Susan Goss, former owners of the shuttered Zinfandel, bring inexpensive contemporary comfort food to West Town via this gracious corner tavern; the dining room, formerly a walk-in cooler, has been warmed up with exposed brick, beaded lamps and sheer fabrics, while a sophisticated Old/New World wine list adds interest.

White Fence Farm S   19 | 17 | 19 | $20

Joliet Rd. (2 mi. south of I-55), Lemont, 630-739-1720

■ "Americana at its best", this Southwest "Suburban legend" remains a "classic" "family gathering place" for "comfort food" like "out-of-this-world fried chicken and corn fritters"; you get "so much for the price" and "sincere service" too, and if "no reservations" for parties under a dozen means "long waits", at least there are "interesting things to see", such as a "car museum and a small zoo."

Wiener's Circle, The ●S⌿   21 | 8 | 13 | $9

2622 N. Clark St. (Wrightwood Ave.), 773-477-7444

■ Dogged devotees worry it "would be an empty world without" this "classic" Lincoln Parker where "great char dogs and cheese fries" draw an "eclectic crowd of yuppies and street people"; the "tacky decor is part of the fun", but wags "warn" beware its "hilarious" "late-night" "shtick" – "deliberately rude staffers" serving up "four-letter words", "insults and fried food."

WILDFIRE S   23 | 21 | 20 | $33

159 W. Erie St. (bet. La Salle & Wells Sts.), 312-787-9000
235 Parkway Dr. (Milwaukee Ave.), Lincolnshire, 847-279-7900
Oakbrook Center Mall, 232 Oakbrook Ctr. (Rte. 83), Oak Brook, 630-586-9000

■ A River North success that's spread to the suburbs, these "casual, clubby" American steakhouses by the Lettuce

Entertain You group keep the "crowds waiting" for "hearty food" from "a wood-burning oven" then "accompanied by wine", "beer flights" and "better-than-sex desserts"; it can be "tough to get reservations", but the memories, like the "wildfire smell" "in your clothes", will linger.

Wishbone S | 20 | 15 | 17 | $19

3300 N. Lincoln Ave. (School St.), 773-549-2663
1001 W. Washington Blvd. (Morgan St.), 312-850-2663
■ "There's always something comforting to eat" at these "casual-but-trendy" chowhouses in the Lakeview and West Loop, where "integrated, happy crowds gorge on" "homey" "Southern- and Cajun-influenced" "diner food with a twist" served at "reasonable prices" amid "funky decor" featuring "crazy artwork" by chef Joel Nickson's talented mother, Lia; weekends are "hectic" – "everyone goes there" – so "be ready to wait."

Wolfgang Puck's Grand Café S | 19 | 19 | 18 | $28

Century Theatre Complex, 1701 Maple Ave. (Church St.), Evanston, 847-869-9653
◪ Proffered by the prolific Puck, this "casual" North Suburban New American in "the Century theater" complex is deemed an "enjoyable spot before or after the movies" by Evanston eaters who enjoy its "unique menu items" (no surprise, "the pizzas are the winners") and "amusing", "eye-catching decor"; those who find it less than grand complain it's "more hype" and "high prices" "than substance."

Xippo S | – | – | – | M

3759 N. Damen Ave. (Grace St.), 773-529-9135
An old-time Roscoe Village corner bar makes good, serving surprisingly sophisticated dinner entrées, updated bar-food classics and custom cocktails to the fresh-faced crowd that flocks there nightly to enjoy the plush red-velvet setting and smooth tunes.

Yoshi's Café S | 23 | 18 | 22 | $38

3257 N. Halsted St. (Belmont Ave.), 773-248-6160
■ Still "a favorite" after 20 years in its Lakeview locale, this French-Asian "fusion-accented bistro" "continues" to be "a perfect blend of East and West"; "inventive" chef Yoshi Katsumura's "innovative preparations" (regulars "love the tofu steak") and "delectable desserts" like "great chocolate espresso crème brûlée" are "served with flair" by a "gracious" staff in a "homey" and "comfortable", if "not elegant", setting.

Zaven's S | ▽ 23 | 21 | 24 | $47

260 E. Chestnut St. (bet. DeWitt Pl. & Lake Shore Dr.), 312-787-8260
■ Still "such a secret place", even after 28 years in its "small" Streeterville setting, this largely "undiscovered treasure" remains a "romantic" and "intimate winner";

though founder Zaven Kodjayan passed away in 2002, new owner Alain Sitbon (ex Carmine's and Rosebud) continues the tradition, overseeing a "seasoned staff" serving "well-prepared and -presented" traditional Continental cuisine with some French touches.

Zealous
22 | 23 | 21 | $62

419 W. Superior St. (bet. Chicago Ave. & New Orleans St.), 312-475-9112

■ The "hushed" "elegance" of its "gorgeous space" has all agreeing this River North New American "is one beautiful restaurant", but there accord ends; fans rate chef-owner Michael Taus "a genius" for the "daring mix of ingredients" in his "complex menu" of "exciting cuisine", but the "unimpressed" say the "overzealous kitchen" "tries too hard" with "off-the-wall recipes", adding the "astronomical prices" "are extreme" for such "small portions."

Zest S
– | – | – | E

Hotel Inter-Continental, 525 N. Michigan Ave. (Grand Ave.), 312-321-8766

This "sophisticated" Eclectic at the Mag Mile's Hotel Inter-Continental serves up a "winning combination" of "excellent service" and "expertly done", "picturesque dishes" – including "fabulous seafood" and tapas-style plates – by chef Josh Young (ex Marché); with floor-to-ceiling windows overlooking Michigan Avenue, its sleek bi-level space is a "quiet place to people-watch."

Zia's Trattoria S
24 | 20 | 22 | $32

6699 N. Northwest Hwy. (bet. Harlem & Touhy Aves.), 773-775-0808

■ The "memorable sauces" of its "creative pasta dishes" and the "vibrant flavors" of its "wonderful selection of fresh fish" plates render this "friendly, casual" Edison Park Italian a "shining light" that's "worth the trip from Downtown"; they still don't take reservations on weekends for fewer than five folks, but "the waits are more comfortable since the expansion" a few years back; P.S. it "won't break the bank."

Zoom Kitchen
17 | 12 | 14 | $13

1646 N. Damen Ave. (bet. Milwaukee & North Aves.), 773-278-7000 S
923 N. Rush St. (bet. Delaware Pl. & Walton St.), 312-440-3500 S
247 S. State St. (Jackson Blvd.), 312-377-9666

■ "When you want fresh and fast", zoom to one of these "casual", "affordable" American spots for "good food" done "your way" by "cheerful" staffers then served "cafeteria-style"; "fantastic sandwiches", "fabulous salads" and "mom's meatloaf and mashed potatoes" are topped off by "great chocolate-chunk cookies" – after all, "even Gen-Xers need comfort food sometimes"; N.B. the Damen Avenue branch was closed for renovation at press time.

Indexes

CUISINES
LOCATIONS
SPECIAL FEATURES

Indexes list the best of many within each category.

CUISINES

Afghan
Kabul House

American (New)
Allen's New Amer.
Ammo
Atwater's
Bandera
Bank Ln. Bistro
Bijan's Bistro
Billy Goat Tav.
Bin 36
Bistro Marbuzet
Blackbird
Black Duck Tav.
Blue Line
Boulevard Café
Brett's
Cab's Wine Bar
Café Absinthe
Cafe Selmarie
Caliterra
Charlie Trotter's
Chef's Station
Cielo
Cité
Cloud 9
Cosí
Courtright's
Currents
David's Bistro
Deleece
d.kelly
D'Vine Rest./Wine
Elaine
erwin
Feast
Frankie J's
Grand Lux Café
Green Dolphin St.
Green Room
Harry's Velvet Rm.
Jack's on Halsted
Jake Melnick's
Jane's
Jilly's Cafe
Kevin
Kit Kat Lounge
Leo's Lunchroom
Lovell's/Lake Forest

Lovitt
Magnolia Cafe
Masck
Menagerie
Meritage/Wine
Milk & Honey
mk
mk North
MOD.
Molive
Montage
Naha
Next Door Bistro
North Pond
Oceanique
One North
one sixtyblue
120 Ocean Place
Outpost
Pepper Lounge
Philander's
Phil & Lou's
Phlair
Prairie Moon
Printer's Row
Puck's at MCA
Rhapsody
Ritz-Carlton Café
Riva
Rivers
RL
Room, The
Rushmore
Saussy
Seasons
1776
She She
Signature Rm.
Spago
Spring
Stained Glass Wine
Tasting Rm.
Tavern
302 West
Thyme
Tomboy
Walter's
Watusi
West Town Tav.
Wolfgang Puck's

Xippo
Zealous
Zoom Kitchen

American (Regional)
Crofton on Wells
Flo
Glory
Jacky's Bistro
Marion St.
Meritage/Wine
Prairie
Red Star Tav.
Soul Kitchen

American (Traditional)
American Girl
Ann Sather
Athenian Rm.
Atwood Cafe
Avenue Ale
Bar Louie
Barn of Barrington
Berghoff
Billy Goat Tav.
Black Duck Tav.
Bongo Room
Boston Blackie's
Breakfast Club
BUtterfield 8
Charlie's Ale
Cheesecake Factory
Chicago Firehse.
Clubhouse
Cornelia's
Cullen's Bar
Dave & Buster's
Dell Rhea's Chicken
Domaine
Duke of Perth
ESPN Zone
Founders Hill Brew.
Four Farthings
Fox & Obel Cafe
Gale St. Inn
Genesee Depot
Glen Ellyn Sports
Goose Island Brew.
Green Door Tav.
Grill on the Alley
Hackney's
Hard Rock Cafe
Heartland Cafe

Hemmingway's
Ina's
Incognito
Inspiration Cafe
John Barleycorn
Johnny Rockets
Lawry's Prime Rib
Lou Mitchell's
L. Woods Tap
Mac's
Maison
Manny's Café
Marché
Margie's Candies
Mike Ditka's
Miller's Pub
Mill Race Inn
Millrose Rest./Brew
Misto
Mity Nice Grill
Moody's Pub
Mrs. Park's Tav.
Nookies
Northside Cafe
Oak Terrace
Oak Tree
Original Pancake
Pauline's
Petterino's
P.J. Clarke's
Public Landing
Rainforest Cafe
Raw Bar
Red Star Tav.
Ritz-Carlton Café
R.J. Grunts
Rock Bottom Brew.
Sarkis Grill
Seasons Café
Silver Cloud
Silver Palm
South Gate Cafe
Southport Saloon
South Water Kit.
Stanley's Kitchen
312 Chicago
Toast
Tommy Nevin's
Twisted Spoke
Walker Bros.
White Fence Farm
Wildfire

Cuisine Index

Argentinean
El Nandu
Tango Sur

Asian
Aria
BD's Mongolian BBQ
Big Bowl
Catch 35
Chinoiserie
Flat Top Grill
Hi Ricky
Joy Yee's Noodle
Karma
L'anne
Le Colonial
Lincoln Noodle
LuLu's Dim Sum
Monsoon
Pasteur
Penang
Penny's Noodle
Red Light
Shanghai Terrace
Stir Crazy
Yoshi's

Austrian
Lutz Continental

Bakeries
Albert's Café
Cafe Selmarie
Corner Bakery
Lutz Continental
Pierrot Gourmet
Pompei Bakery

Barbecue
BD's Mongolian BBQ
Bone Daddy
Carson's Ribs
Dick's Last Resort
Famous Dave's
Fireplace Inn
Freddy's Ribhse.
Joe's Be-Bop
Lem's BBQ
Merle's Smokehse.
Robinson's Ribs
Russell's BBQ
Smoke Daddy
Southport Saloon
Stevie B's

Twin Anchors
Vinh Phat BBQ
Weber Grill

Brazilian
Fogo de Chão
Sal & Carvao

Cafeterias
Fox & Obel Cafe
Manny's Café
Pompei Bakery
Zoom Kitchen

Cajun/Creole
Blue Bayou
Davis St. Fish
Dixie Kitchen
Heaven on Seven
House of Blues
Jambalaya's
Maple Tree Inn
Nola's 32nd Ward
Pappadeaux Seafood
Redfish
Wishbone

Caribbean
Calypso
Ezuli
Julio's Cocina
Watusi

Chinese
Ben Pao
Best Hunan
Dee's Mandarin
Emperor's Choice
Evergreen
Furama
Hai Yen
Happy Chef
Hong Min
Jia's
Lao Sze Chuan
Mars
New Three
Opera
Papajin
P.F. Chang's
Phoenix
Pine Yard
Ping Pong
Shine & Morida

Cuisine Index

Silver Seafood
Sixty-Five
Three Happiness
Vinh Phat BBQ

Coffee Shops/Diners
Cosí
Lou Mitchell's
Manny's Café
Milk & Honey
Nookies
Pauline's
Pompei Bakery
Salt & Pepper Diner
Sarkis Grill
Tempo

Colombian
Flying Chicken
La Fonda Latino
Las Tablas

Continental
Café La Cave
Incognito
Lutnia
Lutz Continental
Narcisse
Restaurant on Park
Trader Vic's
Zaven's

Cuban
Cafe Bolero
Cafe 28
Copa Cubana
Mar y Sol
Rancho Luna
Samba Room

Czech
Czech Plaza

Delis/Sandwich Shops
Bagel
Chicago Flat Sam.
Cold Comfort
Corner Bakery
Cosí
Max's
Mrs. Levy's Deli
Panera Bread
Potbelly Sandwich

Dim Sum
Furama
Happy Chef
Hong Min
LuLu's Dim Sum
New Three
Phoenix
Sixty-Five
Three Happiness

Eclectic
Aria
Big Bowl
Bite
Blind Faith
Cafe Nordstrom
CHIC Cafe
Chinoiserie
Coobah
Corner Bakery
Cru Cafè/Wine
Deleece
Eclectic
Feast
foodlife
Hilary's
Iggy's
Jane's
John's Place
Kitsch'n on Roscoe
La Mora
Lobby, The
Lucky Platter
Lula
Mysore Woodland
Narcisse
Ohba
Orange
Room, The
She She
Sinibar
Stained Glass Wine
Sugar: A Dessert Bar
Tilli's
Toast
Tomboy
Twist
Uncommon Ground
Webster's Wine
Xippo
Zest

Ecuadoran
La Peña

English
Red Lion Pub

Ethiopian
Addis Abeba
Ethiopian Diamond
Ethiopian Village
Mama Desta's

Fondue
Fondue Stube
Geja's Cafe

French (Bistro)
Albert's Café
Bank Ln. Bistro
Barrington Bistro
Bêtise
Bistro Banlieue
Bistro Campagne
Bistro Marbuzet
Bistro 110
Bistrot Margot
Bistrot Zinc
Bistro Ultra
Brasserie Jo
Café Bernard
Cafe Central
Café Le Loup
Cafe Matou
Cafe Pyrenees
Café 36
Cerise
Chez François
Chez Joel
Cochon Sauvage
Cyrano's Bistrot/Wine
D & J Bistro
Firefly
Fond de la Tour
Froggy's
Hemmingway's
KiKi's Bistro
La Crêperie
La Sardine
La Tache
Le Bouchon
Le Passage
Mon Ami Gabi
Ravinia Bistro
Retro Bistro

Tournesol
Yoshi's

French (Classic)
la petite folie
Les Deux Gros
Le Titi de Paris
Le Vichyssois
Oceanique

French (New)
Ambria
Atwater's
Avenues
Brasserie Jo
Café des Architectes
Carlos'
CHIC Cafe
Cité
D'Vine Rest./Wine
Escargot
Everest
Gabriel's
Jacky's Bistro
Jilly's Cafe
Kevin
L'anne
Le Colonial
Le Français
Les Nomades
Le Titi de Paris
Maison
Marché
Mimosa
NoMi
Oceanique
Pasha
Pasteur
Pili.Pili
Pump Room
Ritz-Carlton Din. Rm.
Tallgrass
Thyme
Trio
Tru
Vive La Crepe
Vong's

German
Berghoff
Edelweiss
Lutz Continental
Mirabell

Greek
Artopolis Bakery
Athena
Athenian Rm.
Costa's
Cross-Rhodes
Greek Islands
Noyes St.
Papagus Taverna
Parthenon
Pegasus
Roditys
Santorini

Hamburgers
Billy Goat Tav.
Boston Blackie's
Goose Island Brew.
Green Door Tav.
Hackney's
Johnny Rockets
Pete Miller's Sea/Steak
P.J. Clarke's
R.J. Grunts
Superdawg Drive-In
Twisted Spoke
Wiener's Circle

Hawaiian
Roy's

Hot Dogs
Fluky's
Gold Coast Dogs
Hot Doug's
Superdawg Drive-In
Wiener's Circle

Indian
Gaylord India
Indian Garden
Klay Oven
Monsoon
Moti Mahal
Mt. Everest
Mysore Woodland
Standard India
Tiffin
Udupi Palace
Viceroy of India

Irish
Abbey Pub
Chief O'Neill's
Fadó Irish Pub
Irish Oak
Tommy Nevin's

Italian
(N=Northern; S=Southern)
Angelina (S)
Anna Maria
Antico Posto
a tavola (N)
Aurelio's Pizza
Azuré
Babaluci
Bacchanalia (N)
Bacino's
Bada Bing
Balagio
Basta Pasta (S)
BeccoD'Oro
bella! Bacino's
Bella Notte (S)
Biaggio's
Bice Grill (N)
Bice Rist. (N)
Bruna's
Buca di Beppo (S)
Buona Terra (N)
Cafe Borgia
Café Luciano
Café Spiaggia
Caffé La Scala
Caliterra
Campagnola
Cannella's
Cantare (N)
Carlucci
Carmine's
Cielo (N)
Club Lucky (S)
Coco Pazzo (N)
Coco Pazzo Cafe (N)
Como
Convito Italiano
Cornelia's
Cristiano's (N)
Cucina Bella
Dave's (S)
Del Rio (N)
Dinotto (S)
EJ's Place (N)
Enoteca Piattini
Erie Cafe (N)
Father/Son Pizza

Cuisine Index

Ferrari
Filippo's (S)
Follia
Fortunato
Francesca's Tavola
Francesco's Hole (S)
Gabriel's
Giannotti Steak
Gilardi's
Gioco
Graziano's Pizza
Grotto
Harry Caray's
La Bella Winnetka
La Bocca della Verità
La Borsa (N)
La Cantina Enoteca
La Donna
La Gondola
La Mora
La Rosetta
La Scarola (N)
La Strada
Leona's (S)
Lexi's (S)
Lucca's
Lucia
Maggiano's (S)
Mario's
Merlo (N)
Mia Cucina
Mia Francesca
Mimosa
Misto
Next Door Bistro
Nick & Tony's
Noyes St.
O'Famé
O'Neil's (N)
Palaggi's
Pane Caldo (N)
Papa Milano (S)
Pasha
Pasta Palazzo
Phil Stefani's 437 Rush
Piazza Bella
Pizza Capri (N)
Pompei Bakery
Prego
Privata Café
Red Tomato
Riva

RoSal's
Rose Angelis
Rosebud on Rush
Sabatino's (N)
Salvatore's (N)
Scoozi!
Settimana Café
Sorriso
Sparacino
Spiaggia
Stefani's (N)
Strega Nona
Suparossa
Tarantino's (N)
Topo Gigio
Trattoria Gianni
Trattoria No. 10
Trattoria Roma
Trattoria Trullo (S)
Tucci Benucch
Tufano's Tap (S)
Tuscany
Va Pensiero
Via Carducci (S)
Via Emilia (N)
Via Veneto
Village (N)
Vinci
Vivere
Vivo
Volare
Zia's

Japanese
Akai Hana
Benihana
Bluefin
Bob San
Coast Sushi
CoCoRo/East
Hatsuhana
Heat
Itto Sushi
Jia's
Kamehachi
Kuni's
Kyoto
Lan Sushi/Lobster
Matsuya
Midori
Mirai Sushi
New Japan

Cuisine Index

Ohba
Oysy
Ping Pong
Ringo
Rise
Ron of Japan
Sai Café
Shabu-ya
Shine & Morida
Shiroi Hana
Starfish
Sushi Naniwa
Sushi Wabi
Takkatsu
Tokyo Marina
Tombo Kitchen
Tsunami

Jewish
Bagel
Manny's Café
Max's
Mrs. Levy's Deli

Korean
Amitabul
Chicago Kalbi
Jang Mo Nim
Jin Ju
Ping Pong
San Soo Gab San
Soju

Kosher
Shallots
Slice of Life

Lebanese
Maza

Malaysian
Penang

Mediterranean
Andies
Artopolis Bakery
Avenues
Café des Architectes
Cerise
Cousin's
Currents
Lucca's
Molive
Naha

Pili.Pili
Reza's
Sayat Nova
Shallots
Souk
Tizi Melloul
Wave

Mexican
Abril
Adobo Grill
Cafe 28
Chilpancingo
Chipotle
Dionises
Don Juan
El Jardin
El Presidente
Frontera Grill
Hot Tamales
Ixcapuzalco
Julio's Cocina
La Cazuela Mariscos
Lalo's
Las Bellas Artes
Lindo Mexico
Lupita's
Nuevo Leon
Platiyo
Salbute
Salpicón
Su Casa
Tecalitlan
Topolobampo
Twisted Lizard
Uncle Julio's

Middle Eastern
Andies
Hashalom
Maza
Old Jerusalem
Reza's
Souk

Moroccan
Tizi Melloul

Noodle Shops
Hi Ricky
Joy Yee's Noodle
Lincoln Noodle
Penny's Noodle

Nuevo Latino
Barro Cantina
Coobah
Mambo Grill
Mas
Nacional 27
Otro Mas
Rumba
Sabor
Samba Room

Persian
Noon-O-Kabab

Peruvian
Rinconcito Sudamer.

Pizza
Art of Pizza
Aurelio's Pizza
Bacino's
bella! Bacino's
Bricks
California Pizza
Chicago Pizza/Grinder
Dave's
Edwardo's
Father/Son Pizza
Giordano's
Graziano's Pizza
La Gondola
Leona's
Lou Malnati's Pizzeria
My Pie Pizza
Nancy's Pizza
Original Gino's
Piece
Pie Hole
Pizza Capri
Pizza D.O.C.
Pizzeria Uno
Ranalli's
Red Tomato
Trattoria Roma
Watusi
Wolfgang Puck's

Polish
Lutnia

Polynesian
Trader Vic's

Romanian
Little Bucharest

Russian
Russian Tea

Scottish
Duke of Perth

Seafood
Atlantique
Avenues
Biggs Steak/Wine
Bluepoint Oyster
Bob Chinn's Crab
Bubba Gump Shrimp
Cape Cod Rm.
Catch 35
Chinn's 34th St. Fish.
Cy's Crabhouse
Davis St. Fish
Dick's Last Resort
Don Roth's Blackhawk
Don's Fishmkt.
Dover Straits
Emperor's Choice
Froggy's
Glory
Grillroom
Half Shell
Hugo's Frog/Fish
Joe's Seafood
Keefer's
King Crab
La Cazuela Mariscos
Lan Sushi/Lobster
Lobby, The
McCormick & Schmick's
Nick's Fishmkt.
Nola's 32nd Ward
Oceanique
O'Neil's
120 Ocean Place
Pappadeaux Seafood
Parkers' Ocean
Raw Bar
Redfish
Santorini
Shark Bar
Shaw's Crab
Silver Seafood
Spring

Cuisine Index

Sullivan's Steak
302 West
Tin Fish

South American
El Nandu
Flying Chicken
Julio's Cocina
Las Tablas
Mas
Nacional 27
Otro Mas
Rinconcito Sudamer.
Tango Sur

Southern/Soul
Army & Lou's
BJ's Market
Dixie Kitchen
Edna's
Gladys Luncheon.
House of Blues
Joe's Be-Bop
Shark Bar
Soul Kitchen
Wishbone

Spanish
Arco de Cuchilleros
Cafe Ba-Ba-Reeba!
Café Iberico
Emilio's Tapas
Mesón Sabika
Tapas Barcelona
Twist

Steakhouses
Biggs Steak/Wine
Bogart's Charhse.
Capital Grille
Carmichael's Steak
Chicago Chop Hse.
Chicago Prime
Don Roth's Blackhawk
EJ's Place
Eli's Steaks
Erie Cafe
Gene & Georgetti
Giannotti Steak
Gibsons Steak
Gino's Steak
Grill on the Alley
Grillroom
Grotto

Harry Caray's
Keefer's
Kinzie Chophouse
Las Tablas
Lexi's
Magnum's Steak
Mike Ditka's
Morton's
Myron & Phil's Steak
Nick & Tony's
Nine
Palm
Pete Miller's Sea/Steak
Phil Stefani's 437 Rush
Rosebud Steak
Ruth's Chris
Sal & Carvao
Saloon Steak
Shaw's Crab
Shula's Steak
Smith & Wollensky
Sullivan's Steak
Tango Sur
Tavern on Rush
Wildfire

Swedish
Ann Sather
Tre Kronor

Thai
Always Thai
Amarind's
Arun's
Bangkok
Erawan Thai
Krungthep Thai
Mama Thai
Ping Pong
P.S. Bangkok
Roong
Ruby of Siam
Star of Siam
Thai Classic
Thai Little Home
Thai Pastry
Thai Star Cafe
Vong's

Turkish
A La Turka
Cousin's

Cuisine Index

Vegetarian
Blind Faith
Chicago Diner
Ethiopian Diamond
Ethiopian Village
Heartland Cafe
Mysore Woodland
Reza's

Slice of Life
Udupi Palace
Victory's Banner

Vietnamese
Hai Yen
Le Colonial
Pasteur

Location Index

LOCATIONS

CITY NORTH

Andersonville/Edgewater
Andies
Ann Sather
Atlantique
Charlie's Ale
Ethiopian Diamond
Francesca's Tavola
Hai Yen
Jin Ju
La Donna
La Tache
Moody's Pub
Pasteur
Pauline's
Reza's
Room, The
Tokyo Marina
Tomboy

Lakeview/Wrigleyville
Abbey Pub
Addis Abeba
A La Turka
Always Thai
Angelina
Anna Maria
Ann Sather
Arco de Cuchilleros
Art of Pizza
Bagel
Bangkok
Bar Louie
BD's Mongolian BBQ
Billy Goat Tav.
Blue Bayou
Brett's
Buca di Beppo
Café Le Loup
Cafe 28
Chicago Diner
Chipotle
Coobah
Cornelia's
Cousin's
Cullen's Bar
Cy's Crabhouse
Deleece
Duke of Perth

El Jardin
erwin
Ethiopian Village
Firefly
Flat Top Grill
Flying Chicken
Genesee Depot
Giordano's
Goose Island Brew.
Half Shell
Heaven on Seven
Hi Ricky
Hot Doug's
Irish Oak
Jack's on Halsted
John Barleycorn
Kit Kat Lounge
Kitsch'n on Roscoe
La Crêperie
La Mora
Leona's
Little Bucharest
Lucca's
Mama Desta's
Mars
Matsuya
Menagerie
Mia Francesca
Monsoon
Moti Mahal
Nancy's Pizza
Nookies
Orange
Original Gino's
Otro Mas
Outpost
Panera Bread
Penny's Noodle
Pepper Lounge
Piazza Bella
Pie Hole
Ping Pong
Pizza Capri
Platiyo
Potbelly Sandwich
Prego
P.S. Bangkok
Raw Bar

Heartland Cafe
La Cazuela Mariscos
Leona's
Lincoln Noodle

Uptown/Lincoln Square
Ammo
Andies
Bistro Campagne
Cafe Selmarie
Frankie J's
Furama
Inspiration Cafe

La Bocca della Verità
La Fonda Latino
Magnolia Cafe
Pizza D.O.C.
Ranalli's
San Soo Gab San
She She
Silver Seafood
Thai Pastry
Tournesol
Vinh Phat BBQ

CITY NORTHWEST

Bucktown
Ann Sather
Babaluci
Bar Louie
Bluefin
Café Absinthe
Cafe Bolero
Cafe Matou
Cloud 9
Club Lucky
Coast Sushi
Cold Comfort
Feast
Glory
Hi Ricky
Jambalaya's
Jane's
Le Bouchon
Margie's Candies
Meritage/Wine
My Pie Pizza
Northside Cafe
Papajin
Phlair
Piece
Rinconcito Sudamer.
Roong
Silver Cloud
Toast
Zoom Kitchen

Logan Square
Abril
Boulevard Café
Buona Terra
El Nandu
Father/Son Pizza

Ixcapuzalco
Lula

Northwest Side
Amitabul
Arun's
Chicago Kalbi
Chief O'Neill's
Father/Son Pizza
Gale St. Inn
Giordano's
Indian Garden
Jang Mo Nim
La Peña
Las Tablas
Leona's
Lutnia
Lutz Continental
Midori
Mirabell
Mysore Woodland
Nancy's Pizza
Noon-O-Kabab
Rancho Luna
Sabatino's
Suparossa
Superdawg Drive-In
Thai Little Home
Tiffin
Tre Kronor
Udupi Palace
Via Veneto
Viceroy of India

O'Hare Area/Edison Park
Basta Pasta
Berghoff
Billy Goat Tav.

Location Index

Greek Islands
Parthenon
Pegasus
Roditys
Santorini

Little Italy/ University Village

Caffé La Scala
Chez Joel
Francesca's Tavola
Lao Sze Chuan
Leona's
Pompei Bakery
RoSal's
Rosebud on Rush
Tufano's Tap
Tuscany

Market District

Azuré
Bar Louie
Bluepoint Oyster
d.kelly
Flat Top Grill
Follia
Hi Ricky
Ina's
La Sardine
Marché
Mar y Sol
one sixtyblue
Red Light
Rushmore
Starfish
Sushi Wabi
Tasting Rm.
Vivo

Near West

Bar Louie
Bella Notte

Billy Goat Tav.
Bone Daddy
Breakfast Club
Cannella's
Como
Giordano's
Iggy's
La Borsa
La Scarola
Misto
Pie Hole
Robinson's Ribs
Saussy
Silver Palm
Thyme
Twisted Spoke

Ukrainian Village

a tavola
Bite
Dionises
Fortunato
Leona's
Mac's
Tecalitlan
West Town Tav.

West Loop

Bacino's
Blackbird
Carmichael's Steak
Corner Bakery
Gold Coast Dogs
Green Room
Lexi's
Lou Mitchell's
Nine
Phil & Lou's
Potbelly Sandwich
Shark Bar
Wishbone

DOWNTOWN

Loop

Aria
Atwood Cafe
bella! Bacino's
Berghoff
Billy Goat Tav.
Catch 35
Chipotle

Corner Bakery
Cosí
Currents
Everest
Giordano's
Gold Coast Dogs
Grillroom
Hackney's
Heaven on Seven

Location Index

Chicago Firehse.
Edwardo's
Gioco
Manny's Café
Opera
Oysy
Prairie
Printer's Row
Zoom Kitchen

Streeterville
Bandera
BeccoD'Oro
Benihana
Bice Grill
Bice Rist.
Billy Goat Tav.
Boston Blackie's
Bubba Gump Shrimp
Caliterra
Cantare
Cape Cod Rm.
Capital Grille
Charlie's Ale
Cheesecake Factory
Chipotle
Cité
Coco Pazzo Cafe
Corner Bakery

Dick's Last Resort
Eli's Steaks
Emilio's Tapas
foodlife
Fox & Obel Cafe
Grill on the Alley
Hatsuhana
Indian Garden
Joe's Be-Bop
Kamehachi
Les Nomades
Mity Nice Grill
Mrs. Park's Tav.
Oak Terrace
Puck's at MCA
Ritz-Carlton Café
Ritz-Carlton Din. Rm.
Riva
Ron of Japan
Rosebud Steak
Saloon Steak
Shula's Steak
Signature Rm.
Tru
Volare
Wave
Zaven's

GOLD COAST/NEAR NORTH AREA

Gold Coast
Akai Hana
Albert's Café
Bar Louie
Big Bowl
Biggs Steak/Wine
Bistrot Zinc
Café des Architectes
Café Luciano
Café Spiaggia
Carmine's
Chicago Flat Sam.
Chipotle
Corner Bakery
Cru Café/Wine
Dave & Buster's
Domaine
Edwardo's
Gibsons Steak
Giordano's
Grotto

Hugo's Frog/Fish
Jake Melnick's
Johnny Rockets
Lan Sushi/Lobster
Le Colonial
Le Passage
Mario's
McCormick & Schmick's
Original Pancake
Papa Milano
P.J. Clarke's
Pump Room
Shanghai Terrace
Spiaggia
Tavern on Rush
Tsunami
Tucci Benucch
Zoom Kitchen

Near North
American Girl
Avenues

Location Index

SPECIAL FEATURES

(Restaurants followed by a † may not offer
that feature at every location.)

Additions
Allen's New Amer.
Ammo
Aria
Azuré
Bada Bing
Barro Cantina
Biggs Steak/Wine
Bijan's Bistro
Bistro Campagne
Blue Bayou
Blue Line
Boulevard Café
Buona Terra
Cafe Borgia
Café des Architectes
Caffé La Scala
Chicago Prime
Cloud 9
Coast Sushi
Coobah
Cristiano's
Currents
Dinotto
Dionises
d.kelly
Domaine
Enoteca Piattini
Escargot
Ferrari
Firefly
Flo
Fogo de Chão
Follia
Frankie J's
Glory
Grand Lux Café
Green Room
Grotto
Hemmingway's
Incognito
Inspiration Cafe
Jake Melnick's
Jambalaya's
Krungthep Thai
La Fonda Latino
Lalo's

La Tache
Lovitt
Lucia
Mar y Sol
Menagerie
Milk & Honey
Monsoon
Montage
Nola's 32nd Ward
Ohba
One North
Opera
Oysy
Philander's
Phil & Lou's
Phlair
Pili.Pili
Ping Pong
Platiyo
Prairie Moon
Privata Café
Rancho Luna
Raw Bar
Red Star Tav.
Rumba
Sal & Carvao
Sayat Nova
Shark Bar
Silver Palm
South Water Kit.
Starfish
Sugar: A Dessert Bar
Tin Fish
Tombo Kitchen
Trattoria Trullo
Vive La Crepe
Walter's
West Town Tav.
Xippo

Breakfast
(See also Hotel Dining)
Albert's Café
Ammo
Ann Sather†
Bin 36†
Bite

Blind Faith
Bongo Room
Breakfast Club
Cafe Selmarie
Chicago Diner
Corner Bakery†
David's Bistro
Fox & Obel Cafe
Heartland Cafe
Ina's
John's Place
Lou Mitchell's
Milk & Honey
Nookies
Oak Tree
Original Pancake†
Pauline's
Salt & Pepper Diner
Sarkis Grill
Tempo
Toast
Tre Kronor
Victory's Banner
Walker Bros.†
Wishbone

Brunch

Adobo Grill
Atwood Cafe
Avenues
Barn of Barrington
Bêtise
Biggs Steak/Wine
Bistro 110
Bistrot Margot
Bistrot Zinc
Bite
Bongo Room
Brett's
Cafe Selmarie
Cafe 28
Caliterra
Charlie's Ale†
Chef's Station
CHIC Cafe
Cité
Cochon Sauvage
Coobah
Deleece
erwin
Fortunato
Four Farthings
Frontera Grill

Glory
Heaven on Seven
House of Blues
Ina's
Jane's
John's Place
Kitsch'n on Roscoe
Las Bellas Artes
Lobby, The
Lula
Magnolia Cafe
Menagerie
Milk & Honey
MOD.
North Pond
Northside Cafe
Noyes St.
Oak Terrace
Ohba
Orange
P.J. Clarke's†
Platiyo
Privata Café
Pump Room
Ritz-Carlton Din. Rm.
R.J. Grunts
Salpicón
Seasons
Signature Rm.
Soul Kitchen
Tavern on Rush
312 Chicago
Twisted Spoke
Vinci
Wishbone

Buffet Served

(Check availability)
Bangkok
Barn of Barrington
Dell Rhea's Chicken
Dick's Last Resort
Edwardo's†
El Jardin
Ethiopian Village
Flat Top Grill
Furama†
Gaylord India
Giannotti Steak
Hackney's†
Hilary's
Indian Garden†
John Barleycorn†

Celebrity Chefs

(Chefs are listed under their primary restaurants)
Ambria, *Gabino Sotelino*
Arun's, *Arun Sampanthavivat*
Bistro 110, *Dominique Tougne*
Blackbird, *Paul Kahan*
Campagnola, *M. Altenberg*
Charlie Trotter's, *Charlie Trotter*
Crofton on Wells, *Suzy Crofton*
erwin, *Erwin Drechsler*
Escargot, *Eric Aubriot*

Special Feature Index

Everest, *Jean Joho*
Frontera Grill, *Rick Bayless*
Gioco, *Corcoran O'Connor*
Ixcapuzalco, *Geno Bahena*
Jack's on Halsted, *Jack Jones*
Keefer's, *John Hogan*
Kevin, *Kevin Shikami*
Le Bouchon, *J-C Poilevey*
Le Français, *Don Yamauchi*
Le Titi de Paris, *Pierre Pollin,*
  Michael Maddox
Le Vichyssois, *Bernard Cretier*
Mas, *John Manion*
mk, *Michael Kornick*
Nacional 27, *Randy Zweiban*
Naha, *Carrie Nahabedian*
NoMi, *Sandro Gamba*
North Pond, *Bruce Sherman*
one sixtyblue, *Martial Noguier*
Printer's Row, *Michael Foley*
Ritz-Carlton Din. Rm., *S. Stegner*
Salpicón, *Priscila Satkoff*
Spago, *François Kwaku-Dongo*
Spiaggia, *Tony Mantuano*
Spring, *Shawn McClain*
Tallgrass, *Robert Burcenski*
302 West, *Joel Findlay*
Thyme, *John Bubala*
Topolobampo, *Rick Bayless*
Trio, *Grant Achatz*
Tru, *Rick Tramonto, Gale Gand*
Wave, *Jason Paskewitz*
West Town Tav., *Susan Goss*
Zealous, *Michael Taus*

Child-Friendly
(Besides the normal fast-food
places; *children's menu
available)
American Girl
Ann Sather†
Athenian Rm.
Aurelio's Pizza†
Bacino's†
Bandera
bella! Bacino's†
Berghoff
Big Bowl*
Bin 36†
Bistro 110
Bob Chinn's Crab†
Bricks
Bubba Gump Shrimp*

California Pizza†
Cheesecake Factory
Chicago Flat Sam.
Chicago Pizza/Grinder
Chipotle†
Corner Bakery
Dave & Buster's*
Edwardo's*
El Jardin
ESPN Zone*
Famous Dave's†
Father/Son Pizza†
Flat Top Grill†
Fluky's
foodlife
Frontera Grill
Giordano's†
Glory
Gold Coast Dogs†
Grand Lux Café
Hackney's†
Hard Rock Cafe*
Harry Caray's
Heartland Cafe
Heaven on Seven
Hot Doug's
Ina's
Jambalaya's
Johnny Rockets†
John's Place†
Joy Yee's Noodle
Lawry's Prime Rib
Leona's†
Lindo Mexico
Lou Malnati's Pizzeria†
Lou Mitchell's†
Maggiano's
Max's*
Merle's Smokehse.*
Mity Nice Grill*
Mon Ami Gabi
My Pie Pizza†
Nancy's Pizza
Nookies
Original Gino's†
Original Pancake†
Parthenon
Penny's Noodle
Phoenix
Pizzeria Uno†
Potbelly Sandwich†
Rainforest Cafe†
Ranalli's

...runts*
...son's Ribs†
... Bottom Brew.†
...ll's BBQ*
...is Grill
...ozi!
... Crazy*
...perdawg Drive-In
...mpo
...ast*
...ucci Benucch*
Twin Anchors
Walker Bros.†
Wiener's Circle
Wishbone*

Cigars Welcome

Avenue Ale
Bada Bing
Berghoff†
Bistro 110
BUtterfield 8
Café Luciano†
Caffé La Scala
Caliterra
Capital Grille
Carlucci†
Carmichael's Steak
Carmine's
Carson's Ribs†
Chicago Chop Hse.
Chicago Prime
Cité
Clubhouse
Coco Pazzo
Como
Courtright's
Cru Café/Wine
D & J Bistro
El Nandu
Erie Cafe
ESPN Zone
Gale St. Inn†
Gibsons Steak
Gilardi's
Gino's Steak
Green Dolphin St.
Green Door Tav.
Grillroom
Grotto
Hackney's†
Harry Caray's†

Harry's Velvet Rm.
Hugo's Frog/Fish
Kamehachi†
Karma
Keefer's
Kinzie Chophouse
La Borsa
La Cantina Enoteca
Las Tablas†
La Strada
Le Vichyssois
Lovell's/Lake Forest
Magnum's Steak
Mar y Sol
McCormick & Schmick's
Mike Ditka's
Mill Race Inn
Millrose Rest./Brew
Morton's†
Myron & Phil's Steak
Nick's Fishmkt.†
Nine
120 Ocean Place
Parkers' Ocean
Pasha
Pete Miller's Sea/Steak
Philander's
P.J. Clarke's
Pompei Bakery†
Pump Room
Red Star Tav.†
Retro Bistro
Riva
Rock Bottom Brew.†
Rosebud Steak
Sabatino's
Sabor
Saloon Steak
Samba Room
Shula's Steak†
Signature Rm.
Sinibar
Smith & Wollensky
Stefani's
Sullivan's Steak
Tavern on Rush
Tin Fish
Tommy Nevin's
Tuscany†
Village
Volare
Zaven's

Special Feature Index

Critic-Proof
(Get lots of business, despite so-so food)
Bar Louie†
Billy Goat Tav.†
Bubba Gump Shrimp
Dave & Buster's
Dick's Last Resort
Fadó Irish Pub
John Barleycorn
Rainforest Cafe†

Dancing
Barn of Barrington
Bone Daddy
Dionises
Domaine
Gale St. Inn†
Giannotti Steak
Hard Rock Cafe
Harry's Velvet Rm.
Le Passage
Lutnia
Nacional 27
Nine
Pump Room
Rancho Luna
Rumba
Sayat Nova
Sinibar
Souk
Watusi
Xippo

Delivery/Takeout
(D=delivery, T=takeout)
a tavola (T)
Atlantique (T)
Bacchanalia (T)
BeccoD'Oro†
Bella Notte (D,T)
Bistro Marbuzet (T)
Bob San (T)
Bongo Room (T)
Café Iberico (T)
Café Spiaggia (T)
Café 36 (T)
Cafe 28 (T)
Campagnola (T)
CHIC Cafe (T)
Chilpancingo (T)
Coco Pazzo (T)
Costa's (T)

D & J Bistro (T)
Don Juan (T)
Dover Straits (T)
Emilio's Tapas†
erwin (T)
Filippo's (T)
Francesca's Tavola†
Francesco's Hole (T)
Froggy's (T)
Half Shell (T)
Hatsuhana (D,T)
Hong Min (T)
Ina's (T)
Itto Sushi (D,T)
Ixcapuzalco (T)
Jacky's Bistro (T)
Jilly's Cafe (T)
Joe's Seafood (T)
Kamehachi†
Keefer's (T)
La Bocca della Verità (T)
La Sardine (T)
La Scarola (T)
Las Tablas†
Le Colonial (D,T)
Les Deux Gros (T)
Le Vichyssois (T)
Lou Malnati's Pizzeria†
Lovell's/Lake Forest (T)
Lucca's (T)
Lupita's (T)
Magnum's Steak†
Marché (T)
Margie's Candies (D,T)
Meritage/Wine (T)
Mesón Sabika†
Mimosa (T)
Mirai Sushi (T)
Mon Ami Gabi (T)
Nuevo Leon†
120 Ocean Place (T)
Orange (T)
Parkers' Ocean (T)
Phoenix (T)
Pizza D.O.C. (T)
Pizzeria Uno†
Printer's Row (T)
Retro Bistro (T)
Ritz-Carlton Café (T)
Ritz-Carlton Din. Rm. (T)
Room, The (T)
Rosebud†
Rosebud Steak (T)

Sabatino's (T)
Salbute (D,T)
Shallots (D,T)
She She (T)
Smith & Wollensky (T)
Spiaggia (T)
Stained Glass Wine (T)
Sullivan's Steak†
Superdawg Drive-In (T)
Sushi Naniwa (D,T)
Thai Pastry (D,T)
Tiffin (T)
Tizi Melloul (T)
Topo Gigio (T)
Tre Kronor (T)
Tufano's Tap (T)
Twin Anchors (T)
Va Pensiero (T)
Via Carducci (D,T)
Vong's (T)
Walker Bros.†
Watusi (T)
Wiener's Circle (T)
Wildfire†
Yoshi's (T)
Zia's (T)

Dessert

Albert's Café
Ambria
Avenues
Carlos'
Charlie Trotter's
Courtright's
Crofton on Wells
erwin
Everest
Gabriel's
Grand Lux Café
Jacky's Bistro
La Crêperie
Le Français
Les Nomades
Le Titi de Paris
Lutz Continental
mk
Mon Ami Gabi
North Pond
one sixtyblue
Printer's Row
Rhapsody
Ritz-Carlton Din. Rm.

Seasons
Spiaggia
Spring
Sugar: A Dessert Bar
Tallgrass
302 West
Thyme
Topolobampo
Trio
Tru
Va Pensiero
Zealous

Dining Alone

(Other than hotels and places
with counter service)
Amitabul
Ann Sather†
Aria
Bar Louie†
Bite
Blind Faith
Breakfast Club
Cafe Nordstrom†
Chicago Diner
Chipotle†
Corner Bakery†
Cosí†
Flat Top Grill
Fluky's
foodlife
Fox & Obel Cafe
Gold Coast Dogs†
Heartland Cafe
Hilary's
Hi Ricky
Johnny Rockets†
Leo's Lunchroom
Lula
Manny's Café†
Moody's Pub
Nookies
Noyes St.
Oak Tree
Penny's Noodle†
Pierrot Gourmet
Puck's at MCA
Reza's
Salt & Pepper Diner
Toast
Wiener's Circle
Zoom Kitchen

Entertainment

(Call for days and times)
Abbey Pub (Irish)
A La Turka (belly dancing)
American Girl (show)
Andies†
Avenue Ale (jazz/top 40)
Bada Bing (varies)
Balagio (piano)
Barn of Barrington (piano)
Biggs Steak/Wine (jazz)
Bistro 110 (jazz)
Bistro Ultra (jazz)
Bone Daddy (varies)
Boulevard Café (rock)
Carmichael's Steak (piano)
Carmine's (piano)
Chef's Station (jazz duo)
Chicago Chop Hse. (piano)
Chicago Prime (jazz)
Chief O'Neill's (Irish)
Cyrano's Bistrot/Wine (cabaret)
Dick's Last Resort (varies)
Domaine (DJ)
Dover Straits (bands)
D'Vine Rest./Wine (DJ)
Edelweiss (German)
Eli's Steaks (piano bar)
El Nandu (guitar)
Ethiopian Village (DJ)
Ezuli (DJ)
Fadó Irish Pub (varies)
Fond de la Tour (piano)
Frankie J's (cooking show)
Gale St. Inn†
Geja's Cafe (guitar)
Gibsons Steak (piano)
Gilardi's (piano)
Gino's Steak (jazz piano)
Green Dolphin St. (jazz)
Green Room (DJs)
Hackney's†
Hard Rock Cafe (varies)
Harry's Velvet Rm. (DJ/singers)
House of Blues (band)
Hugo's Frog/Fish (piano)
Irish Oak (Irish)
Joe's Be-Bop (varies)
Julio's Cocina (Brazilian/jazz)
Kabul House†
Kit Kat (female impersonators)
La Fonda Latino (guitar)
Lalo's†
La Peña (Latin)
Las Tablas†
La Strada (piano)
Le Passage (DJ)
Little Bucharest (minstrels)
Lucca's (guitar)
Lula (varies)
Lutnia (piano)
Magnum's Steak (piano)
Mar y Sol (salsa/merengue)
McCormick & Schmick's (piano)
Mesón Sabika†
Mia Cucina (jazz/pop)
Midori (karaoke)
Mill Race Inn (varies)
Millrose Rest./Brew (piano)
Mirai Sushi (DJ)
Montage (jazz)
Myron & Phil's Steak (piano)
Nacional 27 (DJ)
Nine (DJ)
Nola's 32nd Ward (swing)
Palaggi's (jazz)
Parkers' Ocean (jazz/piano)
Pasha (Flamingo)
Pete Miller's Sea/Steak (jazz)
Philander's (jazz)
Piece (DJ)
Prairie Moon (DJ)
Public Landing (jazz)
Pump Room (piano/singer)
Rancho Luna (DJ)
Raw Bar (blues/jazz)
Redfish (blues/jazz)
Ritz-Carlton Din. Rm. (piano)
Rumba (DJ/salsa lessons)
Sabatino's (guitar/piano/violin)
Salvatore's (piano)
Sayat Nova (DJ)
Shark Bar (DJ)
Shaw's Crab (blues/jazz)
Signature Rm. (jazz)
Sinibar (DJ)
Smoke Daddy (blues/jazz)
Sorriso (piano/singer)
Souk (band/belly dancing)
Sugar: A Dessert Bar (DJ)
Sullivan's Steak†
Sushi Wabi (DJ)
Tango Sur (tango)
302 West (jazz)

Special Feature Index

Doubletree Guest Suites
  Mrs. Park's Tav.
Doubletree Hotel
  Gibsons Steak†
Drake Hotel
  Cape Cod Rm.
  Oak Terrace
Embassy Suites Hotel
  Papagus Taverna†
Fairmont, The
  Aria
Fitzpatrick Hotel
  Benihana†
Four Seasons Hotel
  Seasons
  Seasons Café
Homestead Hotel
  Trio
Hotel Allegro
  312 Chicago
Hotel Burnham
  Atwood Cafe
Hotel Inter-Continental
  Zest
Hotel Monaco
  South Water Kit.
Le Meridien Hotel
  Cerise
Omni Ambassador East
  Pump Room
Omni Chicago Hotel
  Cielo
Park Hyatt Chicago
  NoMi
Peninsula Hotel
  Avenues
  Lobby, The
  Pierrot Gourmet
  Shanghai Terrace
Radisson Hotel & Suites
  BeccoD'Oro†
Ritz-Carlton Hotel
  Ritz-Carlton Café
  Ritz-Carlton Din. Rm.
Seneca Hotel
  Saloon Steak
Sheraton Chicago
  Shula's Steak†
Sofitel Chicago Water Tower
  Café des Architectes
Swissôtel
  Currents
  Palm

Tremont Hotel
  Mike Ditka's
W Chicago Lakeshore
  Wave
Westin Hotel
  Grill on the Alley
Whitehall Hotel
  Molive
Wyndham Hotel
  Caliterra

"In" Places

Adobo Grill
Bin 36
Bistro Campagne
Bistrot Margot
Blackbird
Bob San
Bongo Room
Café Iberico
Coobah
Follia
Fortunato
Frontera Grill
Gibsons Steak†
Gioco
Green Room
Heat
Jin Ju
Joe's Seafood
Keefer's
Kevin
Marché
Mas
Mia Francesca
Mirai Sushi
mk
mk North
MOD.
Naha
Nine
NoMi
Ohba
one sixtyblue
Opera
Otro Mas
Oysy
Ping Pong
Platiyo
Red Light
Roy's
Shaw's Crab†
Soul Kitchen

get updates at zagat.com 203

Spring
Starfish
Sushi Wabi
Tavern on Rush
Tombo Kitchen
Tournesol
Trio
Tru
Wave

Jacket Required

Ambria
Cape Cod Rm.
Carlos'
Charlie Trotter's
Cité
Everest
Fond de la Tour
Le Français
Les Nomades
Little Bucharest
Ritz-Carlton Din. Rm.
Seasons
Spiaggia
Tallgrass
Trio
Tru

Late Dining

(Weekday closing hour)
Bar Louie†
Bijan's Bistro (2 AM)
Billy Goat Tav.†
Bistro 110 (1 AM)
Bone Daddy (2 AM)
Coobah (1 AM)
El Presidente (24 hrs.)
Father/Son Pizza†
Firefly (1:30 AM)
Gibsons Steak†
Happy Chef (2 AM)
Harry's Velvet Rm. (3 AM)
Hong Min†
Hugo's Frog/Fish (1 AM)
Jang Mo Nim (6 AM)
Kit Kat Lounge (1:30 AM)
Miller's Pub (3 AM)
Moody's Pub (1 AM)
Mrs. Park's Tav. (1:30 AM)
Narcisse (1 AM)
Northside Cafe (1 AM)
Pasha (3 AM)
Penang (1 AM)

Pepper Lounge (1 AM)
Pizzeria Uno†
P.J. Clarke's†
Ranalli's†
Raw Bar (1 AM)
Rosebud Steak (1 AM)
San Soo Gab San (6 AM)
Silver Seafood (1 AM)
Sinibar (1 AM)
Smoke Daddy (1 AM)
Suparossa†
Superdawg Drive-In (1 AM)
Tempo (24 hrs.)
Three Happiness (2 AM)
Twisted Spoke (1 AM)
Wave (2 AM)
Webster's Wine (2 AM)
Wiener's Circle (4 AM)

Meet for a Drink

(Most top hotels and the
following standouts)
Allen's New Amer.
Bandera
Bar Louie†
Biggs Steak/Wine
Billy Goat Tav.†
Bin 36
Bistro 110
Blue Bayou
Blue Line
Brasserie Jo
BUtterfield 8
Cab's Wine Bar
Café des Architectes
Catch 35
Charlie's Ale†
Chicago Prime
Chief O'Neill's
Coobah
Cru Café/Wine
Enoteca Piattini
Firefly
Frontera Grill
Gibsons Steak†
Goose Island Brew.
Green Room
Harry Caray's†
Iggy's
Jake Melnick's
Joe's Seafood
John Barleycorn
Keefer's

Le Passage
Marché
McCormick & Schmick's
mk
Moody's Pub
Nacional 27
Naha
Nine
One North
one sixtyblue
P.J. Clarke's†
Platiyo
Red Light
Rhapsody
RL
Rosebud Steak
Rumba
Scoozi!
Shark Bar
Shaw's Crab
Signature Rm.
Sinibar
Smith & Wollensky
South Water Kit.
Stained Glass Wine
Sugar: A Dessert Bar
Tasting Rm.
Tavern on Rush
Tizi Melloul
Trader Vic's
Trattoria No. 10
Twisted Spoke
Webster's Wine

Microbreweries
Founders Hill Brew.
Glen Ellyn Sports
Goose Island Brew.
Hard Rock Cafe
Millrose Rest./Brew
Piece
Rock Bottom Brew.

Offbeat
Billy Goat Tav.†
Bite
Bone Daddy
CHIC Cafe
Dell Rhea's Chicken
Edna's
Gladys Luncheon.
Heat
Inspiration Cafe

Kabul House†
Kit Kat Lounge
Kitsch'n on Roscoe
Leo's Lunchroom
Little Bucharest
Lovitt
MOD.
Mt. Everest
Narcisse
Sayat Nova
Shabu-ya
Silver Palm
Superdawg Drive-In
Twisted Spoke
Victory's Banner
Vinh Phat BBQ
White Fence Farm
Wiener's Circle
Zoom Kitchen†

Outdoor Dining
(G=garden; P=patio;
S=sidewalk; T=terrace;
W=waterside)
Athena (P)
Atwater's (P)
Azuré (P)
Barrington Bistro (P)
BeccoD'Oro†
Bice Grill (S)
Bice Rist. (S)
Bijan's Bistro (P)
Billy Goat Tav.†
Bistro Banlieue (P)
Bistro Campagne (G)
Bistro 110 (S)
Bistrot Margot (S)
Blackbird (S)
Bob Chinn's Crab†
Brasserie Jo (S)
Bubba Gump Shrimp (P)
Cafe Ba-Ba-Reeba! (P)
Cafe Borgia (P)
Café Le Loup (P)
Campagnola (G)
Carmichael's Steak (G)
Carmine's (P,S)
Carson's Ribs†
Charlie's Ale†
Chez Joel (P)
Chicago Firehse. (P)
Cochon Sauvage (P)
Coco Pazzo (P)

Coco Pazzo Cafe (P)
Como (P)
Convito Italiano (T)
Cornelia's (P)
Cosí†
Cru Café/Wine (S)
Cyrano's Bistrot/Wine (S)
D & J Bistro (S)
Dick's Last Resort (S,W)
Dinotto (P)
Dixie Kitchen†
d.kelly (P)
Domaine (P)
Elaine (P,S)
El Jardin (P)
Emilio's Tapas†
Feast (G)
Firefly (S)
Follia (P)
Four Farthings (P)
Frontera Grill (S)
Gabriel's (T)
Gioco (S)
Glory (P)
Greek Islands†
Green Dolphin St. (P,W)
Hackney's†
Harry Caray's†
Heartland Cafe (P)
Ina's (P)
Jacky's Bistro (S)
Jake Melnick's (P)
Jane's (S)
John Barleycorn†
John's Place (S)
Kamehachi†
Keefer's (S)
Kinzie Chophouse (S)
Kitsch'n on Roscoe (G,P,S)
La Bella Winnetka (G)
La Borsa (P)
La Crêperie (G)
Le Colonial (S,T)
Lou Malnati's Pizzeria†
Lucca's (G)
Lula (S)
Lutz Continental (G)
Mambo Grill (S)
Maple Tree Inn (G,P)
Mar y Sol (S)
Menagerie (P)
Meritage/Wine (G)
Mesón Sabika†

Mia Cucina (P,S)
Mia Francesca (G)
Milk & Honey (S)
Mill Race Inn (P,W)
Millrose Rest./Brew (P)
mk North (P)
Mon Ami Gabi (P)
Monsoon (P)
Montage (P)
Moody's Pub (G)
My Pie Pizza†
Nacional 27 (S)
Nick & Tony's†
Nola's 32nd Ward (P)
NoMi (T,W)
Northside Cafe (G)
O'Neil's (S)
One North (P)
120 Ocean Place (P)
Otro Mas (P)
Papagus Taverna (S)
Parkers' Ocean (P)
Pasha (S)
Pegasus†
Petterino's (S)
Philander's (S)
Phil & Lou's (P)
Phil Stefani's 437 Rush (S)
Ping Pong (P)
Pizzeria Uno†
P.J. Clarke's†
Platiyo (P)
Prairie Moon (P)
Prego (G)
Public Landing (T)
Puck's at MCA (P,W)
Ranalli's†
Red Light (P)
Red Star Tav. (P)
Retro Bistro (S)
Reza's†
Rhapsody (P)
Riva (P,W)
Rivers (P,W)
Robinson's Ribs†
Rock Bottom Brew.†
Room, The (S)
Rose Angelis (P)
Rosebud on Rush†
Roy's (P)
Sabor (P)
Salvatore's (G,P)
Sarkis Grill (P)

Settimana Café (P,S)
Shaw's Crab†
She She (P)
Silver Cloud (P)
Smith & Wollensky (P,T,W)
Sorriso (P,W)
South Gate Cafe (P,S)
Southport Saloon (P)
Stained Glass Wine (S)
Starfish (P)
Star of Siam (P)
Stefani's (P)
Strega Nona (S)
Sullivan's Steak†
Sushi Naniwa (P)
Takkatsu (S)
Tango Sur (P,S)
Tapas Barcelona (G,P)
Tarantino's (P)
Tavern on Rush (P,S)
Tempo (P)
Thyme (G,P,T)
Tilli's (P)
Tommy Nevin's (P)
Topo Gigio (G,S)
Topolobampo (S)
Trattoria Roma (S)
Trattoria Trullo (S)
Tre Kronor (G,S)
Tsunami (P,S)
Tufano's Tap (S)
Tuscany†
Twist (S)
Twisted Lizard (P,S)
Twisted Spoke (P)
Uncommon Ground (S)
Va Pensiero (T)
Via Veneto (S)
Vinci (S,T)
Vivo (S)
Volare (S)
Watusi (P)
Wave (S)
Xippo (S)
Yoshi's (P)

People-Watching
Adobo Grill
Berghoff
Bice Rist.
Bin 36
Blackbird
Brasserie Jo

Carmine's
Chicago Chop Hse.
Coco Pazzo
Coobah
Ferrari
Follia
Gibsons Steak†
Grill on the Alley
Harry Caray's†
Harry's Velvet Rm.
Iggy's
Keefer's
Le Colonial
Le Passage
Marché
Mirai Sushi
mk
MOD.
Naha
Narcisse
Nine
NoMi
Ohba
one sixtyblue
Opera
Pasha
Rosebud on Rush†
Rosebud Steak
Scoozi!
Shark Bar
Sinibar
Spring
Tavern on Rush
Wave

Power Scenes
Ambria
Avenues
Bice Rist.
Capital Grille
Catch 35
Charlie Trotter's
Chicago Chop Hse.
Coco Pazzo
Everest
Gene & Georgetti
Gibsons Steak
Grill on the Alley
Hugo's Frog/Fish
Keefer's
Le Français
Les Nomades
mk

Morton's†
Naha
NoMi
Ritz-Carlton Café
Ritz-Carlton Din. Rm.
RL
Ruth's Chris
Seasons
Smith & Wollensky
Spago
Spiaggia
Spring
Tru
Zealous

Private Rooms Available

(Restaurants charge less at off times; call for capacity)

Allen's New Amer.
Ambria
Aria
Arun's
a tavola
Avenues
Azure
Bagel†
Barrington Bistro
Bijan's Bistro
Bistro Marbuzet
Bistrot Margot
Blue Bayou
Bob Chinn's Crab†
Bob San
Buona Terra
Cafe Borgia
Café La Cave
Cafe Pyrenees
Café Spiaggia
Caliterra
Campagnola
Cape Cod Rm.
Capital Grille
Carlos'
Carmichael's Steak
Catch 35
Charlie Trotter's
Chicago Chop Hse.
Chicago Prime
Cloud 9
Costa's
Courtright's
Cristiano's
Crofton on Wells

D & J Bistro
d.kelly
Domaine
Don Roth's Blackhawk
Erie Cafe
Escargot
Everest
Fogo de Chão
Fond de la Tour
Francesca's Tavola†
Froggy's
Frontera Grill
Gabriel's
Gene & Georgetti
Giannotti Steak
Gibsons Steak
Gioco
Goose Island Brew.
Grand Lux Café
Green Room
Grotto
Hatsuhana
Ixcapuzalco
Jack's on Halsted
Jacky's Bistro
Jake Melnick's
Kamehachi†
Keefer's
Lao Sze Chuan†
Las Tablas†
Lawry's Prime Rib
Le Colonial
Le Français
Les Deux Gros
Le Titi de Paris
Le Vichyssois
Lou Malnati's Pizzeria†
Magnum's Steak
Marché
Menagerie
Mesón Sabika†
Mia Francesca
Midori
mk
MOD.
Mon Ami Gabi†
Montage
Morton's†
Mysore Woodland†
Naha
Nick's Fishmkt.
Nine
NoMi

Oceanique
one sixtyblue
120 Ocean Place
Opera
Original Gino's†
Palm
Parkers' Ocean
Pasteur
Philander's
Phoenix
Pili.Pili
Prairie Moon
Printer's Row
Red Star Tav.†
Rhapsody
Rock Bottom Brew.
Rose Angelis
Ruth's Chris†
Sabatino's
Sal & Carvao
Seasons
Shark Bar
Shaw's Crab
Spago
Spiaggia
Sugar: A Dessert Bar
Tallgrass
Thyme
Tombo Kitchen
Topolobampo
Trattoria No. 10
Trio
Tru
Tuscany†
Va Pensiero
Via Carducci
Vinci
Vivere
Walker Bros.†
Wildfire
Zealous
Zia's

Prix Fixe Menus
(Call for prices and times)
Ambria
American Girl
Arun's
Bin 36†
Café Le Loup
Cafe Pyrenees
Caliterra
Campagnola

Carlos'
Charlie Trotter's
CHIC Cafe
Cielo
Cyrano's Bistrot/Wine
D & J Bistro
Dick's Last Resort
El Jardin
Erawan Thai
Ethiopian Village
Everest
Froggy's
Jilly's Cafe
Lan Sushi/Lobster
la petite folie
La Sardine
Las Bellas Artes
La Strada
Le Français
Les Deux Gros
Les Nomades
Le Titi de Paris
Le Vichyssois
Lexi's
Lobby, The
Marché
one sixtyblue
Papagus Taverna†
Pump Room
Retro Bistro
Reza's†
Ritz-Carlton Din. Rm.
Riva
Rushmore
Seasons
Sorriso
Spiaggia
Sushi Naniwa
Tallgrass
Thyme
Tizi Melloul
Trio
Tru

Quick Fix
Albert's Café
Art of Pizza
Artopolis Bakery
Bagel
Bar Louie†
BD's Mongolian BBQ†
Berghoff†
Bice Grill

Special Feature Index

Big Bowl
Billy Goat Tav.†
Bin 36
Cafe Nordstrom
Cafe Selmarie
Chicago Flat Sam.
Chicago Pizza/Grinder
Chipotle†
Cold Comfort
Corner Bakery†
Cosí†
Cru Café/Wine
El Presidente
Flat Top Grill
Fluky's
Flying Chicken
foodlife
Fox & Obel Cafe
Gold Coast Dogs†
Hi Ricky
Hot Doug's
Jambalaya's
Johnny Rockets†
Lem's BBQ
Lincoln Noodle
Manny's Café
Max's
Mrs. Levy's Deli
Noon-O-Kabab
Oak Tree
Old Jerusalem
Panera Bread†
Pegasus†
Penny's Noodle†
Pierrot Gourmet
Pompei Bakery†
Potbelly Sandwich†
Puck's at MCA
Russell's BBQ
Salt & Pepper Diner
Sarkis Grill
Stained Glass Wine
Stevie B's
Stir Crazy
Superdawg Drive-In
Tasting Rm.
Tempo
Uncommon Ground
Vinh Phat BBQ
Webster's Wine
Wiener's Circle
Zoom Kitchen

Quiet Conversation
Akai Hana†
Albert's Café
Amitabul
Aria
Arun's
Bank Ln. Bistro
Barn of Barrington
Barrington Bistro
Best Hunan
Bêtise
Biggs Steak/Wine
Bistro Banlieue
Café Bernard
Café des Architectes
Café La Cave
Cafe Matou
Cafe Pyrenees
Cafe Selmarie
Café Spiaggia
Caliterra
Cape Cod Rm.
Carlos'
Charlie Trotter's
Chicago Prime
Chinoiserie
Cité
CoCoRo/East
Convito Italiano
D & J Bistro
d.kelly
Don Roth's Blackhawk
Dover Straits†
Eli's Steaks
erwin
Everest
Fond de la Tour
Fondue Stube
Gale St. Inn†
Gaylord India
Geja's Cafe
Genesee Depot
Hashalom
Hatsuhana
Hong Min
Itto Sushi
Jilly's Cafe
Kevin
Klay Oven
Kyoto†
La Crêperie
La Gondola

Special Feature Index

Las Bellas Artes
Lawry's Prime Rib
Le Français
Les Nomades
Le Titi de Paris
Le Vichyssois
Lobby, The
Lovell's/Lake Forest
Lucca's
Mill Race Inn
Mimosa
Molive
New Japan
North Pond
Oak Terrace
Oceanique
One North
120 Ocean Place
Pierrot Gourmet
Prairie
Printer's Row
Pump Room
Ravinia Bistro
Restaurant on Park
Rhapsody
Ritz-Carlton Café
Ritz-Carlton Din. Rm.
Rivers
RL
Ron of Japan
Russian Tea
Salvatore's
Seasons
Seasons Café
1776
Shanghai Terrace
Shiroi Hana
Signature Rm.
Slice of Life
South Gate Cafe
South Water Kit.
Takkatsu
Tallgrass
Tasting Rm.
Tavern
Thai Little Home
302 West
Trattoria No. 10
Tre Kronor
Trio
Tru
Va Pensiero
Via Veneto

Village
Vinci
Vivere
Vong's
Zaven's
Zealous

Raw Bars
Akai Hana
Benihana†
Bijan's Bistro
Bin 36†
Bluefin
Bluepoint Oyster
Bob Chinn's Crab
Brasserie Jo
Cape Cod Rm.
Catch 35
CoCoRo/East
Cy's Crabhouse
Davis St. Fish
Half Shell
Kamehachi†
Midori
Montage
Nola's 32nd Ward
NoMi
120 Ocean Place
Oysy
Pappadeaux Seafood
Raw Bar
Riva
Sai Café
Shine & Morida
Sushi Naniwa
Takkatsu
Tin Fish

Reserve Ahead
Abbey Pub
Ambria
Aria
Arun's
Atwater's
Atwood Cafe
Avenues
Biggs Steak/Wine
Bistrot Margot
Blackbird
BUtterfield 8
Café Le Loup
Café 36
Carlos'

subscribe to zagat.com

Romantic Places

Topo Gigio
Tru
Va Pensiero
Vinci
Webster's Wine

Tre Kronor
Twin Anchors
Via Veneto
Village
Zaven's

Senior Appeal
Albert's Café
Andies†
Ann Sather†
Army & Lou's
Berghoff†
Biaggio's†
Bogart's Charhse.
Bruna's
Buca di Beppo†
Café Luciano
Cannella's
Cape Cod Rm.
Carson's Ribs†
Czech Plaza
Dave's
Davis St. Fish
Don Roth's Blackhawk
Don's Fishmkt.
Dover Straits
Edelweiss
Father/Son Pizza†
Fireplace Inn
Francesco's Hole
Gale St. Inn
Genesee Depot
La Bella Winnetka
La Cantina Enoteca
La Gondola
Las Tablas†
La Strada
Lawry's Prime Rib
Leona's†
Little Bucharest
Lou Mitchell's†
Lutnia
Lutz Continental
Mill Race Inn
Mirabell
Myron & Phil's Steak
Next Door Bistro
Oak Terrace
Oak Tree
Papa Milano
Pump Room
Russian Tea
Sabatino's
South Gate Cafe

Singles Scenes
Adobo Grill
Bar Louie†
BUtterfield 8
Café Iberico
Charlie's Ale†
Clubhouse
Cullen's Bar
Dick's Last Resort
ESPN Zone
Fadó Irish Pub
Four Farthings
Glen Ellyn Sports
Green Room
House of Blues
Joe's Be-Bop
John Barleycorn
Le Passage
Moody's Pub
Nacional 27
Nine
Northside Cafe
Otro Mas
Pasha
Piece
Ping Pong
P.J. Clarke's†
Ranalli's
Redfish
Red Light
Red Lion Pub
Rock Bottom Brew.
Scoozi!
Shark Bar
Sinibar
Southport Saloon
Stanley's Kitchen
Sugar: A Dessert Bar
Tavern on Rush
Tilli's
Wave

Sleepers
(Good to excellent food, but
little known)
Amarind's
Army & Lou's
Bagel

subscribe to zagat.com

Special Feature Index

Elaine
Enoteca Piattini
Erawan Thai
Everest
Gabriel's
Geja's Cafe
La Sardine
Le Français
Les Nomades
Le Titi de Paris
Meritage/Wine
mk
MOD.
Molive
Naha
NoMi
North Pond
Oceanique
one sixtyblue
Pane Caldo
Pasteur
Printer's Row
Rhapsody
Ritz-Carlton Din. Rm.
Salpicón
Seasons
1776
Signature Rm.
Spiaggia
Spring
Stained Glass Wine
Tallgrass
Tasting Rm.
302 West
Thyme
Topolobampo
Trattoria No. 10
Trio
Tru
Va Pensiero
Vivere

West Town Tav.
Zealous
Zest

Worth a Trip

Arlington Heights
   Le Titi de Paris
Evanston
   Campagnola
   Jacky's Bistro
   Trio
   Va Pensiero
Geneva
   302 West
Highland Park
   Carlos'
Highwood
   Del Rio
   Froggy's
   Gabriel's
Hinsdale
   Salbute
Lake Zurich
   D & J Bistro
Lakemoor
   Le Vichyssois
Lockport
   Tallgrass
Mt. Prospect
   Retro Bistro
Northfield
   mk North
Tinley Park
   Tin Fish
Wheaton
   120 Ocean Place
Wheeling
   Le Français
Willow Springs
   Courtright's

Wine Vintage Chart

This chart is designed to help you select wine to go with your meal. It is based on the same 0 to 30 scale used throughout this *Survey*. The ratings (prepared by our friend **Howard Stravitz**, a professor at the University of South Carolina) reflect both the quality of the vintage and the wine's readiness for present consumption. Thus, if a wine is not fully mature or is over the hill, its rating has been reduced. We do not include 1987, 1991–1993 vintages because they are not especially recommended for most areas.

	'85	'86	'88	'89	'90	'94	'95	'96	'97	'98	'99	'00	'01
WHITES													
French:													
Alsace	24	18	22	28	28	26	25	23	23	25	23	25	26
Burgundy	26	25	17	25	24	15	29	28	25	24	25	22	20
Loire Valley	–	–	–	–	25	23	24	26	24	23	24	25	23
Champagne	28	25	24	26	29	–	26	27	24	24	25	25	–
Sauternes	21	28	29	25	27	–	20	23	27	22	22	22	28
California (Napa, Sonoma, Mendocino):													
Chardonnay	–	–	–	–	–	22	27	23	27	25	25	23	26
Sauvignon Blanc/Semillon	–	–	–	–	–	–	–	–	24	24	25	22	26
REDS													
French:													
Bordeaux	25	26	24	27	29	22	26	25	23	24	23	25	23
Burgundy	23	–	21	25	28	–	26	27	25	22	27	22	20
Rhône	25	19	27	29	29	24	25	23	25	28	26	27	24
Beaujolais	–	–	–	–	–	–	–	–	23	22	25	25	18
California (Napa, Sonoma, Mendocino):													
Cab./Merlot	26	26	–	21	28	29	27	25	28	23	26	23	26
Pinot Noir	–	–	–	–	27	24	24	26	25	26	25	27	
Zinfandel	–	–	–	–	25	22	23	21	22	24	19	24	
Italian:													
Tuscany	26	–	24	–	26	22	25	20	28	24	27	26	25
Piedmont	26	–	26	28	29	–	23	26	28	26	25	24	22